Palgrave Macmillan Studies in Banking and Financial Institutions
Series Editor: **Professor Philip Molyneux**
The Palgrave Macmillan Studies in Banking and Financial Institutions are international in orientation and include studies of banking within particular countries or regions, and studies of particular themes such as Corporate Banking, Risk Management, Mergers and Acquisitions, etc. The books' focus is on research and practice, and they include up-to-date and innovative studies on contemporary topics in banking that will have global impact and influence.

Titles include:
Yener Altunbaş, Blaise Gadanecz and Alper Kara
SYNDICATED LOANS
A Hybrid of Relationship Lending and Publicly Traded Debt

Yener Altunbaş, Alper Kara and Öslem Olgu
TURKISH BANKING
Banking under Political Instability and Chronic High Inflation

Steffen E. Andersen
THE EVOLUTION OF NORDIC FINANCE

Elena Beccalli
IT AND EUROPEAN BANK PERFORMANCE

Paola Bongini, Stefano Chiarlone and Giovanni Ferri (*editors*)
EMERGING BANKING SYSTEMS

Vittorio Boscia, Alessandro Carretta and Paola Schwizer
COOPERATIVE BANKING: INNOVATIONS AND DEVELOPMENTS

COOPERATIVE BANKING IN EUROPE: CASE STUDIES

Roberto Bottiglia, Elisabetta Gualandri and Gian Nereo Mazzocco (*editors*)
CONSOLIDATION IN THE EUROPEAN FINANCIAL INDUSTRY

Alessandro Carretta, Franco Fiordelisi and Gianluca Mattarocci (*editors*)
NEW DRIVERS OF PERFORMANCE IN A CHANGING FINANCIAL WORLD

Dimitris N. Chorafas
CAPITALISM WITHOUT CAPITAL

Dimitris N. Chorafas
FINANCIAL BOOM AND GLOOM
The Credit and Banking Crisis of 2007–2009 and Beyond

Violaine Cousin
BANKING IN CHINA

Vincenzo D'Apice and Giovanni Ferri
FINANCIAL INSTABILITY
Toolkit for Interpreting Boom and Bust Cycles

Peter Falush and Robert L. Carter OBE
THE BRITISH INSURANCE INDUSTRY SINCE 1900
The Era of Transformation

Franco Fiordelisi
MERGERS AND ACQUISITIONS IN EUROPEAN BANKING

Franco Fiordelisi, Philip Molyneux and Daniele Previati (*editors*)
NEW ISSUES IN FINANCIAL AND CREDIT MARKETS

Franco Fiordelisi, Philip Molyneux and Daniele Previati (*editors*)
NEW ISSUES IN FINANCIAL INSTITUTIONS MANAGEMENT

Franco Fiordelisi and Philip Molyneux
SHAREHOLDER VALUE IN BANKING

Hans Genberg and Cho-Hoi Hui
THE BANKING CENTRE IN HONG KONG
Competition, Efficiency, Performance and Risk

Carlo Gola and Alessandro Roselli
THE UK BANKING SYSTEM AND ITS REGULATORY AND SUPERVISORY FRAMEWORK

Elisabetta Gualandri and Valeria Venturelli (*editors*)
BRIDGING THE EQUITY GAP FOR INNOVATIVE SMEs

Kim Hawtrey
AFFORDABLE HOUSING FINANCE

Otto Hieronymi (*editor*)
GLOBALIZATION AND THE REFORM OF THE INTERNATIONAL BANKING AND MONETARY SYSTEM

Munawar Iqbal and Philip Molyneux
THIRTY YEARS OF ISLAMIC BANKING
History, Performance and Prospects

Sven Janssen
BRITISH AND GERMAN BANKING STRATEGIES

Kimio Kase and Tanguy Jacopin
CEOs AS LEADERS AND STRATEGY DESIGNERS
Explaining the Success of Spanish Banks

Alexandros-Andreas Kyrtsis (*editor*)
FINANCIAL MARKETS AND ORGANIZATIONAL TECHNOLOGIES
System Architectures, Practices and Risks in the Era of Deregulation

M. Mansoor Khan and M. Ishaq Bhatti
DEVELOPMENTS IN ISLAMIC BANKING
The Case of Pakistan

Mario La Torre and Gianfranco A. Vento
MICROFINANCE

Roman Matousek (*editor*)
MONEY, BANKING AND FINANCIAL MARKETS IN CENTRAL AND EASTERN EUROPE
20 Years of Transition

Philip Molyneux and Eleuterio Vallelado (*editors*)
FRONTIERS OF BANKS IN A GLOBAL WORLD

Imad Moosa
THE MYTH OF TOO BIG TO FAIL

Simon Mouatt and Carl Adams (*editors*)
CORPORATE AND SOCIAL TRANSFORMATION OF MONEY AND BANKING
Breaking the Serfdom

Anastasia Nesvetailova
FRAGILE FINANCE
Debt, Speculation and Crisis in the Age of Global Credit

Anders Ögren (*editor*)
THE SWEDISH FINANCIAL REVOLUTION

Dominique Rambure and Alec Nacamuli
PAYMENT SYSTEMS
From the Salt Mines to the Board Room

Catherine Schenk (*editor*)
HONG KONG SAR's MONETARY AND EXCHANGE RATE CHALLENGES
Historical Perspectives

Noël K. Tshiani
BUILDING CREDIBLE CENTRAL BANKS
Policy Lessons for Emerging Economies

Ruth Wandhöfer
EU PAYMENTS INTEGRATION
The Tale of SEPA, PSD and Other Milestones along the Road

The full list of titles available is on the website: www.palgrave.com/finance/sbfi.asp

---

Palgrave Macmillan Studies in Banking and Financial Institutions
Series Standing Order ISBN 978–1–4039–4872–4

You can receive future titles in this series as they are published by placing a standing order. Please contact your bookseller or, in case of difficulty, write to us at the address below with your name and address, the title of the series and the ISBN quoted above.

Customer Services Department, Macmillan Distribution Ltd, Houndmills, Basingstoke, Hampshire RG21 6XS, England

---

Money, Banking and Financial Markets in Central and Eastern Europe

20 Years of Transition

Edited by

Roman Matousek

Director, Centre for EMEA Banking, Finance and Economics, London Metropolitan University, UK

palgrave
macmillan

First published 2010 by
PALGRAVE MACMILLAN

Palgrave Macmillan in the UK is an imprint of Macmillan Publishers Limited, registered in England, company number 785998, of Houndmills, Basingstoke, Hampshire RG21 6XS.

Palgrave Macmillan in the US is a division of St Martin's Press LLC, 175 Fifth Avenue, New York, NY 10010.

Palgrave Macmillan is the global academic imprint of the above companies and has companies and representatives throughout the world.

Palgrave® and Macmillan® are registered trademarks in the United States, the United Kingdom, Europe and other countries.

ISBN 978–0–230–23168–9 hardback

This book is printed on paper suitable for recycling and made from fully managed and sustained forest sources. Logging, pulping and manufacturing processes are expected to conform to the environmental regulations of the country of origin.

A catalogue record for this book is available from the British Library.

A catalog record for this book is available from the Library of Congress.

10 9 8 7 6 5 4 3 2 1
19 18 17 16 15 14 13 12 11 10

Printed and bound in Great Britain by
CPI Antony Rowe, Chippenham and Eastbourne

Contents

List of Figures and Tables

Figures

Tables

Notes on Contributors

Jan Babecký, Ph.D. studied in the Czech Republic and France. He has held the following positions at the Czech National Bank, Prague: economic analyst in the International Relations Division (2003–7), Deputy Head of the Foreign Research Unit (2007), and Senior Economist at the Research and Financial Stability Department. He also serves as member of the ECB Wage Dynamic Network Working Paper Team and member of the Editorial Board of the Czech Economic Review.

Fabrizio Coricelli, Ph.D. is Professor of Economics at the University of Paris 1, Panthéon-Sorbonne. He is a research fellow at the Paris School of Economics and the Centre for Economic Policy Research (CEPR), London. He has been Professor of Economics at the University of Siena and has worked in London as Director of Policy Studies at the European Bank for Reconstruction and Development (EBRD); in Washington at the International Monetary Fund and at the World Bank, and in Brussels as Economic Advisor at the European Commission.

Dan Gabriel Dumitrescu is Lecturer at the University of Economics, Bucharest, Romania. The research topic of his thesis focused on European capital markets and his main research interests revolve around quantitative economic analysis in financial markets and international macroeconomics with application to the EU policies. He is involved in various national and international research projects and author or co-author of numerous research papers, published in Romania and abroad.

Sorin Dumitrescu is Lecturer at the University of Economic Studies in Bucharest, Romania, where he teaches finance-related disciplines and econometrics at the Faculty of International Business and Economics. He is a Ph.D. candidate in International Finance. Sorin has worked at the National Centre for Social Research in Athens on a Leonardo da Vinci grant and has spent a semester at the Polytechnic University in Braganca, Portugal, in the Erasmus programme.

Jan Frait, Ph.D. is Professor of Economics Technical University of Ostrava, Czech Republic. In 2002–3 he served as the president of the Czech Economic Society. In 2000, Jan was appointed as a member of the Czech National Bank Board for the period 2000–6. In this capacity, he was a member of the OECD Economic Policy Committee in 2005 and 2006. Since 2007 he has been the advisor to the board of the Czech National Bank and Deputy Head of the Research and Financial Stability Department. He also acts as a member of the ECB's Banking Supervision Committee.

Barry Harrison is a graduate of Nottingham and Sheffield universities. He has held teaching appointments at the Universities of Sheffield and Loughborough and is currently at Nottingham Business School, where he teaches on both undergraduate and postgraduate courses. In addition to teaching in the UK, he has lectured on postgraduate courses in The Netherlands, Germany, France, Azerbaijan, Estonia and Russia. He is a faculty professor at TiasNimbas Business School in the Netherlands and is also Visiting Professor at the European University at St Petersburg in Russia. He has worked as a consultant for the National Institute for Management of the Economy in Baku, Azerbaijan and the Training Board of the Clothing and Allied Products Industry. He has also appeared on TV and radio. His current research interests focus primarily on Central and Eastern European economies and his recent publications have appeared in Economics Letters, Applied Financial Economics and Economic Issues.

Iraj Hashi, Ph.D., is Professor of Economics and the Director of the Centre for Research on Emerging Economies at Staffordshire University Business School. His research has focused on microeconomic problems of transition to a market economy in Central and Eastern Europe. He has worked with research and consultancy institutions in Albania, Bosnia-Herzegovina, Croatia, the Czech Republic, Kosovo, Macedonia, Poland, Romania and Russia on projects funded by national, EU and international institutions.

Alexandra Horobet, Ph.D. is Full Professor at the University of Economic Studies in Bucharest, Romania. She is also Visiting Lecturer at another two Romanian universities: University Al.I. Cuza Iaşi and University Lucian Blaga of Sibiu. Throughout her career she has worked on various research grants in Europe and Canada. Her main research interests focus on financial integration, including the impact of financial crises, currency risk assessment and management, dynamic links between financial and real markets and financial stability in emerging markets.

Luboš Komárek, Ph.D. is Director of the External Economic Relations Division at the Czech National Bank, Prague. In 2006 he became associate professor, teaching at the Faculty of Finance and Accounting at the Prague School of Economics, and at the Faculty of Economics at the Technical University in Ostrava. In 2008–9 he served as the president of the Czech Economic Society. He is a member of the ECB's Monetary Policy Committee. His research is oriented towards the analysis of exchange rates and FX interventions, monetary policy transmission mechanisms, financial integration and asset prices.

Zlatuše Komárková. After her university studies, she worked as an economic analyst at the Ministry of Industry and Trade of the Czech Republic. She is a senior analyst and the advisor to the Bank Board Members at the Czech National Bank. She is mainly responsible for financial stability analysis. Her research is primarily oriented towards the analysis of capital markets, financial integration, liquidity and tools for financial stability.

Ladislav Krištoufek is a Ph.D. candidate at the Institute of Economic Studies at Charles University in Prague, Czech Republic. During his undergraduate studies, he studied economics at London Metropolitan University, UK (Erasmus Exchange Programme). He is also a member of the econometrics department of the Institute of Information Theory and Automation of the Academy of Sciences of the Czech Republic. In his research, Ladislav focuses on financial economics, financial econometrics and econophysics.

Mojca Marc, Ph.D. is a teaching and research assistant collaborating since 2001 on undergraduate and postgraduate courses at the Faculty of Economics, University of Ljubljana (Slovenia). She studied her Ph.D. at the University of Siena and Nuffield College, Oxford University (UK). Her research interests range from banking and financing of companies, performance measurement in companies to the intellectual and innovation activity of companies. She has published in the *International Business and Economics Research Journal* and in the *Journal of Business and Economics Research*.

Dubravko Mihaljek, Ph.D., is a Senior Economist in the Emerging Market Issues group of the Monetary and Economic Department, Bank for International Settlements. From 1990 to 1999 he worked at the IMF in Washington, DC. From 1982 to 1989 he was a researcher at the Economics Institute in Zagreb, Croatia. He studied economics at the University of Pittsburgh (PhD, 1990), University of Minnesota (MA, 1986) and University of Zagreb (BA, 1981). He has published empirical and policy-oriented papers on a broad range of topics, including recently on international capital flows; the banking industry; determinants of house prices; the Balassa–Samuelson effect; and a number of fiscal policy issues.

Winston Moore, Ph.D. is a Lecturer in Economics at the University of the West Indies, Cave Hill Campus (2006–present). Prior to joining the department, he was Senior Economist at the Central Bank of Barbados. Dr Moore's research has focused on three major areas in economics: Industrial Economics, Tourism Economics and International Macroeconomics. He has published more than 50 articles in peer-reviewed journals and books. His research has appeared in major journals such as the *Journal of Forecasting, Journal of Policy Modeling, Annals of Tourism Research, Applied Economics* and *Contemporary Economic Policy*. Dr. Moore holds a PhD in Economics from the University of Surrey.

Shahdad Naghshpour, Ph.D. is Professor of International Economics and Statistics in the Department of Political Science, International Development and International Affairs PhD Program at the University of Southern Mississippi (USA). He has taught numerous courses in all levels of statistics and economics. He has published over 41 journal papers, book chapters, monographs, and translations. His current research interests include globalisation, ethnic conflict, and monetary theory applications in macroeconomics.

Marjan Senjur, Ph.D. is Full Professor of Economics at the Faculty of Economics, University of Ljubljana, Slovenia. He does research in economic growth and development and macroeconomics of transition countries. He has recently published in the journals *Comparative Economic Studies* and *Post-Communist Economies* (2009). He served as a Minister for Economic Relations and Development in the Slovenian government. He served as the ambassador of the Republic of Slovenia to the United Kingdom. In 2009 he became the Chairman of the Fiscal Council.

Bruno S. Sergi, Ph.D. is Professor of International Economics at the University of Messina, Italy. He has taught international classes and has been Guest Lecturer at central banks' research departments and universities in several countries around the world, including the International Monetary Fund, several central banks in Europe, and New York University. He has published over 80 journal papers and is the author or co-editor of several books on transition economics and global business.

Alina M. Spiru, Ph.D., has been a Lecturer in Economics at Lancaster University Management School since 2007. Prior to that, she taught at the University of Reading and at the Academy of Economic Studies Bucharest, where she is a Visiting Research Associate. She holds a PhD in Economics from the University of Reading. Her research interests lie in the area of applied time series econometrics, with a focus on inflation and exchange rate modelling, convergence and integration in Central and Eastern Europe.

Menbere Workie Tiruneh, Ph.D. is Associate Professor at City University of Seattle and the College of Management in Bratislava, and Researcher at the Institute of Economics at the Slovak Academy of Sciences. Dr Workie's research is in the areas of economic growth, external debt and financial development. He has published several articles in the *Journal of Economics* of the Slovak Academy of Sciences and the Czech *Journal of Economics and Finance*. Dr Workie's book *From Debt Crisis to Growth Crisis: Is External Debt the Cause or the Effect of Africa's Marginalization?* was published in 2007.

Valentin Z. Toçi, Ph.D. is the Chief Economist of the Central Bank of the Republic of Kosovo and has directed the economic analysis and statistics work of the bank since 2004. He is also the editor of the periodical and occasional publications of the Central Bank. He completed many professional training programmes, including Financial Programming and Policies at the IMF. Toçi is also Assistant Professor at the University of Prishtina and teaches economics and econometrics. His fields of interest include financial economics, institutional economics and macroeconomics.

1
Introduction

Roman Matousek

This book is an outcome of the Research Conference organised by the London Metropolitan Business School in London on the occasion of 20 Years of Transition in Central and Eastern Europe (CEE). The main research themes were focused on Money, Banking and Financial Markets in transition economies. The book consists of 11 research chapters written by practitioners and academics. The selected chapters evaluate the changes and policy challenges that transition economies have undergone in the past 20 years.

The first chapter, written by Dubravko Mihaljek, analyses the spread of the global financial crisis to Central and Eastern Europe and the patterns of cross-border bank flows in the region. Mihaljek argues that despite pronounced vulnerabilities on the eve of the crisis, the CEE countries did not experience a sudden cessation of cross-border bank flows. He supports his arguments by showing that foreign bank ownership provided some insulation from reversals in cross-border bank flows and the drop in domestic financing. The chapter concludes that some aspects of the crisis in CEE countries are similar to those observed in past emerging market crises.

Fabrizio Coricelli and Mojca Marc, in their chapter, 'Are Product Market Structures Affected by Banking Concentration: Evidence from Transition Countries', rigorously analyse the relationship between banking and product market structure in transition countries. They try to validate this relationship for different geographical and time domains. Their findings contrast with the results from other empirical research applied in developed economies. Coricelli and Marc show that greater banking concentration has no significant effect on product market structure in transition countries, whereas it is negatively related to product market structure in advanced countries. The chapter concludes with relevant policy recommendations.

Chapter 4 is geographically focused on South-Eastern Europe. Iraj Hashi and Valentin Z. Toçi address in their chapter the issue linked to financing constraints, credit rationing and financing obstacles. Hashi and Toçi stress that financing constraints have been one of the major impediments to doing business in this region. They provide new evidence on financing constraints, credit rationing and financing obstacles for firms in Albania, Bosnia and Herzegovina, Bulgaria, Croatia, Macedonia, Romania, and Serbia and Montenegro. Based on their findings, a number of policy implications aimed at reducing financing constraints for the small business sector are derived.

Chapters 5 and 6 then focus on stock markets in Central and Eastern Europe. Ladislav Krištoufek's chapter analyses an interesting research topic on the efficiency, persistence and predictability of stock markets in the Czech Republic, Hungary, Poland and Slovakia. He validates the imposed working hypothesis that stock markets in Poland and Hungary are the most efficient, whereas the Czech Republic remains very close to significant long-range dependent behaviour. Finally, in the case of Slovakia, Krištoufek shows that this market lacks the liquidity needed to be described correctly by Hurst exponent.

Barry Harrison and Winston Moore's chapter investigates the stock market convergence in those Central and Eastern European countries that have recently joined the European Union with the developed stock markets of London and Frankfurt. They argue that most investigations into stock market convergence assume a linear co-integrating relationship. However, the relationship between two series might not always be linear and in this chapter they test whether a non-linear relationship exists between our series and evaluate whether the results from testing for stock market integration are significantly affected by the frequency of observations employed. Their findings suggest that linear co-integration tests may provide misleading results.

The next chapter deals with the interesting issue of cross-country versus regional convergence in the European Union (EU). Menbere Workie Tiruneh shows that the high growth dynamics of Central and Eastern European economies over the past two decades helped to achieve modest but consistent convergence towards the living standards of advanced EU member states (EU 15). Furthermore, Tiruneh argues that there was a convergence process across EU member states during these periods, as indicated by a declining dispersion of income per capita measured using a standard deviation. Finally, he shows that regional disparities within countries remain a persistent problem in most of the transition economies of the EU.

The issue of financial integration among New EU countries and the Euro Area is presented by Jan Babecký, Jan Frait, Luboš Komárek, Zlatuše Komárková. The study sheds light on the integration of financial markets (money, foreign exchange, and bond and stock markets) in five new EU member states (Czech Republic, Hungary, Poland, Slovakia and Slovenia) and selected old EU members (Germany, Austria, Portugal and Sweden) in comparison with the Euro Area. Babecký et al. test for the existence and determine the degree of financial integration among these economies relative to the Euro Area aggregate over the past decade. Their results show an increase in financial market integration of the new EU members' markets with the old EU members in the Euro Area economies. Furthermore, they argue that the group of new EU member states is far from homogeneous.

Shahdad Naghshpour and Bruno S. Sergi examine the contribution of export to growth in the East European countries. This study uses Maizels' model that exports could be an engine of growth and considers four alternative models; the data are combined to take advantage of the panel data analysis. Although the idea of export as a growth engine is theoretically feasible, it is nevertheless unclear how the expansion of exports would translate to the overall growth of a country. Naghshpour and Sergi empirically consider four alternative models, starting with the Balassa (1985) model. In this model the export variables fail statistical significance. All subsequent models confirm Maizels' hypotheses.

Alina M. Spiru examines the degree of convergence of inflation rates of Central and East European economies. A variety of measures of European norm inflation is assessed using a range of techniques. These include unit root testing based upon panels of data and – an innovation to the pertinent literature – tests of nonlinear convergence. The results suggest that whereas convergence can be revealed in a number of cases, there is some sensitivity associated with the testing framework, in particular whether time series or panel methods are used. Furthermore, the inflation convergence performance of the CEE countries is conditional on the chosen inflation benchmark, the composition of the panel and the correlations among members. Moreover, by conducting a battery of linearity tests, it is found that nonlinear inflation convergence is virtually ubiquitous for the period that includes the accession of the Central and Eastern European former transition economies into the EU.

Marjan Senjur investigates inflation in CEE countries from a different perspective. In his chapter, 'Persistent Differential Inflation Rates in the New Euro Member Countries: The Phillips Curve before and after Adopting the Euro', the inflation process is analysed by exploring the Phillips curve before and after Slovenia joined the Eurozone.

The imposed hypothesis of the article is that the basic macroeconomic model does not reflect changes once a country in question has adopted the euro. This hypothesis springs from the assumption that the inflationary process in a national economy has changed since the euro was adopted. Senjur concludes that empirical evidence is not robust due to the short time periods involved. However, on the basis of analytical considerations it is further argued that the Phillips curve will have to be modified. The mechanism for adjusting to asymmetric shocks has to be changed since exchange rate policy is not available anymore.

The last chapter of this volume is focused on testing the volatility of uncovered interest parity (UIP). Alexandra Horobet, Sorin Dumitrescu, and Dan Gabriel Dumitrescu investigate the relationship between exchange rate changes and interest rate differentials in the UIP framework by taking into account capital market and foreign exchange market volatility. They empirically test the UIP framework on Polish zloty (PLZ), Czech koruna (CZK), Romanian leu (RON), Turkish Lira (NTL), Russian ruble (RUR), Japanese yen (JPY), Swiss franc (SWF) and British pound (GBP). They find that UIP is not validated in times of high volatility, but the direction in the exchange rate change indicated by the interest rate differential follows the UIP framework.

2

The Spread of the Financial Crisis to Central and Eastern Europe: Evidence from the BIS Data

Dubravko Mihaljek

2.1 Introduction

Like other emerging markets, central and eastern European (CEE) economies weathered the financial crisis relatively well for over a year after it had started in major financial centres in August 2007. Growth and capital inflows were generally strong and financial markets for the most part performed well. But, starting in October 2008, the region got increasingly sucked into the global financial and economic maelstrom. As credit markets around the globe became dysfunctional in the aftermath of the collapse of Lehman Brothers, there was heavy and at times indiscriminate selling of emerging market assets, including CEE equities and bonds. There were also widespread expectations of a sudden stop in cross-border bank flows, drawing on the experience from previous emerging market crises. CEE appeared particularly vulnerable because it had financed its long expansion since 2002 to a major extent with foreign bank loans, which over time resulted in large external and internal imbalances in many countries. These vulnerabilities were starkly exposed in a bout of severe financial turmoil in February 2009, when it seemed likely that the CEE region would become another sad case in a long series of emerging market crises.

In the event, although CEE financial markets were hit severely and virtually the whole region (with the exception of Poland) plunged into deep recession, cross-border bank flows were not disrupted as seriously as had been feared. In March 2009 financial markets began to stabilise, and by the end of October 2009 the worst phase of the crisis was over.

This chapter analyses the evolution of capital flows to the region during the critical phase of the global financial and economic crisis, from Q3:2008 to Q3:2009. The international banking statistics of the

Bank for International Settlements (BIS) suggests that credit flows to the region remained fairly stable during this period. Preliminary evidence also suggests that this stability can be at least partly attributed to the high share of foreign bank ownership in the region. Nevertheless, capital flows to CEE are not likely to return to the pre-crisis levels over the medium term. One reason is that international banks are expected to modify their business model as a result of the crisis. Another is that investment and consumption in CEE are not likely to return to the high pre-crisis growth path for some time.

This chapter is organised as follows. Section 2.1 highlights the build-up of vulnerabilities related to large capital inflows in CEE from 2002 to 2007. Section 2.2 describes how the crisis spread through CEE financial markets. Section 2.3 looks in more detail at the pattern of cross-border flows during 2008 and the first half of 2009. Section 2.4 makes a preliminary assessment of some special features of the current crisis. Section 2.5 concludes with a brief discussion of likely changes in the pattern of capital flows to CEE over the medium term.

2.2 Build-up of vulnerabilities

Between 2002 and 2007, the CEE region attracted a staggering amount of $515 billion in net private capital inflows, the second highest amount only to emerging Asia, and far more – that is, 30 per cent of the Emerging Market Economies (EME) total – than the CEE's 11 per cent share in total emerging market output (Figure 2.1). Around 46 per cent of cumulative net inflows consisted of cross-border loans to banks and the non-bank sector ('other investment' in the balance of payments statistics), 47 per cent were foreign direct investments, and 7 per cent net portfolio (equity and bond) investments.

To obtain additional insights into trends in capital flows, the rest of this chapter will focus on *gross* inflows, which are a better measure of financial integration and a more useful source of information for macroeconomic and financial stability analysis than net inflows, which have been traditionally discussed in the literature (see Mihaljek, 2008). In particular, the chapter will focus on external (or 'cross-border') loans of parent banks from western Europe to banks and the non-bank sector in CEE. The main source of the data for these loans is the BIS locational banking statistics, which is consistent with the balance of payments data.[1]

Between 2002 and 2007, the CEE region experienced a genuine deluge of cross-border bank inflows: external loans of BIS reporting

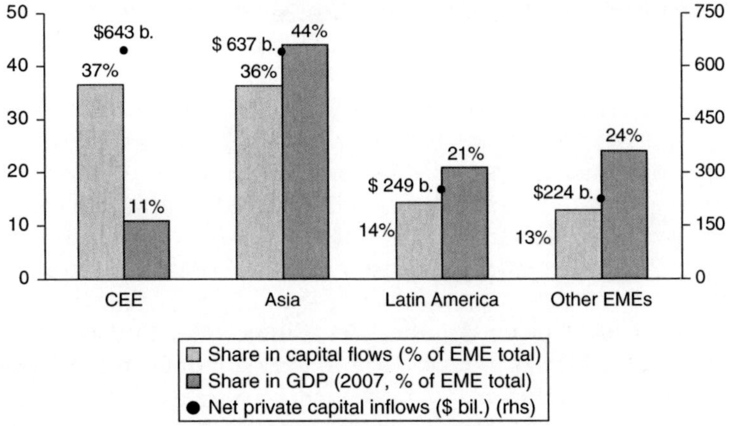

Figure 2.1 Net private capital flows to EMEs (Cumulative net inflows, 2002–7)
Source: IMF, *World Economic Outlook*, October 2009.

Table 2.1 External loans of BIS reporting banks vis-à-vis CEE countries

	Amount outstanding					
	USD billions			**Percent of GDP**		
	1998	**2002**	**2007**	**1998**	**2002**	**2007**
Central and eastern Europe						
Vis-à-vis all sectors	72	90	439	10.1	11.7	22.6
Vis-à-vis banks	33	36	228	4.7	4.7	11.7
Vis-à-vis the non-bank sector	39	54	211	5.5	7.0	10.9

Note: External loans of BIS reporting banks vis-à-vis Albania, Bosnia and Herzegovina, Bulgaria, Croatia, the Czech Republic, Estonia, Hungary, Latvia, Lithuania, Macedonia, Montenegro, Poland, Romania, Serbia, Slovakia, Slovenia and Turkey; end of period; totals for the region as a whole.
Source: BIS locational banking statistics; IMF.

banks to 17 countries in CEE increased roughly five times, from $90 billion to $440 billion as at end-2007 (Table 2.1). These huge inflows went in roughly equal proportions to banks and the non-bank sector in CEE. Relative to regional GDP, external loans vis-à-vis CEE countries doubled between 2002 and 2007, to almost a quarter of the region's GDP in 2007. In comparison, in Latin America gross cross-border bank inflows *decreased* between 2002 and 2007, by 4 per cent of the region's

GDP; while in emerging Asia they increased by just 2 per cent of GDP. The large inflows alone exposed the CEE region to the risk of capital flow reversals.

Based on standard indicators, the Baltic states, countries in south-eastern Europe (SEE) as well as Hungary and Turkey appeared to be particularly vulnerable to a possible reversal in capital inflows on the eve of the crisis in 2007 (Table 2.2). The Baltic and SEE countries had current account deficits from 15 to 17 per cent of GDP on average in 2007, and financed these deficits only partly with foreign direct investment (FDI), usually considered a more stable form of foreign financing than cross-border loans or portfolio inflows. Hungary and Turkey had current account deficits of around 6 per cent of GDP, but compared to the smaller economies they had to raise a much larger amount of funds in international debt and credit markets – a combined total of $66 billion vs $15 billion for the Baltic states and $43 billion for SEE in 2007. The Baltic and SEE countries also had a very high proportion of short-term external debt (up to 135 per cent of foreign exchange reserves in the Baltic states), and cross-border loans accounted for up to 70 per cent of their domestic credit. In addition, Hungary had no net FDI inflows at the time and faced a chronically high fiscal deficit (–5½% of GDP in 2007).

The uses of cross-border credit in CEE countries gave rise to further pronounced vulnerabilities. First, the CEE corporations that borrowed directly from foreign banks were often active in real estate or wholesale and retail trade, that is, non-tradable sectors that for the most part did not generate foreign currency income. Second, the CEE banks that borrowed abroad on-lent a large share of these funds to local households for the purchase of housing and consumer durables. Third, many housing loans – virtually all of them in the Baltic states, Croatia, Hungary, Poland and Romania in 2007–8 – were denominated in foreign currencies, typically euro or Swiss francs, or were linked to local currency exchange rates vis-à-vis major international currencies (including, in some cases, the Japanese yen). As a result, gross external debt rose to 40–50 per cent of total debt outstanding in the Baltic states, Romania and Bulgaria in 2008 (Table 2.3). Net external debt rose to 50 per cent of GDP in Hungary and Latvia in 2008; and almost 40 per cent of GDP in Estonia and Lithuania. As exports of goods and services expanded much more slowly than foreign borrowing, significant currency mismatches developed at the aggregate level and on many private sector balance sheets.

Table 2.2 Selected external vulnerability indicators, 2007

	Current account	Net FDI	Net portfolio investment	Short-term foreign debt[a]	Cross-border loans[a,b]
	Percent of GDP	Percent of current account balance[c]		Percent of forex reserves	Percent of domestic credit
Baltic states[d]	–17.4	31	–10	135	68
South-eastern Europe[e]	–15.0	67	2	108	61
Hungary	–5.6	–3	10	110	58
Turkey	–5.7	52	2	74	23

Note: a. Data as of Q3:2007.
b. Consolidated cross-border claims of BIS reporting banks (ultimate risk basis); in all currencies, excluding local claims in non-local currencies; amounts outstanding.
c. Ratios are taken over the absolute value of the current account balance; negative numbers indicate net outflows.
d. Simple average of Estonia, Latvia and Lithuania.
e. Simple average of Bulgaria, Croatia, Romania and (except for cross-border loans) Serbia.
Source: BIS and IMF

2.3 The crisis spreads

The crisis began in the main financial centres in August 2007, but for over a year it had only a moderate impact on CEE. Since October 2008, however, CEE has become one of the most affected emerging market regions. The crisis has spread in a rapid succession through equity, bond, foreign exchange and interbank markets, leading to a significant tightening of external financing conditions and a large-scale withdrawal of cross-border loans.

The first to feel the full force of the crisis were the equity markets. The slide in equity prices that began in different markets in mid- or late 2007, and continued at a more or less gradual pace through August 2008, turned into a veritable plunge in September and October, when prices fell by 50 per cent on average (Figure 2.2). From November 2008 to mid-February 2009, prices in most markets moved sideways, amid very thin trading volumes. But in mid-February they fell by another 10–15 per cent amid renewed uncertainty about the prospects for the region. By mid-February 2009, CEE equities lost on average 75 per cent from peak values realised in 2007, and were back to the levels from 2004 or earlier.

The next domino that fell was the CEE sovereign eurobond market. After the onset of the crisis, spreads of widely traded central European sovereign bonds moved up gradually, from around 30–45 basis points in August 2007 to 50–100 basis points in September 2008 (Figure 2.3, left-hand panel). In SEE and the Baltics, the spreads had widened by an additional 50–100 basis points over this period, reflecting somewhat

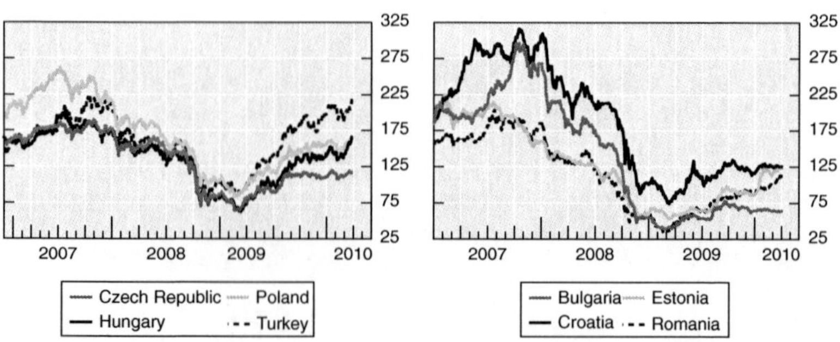

Figure 2.2 Equity prices
Note: January 2005 = 100; in local currency terms.
Source: Datastream.

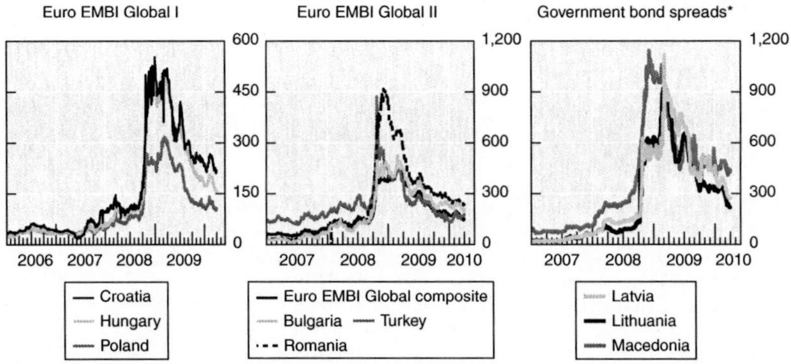

Figure 2.3 Bond spreads for selected countries
Note: Spreads over benchmark euro area bonds, in basis points.
* For Latvia, 5-year bond; for Lithuania, 4-year bond; for Macedonia, 6-year bond.
Source: Datastream; JPMorgan Chase.

greater concerns over external financing (Figure 2.3, centre and right-hand panels). But the worsening of the crisis in September and October 2008 led to an unprecedented widening of sovereign spreads. Countries with larger external imbalances were affected particularly hard: within a couple of weeks their spreads tripled in most cases, reflecting to a considerable degree the escalating problems on the Hungarian forint market. In comparable emerging markets in Asia and Latin America the spreads initially widened by amounts similar to those in CEE countries with high external deficits, but subsequently came down faster and to lower levels than in CEE.

In credit insurance markets, credit default swap (CDS) spreads for sovereign bonds of highly indebted countries such as Croatia, Hungary, Romania and Turkey doubled within days to 400–750 basis points (Figure 2.4). The CDS spreads also rose sharply – albeit to much lower levels – for Slovenia (which has been a Euro Area member since 2007), Slovakia (which was preparing to join the Euro Area in January 2009) and the Czech Republic (which is a net external creditor). This clearly suggested that an element of contagion was present in CEE financial markets at the time.

As with bond spreads, the CDS spreads for comparable sovereigns from emerging Asia and Latin America initially widened by similar amounts, but then quickly narrowed and stayed at lower levels than in CEE (e.g., around 250 basis points in Chile, Malaysia and Thailand;

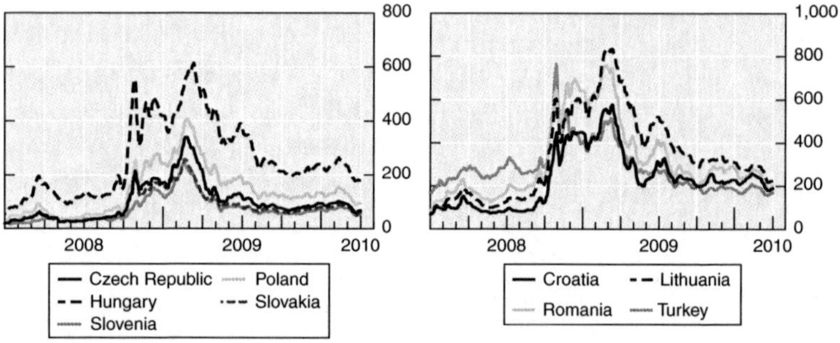

Figure 2.4 CDS spreads
Note: Senior five-year CDS mid spread, in euros. Five-day moving averages; in basis points.
Source: Datastream.

400 points in Brazil and Mexico). This indicates that, since October 2008, investors have become more concerned about creditworthiness of borrowers in the CEE region relative to other emerging markets.

The turmoil in October quickly spread to the foreign exchange markets. After the Lehman collapse there was a big increase in demand for major currencies in both onshore cash markets and short-term credit markets. As several central banks in CEE initially adopted a hands-off policy towards exchange rates, the scale and speed of exchange rate decline came as a shock: the Polish zloty, for instance, depreciated by over 20 per cent against the euro over the fourth quarter of 2008, despite the relatively good performance of the economy (Figure 2.5, left-hand panel). Household and corporate borrowers with large foreign exchange exposures suffered heavy losses as local currencies fell against the dollar, the euro and the Swiss franc. Those with leveraged exposures were forced to raise foreign exchange by selling local currency assets at much-depreciated prices, magnifying the decline in exchange rates and equity prices in very thin markets.

Depreciation pressures also brought to light large non-linear foreign exchange exposures, in particular in Poland, where many companies entered the hedging contracts in mid-2008 to protect their export earnings against the sharp appreciation of the zloty and, in some cases, to speculate on a continuing appreciation. As banks called these options, they triggered a self-reinforcing downward spiral of depreciation – the zloty weakened the more the demand for the euro increased. The Polish authorities estimated the total size of these options at about 15 billion zloty (about 1.2 per cent of GDP), of which about 2.3 billion had to be written off.[2]

The foreign exchange markets in CEE were also affected by the fact that the operation of international currency swap markets became severely impaired. As the lack of foreign currency swaps and contagion from the Icelandic banking crisis hit Hungary in the first weeks of October, the share price of OTP Bank (which was viewed as vulnerable because it is not majority foreign-owned) and foreign demand for forint government securities both collapsed. At government bond auctions in mid-October, for instance, there were no bidders, sending local currency bond spreads close to 600 basis points (Figure 2A.2). As banks were no longer prepared to exchange euros for forints in foreign currency swap markets, the forint depreciated sharply, triggering contagion effects throughout the region (Figure 2.5). This prompted several central banks to step in as counterparties in swap transactions and to lend euros to their banks. The central banks of Hungary and Poland obtained in turn euro refinancing from the European Central Bank (ECB) (against high-quality collateral), and Swiss franc refinancing from the Swiss National Bank (via Swiss franc/euro swap arrangements). The central banks of Denmark and Sweden similarly established a temporary swap facility for Latvia. The Swiss franc swap lines were discontinued in January 2010.

The sale of CEE currencies, growing concerns over external financing gaps, and rating downgrades of some countries in the region added to illiquidity in external funding markets. But liquidity was also drained from the interbank markets, with money market rates occasionally spiking at around 40 per cent in Croatia and Romania.

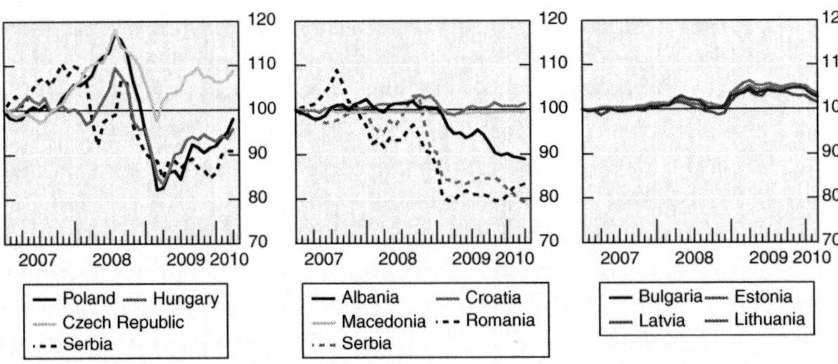

Figure 2.5 Exchange rates

Note: December 2006 = 100; euro per unit of local currency (nominal effective exchange rates for Bulgaria, Estonia, Latvia and Lithuania). An increase indicates an appreciation; monthly averages.

Source: ECB; Datastream; national data; BIS.

The biggest threat to financial stability started, however, in mid-February 2009, when the rating agency Moody's (2009) warned that it might downgrade banks active in CEE because of their heavy exposure to the region. Although the report revealed no new information about the vulnerabilities of parent banks or their subsidiaries, it shook investor confidence. Equity prices plunged by more than 10 per cent on average within a week (Figure 2.2); bond spreads soared to 300 basis points in Poland, close to 500 points in Hungary, and 850 points in Lithuania (Figure 2.3); and currencies again came under pressure (Figure 2.5). These developments gave rise to widespread concerns about the imminent onset of a financial crisis in the region. Together with fears of the impact on their banking systems, these concerns have led Bosnia and Herzegovina, Hungary, Latvia, Serbia, Romania and Ukraine to seek IMF assistance.

As it turned out, the Moody's report and the subsequent reporting in the press contained errors that may have influenced market decisions. In particular, figures on foreign bank lending were misinterpreted by including not only cross-border loans from parent banks to their subsidiaries in CEE, but also loans that the subsidiaries granted on the basis of deposits in domestic and foreign currencies raised from their local customers in CEE. This prompted central banks of the Czech Republic, Hungary, Poland and Romania to coordinate the issuance of press statements informing the markets about the actual state of foreign bank lending in their countries.[3] On 23 February 2009, the rating agency Standard and Poor's issued a report (2009) that introduced somewhat greater differentiation among the countries in the region. Around the same time, the Austrian National Bank clarified several key arguments behind its pan-European initiative launched in late January 2009 (latter dubbed the Vienna Initiative; see EBRD, 2009), which was aimed at helping the CEE countries to avoid a crisis (OeNB, 2009).

In mid-March 2009, financial markets in CEE began to stabilise. However, the pace of the recovery has been much slower than in other emerging market regions. The rebound has been somewhat more pronounced only in Turkey, which seems to have decoupled from CEE and is recovering at a similar pace as the Asian emerging markets. For instance, in Bulgaria, Croatia and the Czech Republic there have been no further gains in equity prices since October 2009 (Figure 2.2). In the sovereign eurobond market, the spreads have narrowed since February 2009 but remain above pre-Lehmann levels (Figure 2.3). Similar developments have been observed in sovereign CDS markets (Figure 2.4) and local currency bond markets (Figure 2A.1). In particular, with the exception of Turkey and Lithuania, the CDS spreads have trended upwards since mid-2009. Likewise, none of the CEE currencies has yet reversed the losses from depreciation against the euro experienced between October 2008 and March 2009 – most remained 10–25 per cent weaker in early 2010 than in September 2008 (Figure 2.5). More recently, the spreads widened in several countries as a result of spillovers from the Greek fiscal crisis (Figures 2.3 and 2.4). In summary, financial markets in CEE have not yet fully recovered from the global financial crisis.

2.4 Impact on capital flows

Most emerging market crises of the 1980s and the 1990s were associated with sudden stops in private capital inflows. The stops typically took place once international investors had lost confidence that governments would follow policies to correct large external and internal imbalances. Although CEE was clearly in a vulnerable position, in the first half of 2008, when credit flows to other emerging markets had already started to contract, the external loans of BIS reporting banks to CEE were equivalent to more than 70 per cent of the total for 2007 (Table 2.3).

But during Q3:2008, as disruptions in international credit markets mutated into a full-scale global financial crisis, major international banks started to reduce their loans to banks in CEE. Countries initially affected were those with more liquid banking systems (as measured, for instance, by the ratio of deposits to loans; see Figure 2A.1), and included Croatia, the Czech Republic and Poland (Table 2A.1). In Q4:2008, international banks further withdrew from the Czech Republic and Poland, and started reducing their exposure to banks in Turkey.

Q4:2008 also saw a widespread reduction in cross-border loans to the non-bank sector in CEE (Table 2A.2). But banks and the non-bank sector in many smaller CEE countries with a large share of foreign bank ownership (including Croatia, Estonia, Lithuania, Romania and Serbia) received additional cross-border loans during this period, indicating that a foreign bank presence provided some stability to cross-border loans.

Total cross-border financing was hit much harder in 2009. Cross-border loans to banks and the non-bank sector in CEE fell by $37 billion over Q1–Q3:2009, compared to an increase of $110 billion over the same period a year before (Table 2.3). Loans to banks accounted for more than 80 per cent of the decrease ($30 billion). Most of the decrease took place in Q1:2009 ($24 billion). In Q2 the decrease was smaller

Table 2.3 Cross border financing of CEE economies[a] (in billions of US dollars)

	2007	2008	2008				2009		
			Q1	Q2	Q3	Q4	Q1	Q2	Q3
Cross border loans[b]	125	107	49	41	20	–4	–24	–5	–8
To banks	70	53	32	18	7	–4	–20	–1	–9
To the non-bank sector	55	53	17	23	13	0	–4	–4	1
International debt securities[c]	21	23	2	15	7	0	5	10	10

Note: a. Includes 17 CEE countries listed in Tables 2A.1 and 2A.2.
b. External loans of BIS reporting banks vis-à-vis individual countries; exchange rate adjusted changes in gross amounts outstanding.
c. Net issuance of all issuers (sovereign and corporate), by nationality of issuer.
Source: BIS, locational banking statistics and international securities statistics.

($5 billion), raising hopes that later in the year cross-border loans would start growing. But Q3 saw a further reduction in loans to the banks (of $9 billion), which offset a small increase in loans to the non-bank sector. This suggests that parent banks may have started restructuring their operations in CEE after the worst impact of the crisis was over.

In contrast to cross-border loans, data on international debt issuance depict a more positive picture. After strong issuance of sovereign and corporate debt securities in Q1–Q3:2008, net bond issuance in CEE stopped in Q4:2008, with only Slovakia and Slovenia issuing larger amounts of new debt, and all other countries repaying maturing debt. In Q1–Q3:2009, however, international bond issuance resumed. Croatia, the Czech Republic, Lithuania, Macedonia, Poland, Slovakia, Slovenia and Turkey made a total of $25 billion in new net placements of sovereign bonds, more than the total annual issuance of the region in 2007 and 2008 (Table 2.3).

Foreign direct investment inflows also held up somewhat better than feared in early 2009. Total net inflows to the region fell by more than half (to about $32 billion); Hungary and Slovenia had zero net FDI inflows; and Estonia and Slovakia experienced net outflows. But in a number of countries net FDI was sufficient to finance the entire current account deficit (Czech Republic, Lithuania, Poland) or a large part of it (Albania, Bulgaria, Croatia, Romania, Turkey). Reports from early 2010 indicate that foreign investors are regaining interest in the region, including through mergers and privatisations (e.g. in Poland and SEE) and the relocation of production facilities to CEE.

Although aggregate figures on cross-border bank flows appear unfavourable, during the critical phase of the crisis, from Q4:2008 to Q2:2009, they decreased less in CEE than in emerging Asia or Latin America. In particular, cross-border bank flows fell during this period by $54 billion in CEE (6.5 per cent of GDP), $52 billion in Latin America (6.7 per cent of GDP), and $203 billion in emerging Asia (12.4 per cent of GDP).

Moreover, as already noted, the decrease was concentrated in a few countries with more liquid banking systems. For instance, in Q1:2009, cross-border loans to banks in the Czech Republic decreased by $2.5 billion and in Slovakia by as much as $9.1 billion (Table 2A.1). This suggests that some parent banks may have temporarily used these markets to maintain liquidity at home or to reallocate funds to other banking systems in the region that were hit harder by the crisis. This seems to be the case in particular with Slovakia, where banks had fairly low loan to deposit ratios and the euro was introduced in January 2009.[4] The same apparently happened with Poland in Q4:2008, when cross-border loans to the Polish banks were reduced by $4.6 billion. However, as Poland was the only EU economy with positive growth in Q1:2009, parent banks increased their positions vis-a-vis Polish banks in Q1:2009. Bilateral data from the BIS locational banking statistics (which are not published) confirm that the largest reductions in cross-border loans to the Czech Republic and Slovakia took place from those western European countries where banks faced major difficulties in maintaining liquidity in Q4:2008 and Q1:2009.

It is also worth noting that cross-border loans to the non-bank sector decreased much less than those to the banks (Table 2.3). Loans to the non-bank sector in Turkey decreased the most, with other larger reductions having been made to the non-bank sector in Bulgaria, Croatia, Romania, Slovakia and Slovenia (Table 2A.2). Elsewhere, international banks mostly maintained their loans at similar or higher levels as in Q4:2008 (especially in Hungary).

2.5 Is this crisis different?

The prevailing view on the nature of financial crises among academics currently seems to be that all crises are essentially the same or, to paraphrase Reinhart and Rogoff (2009), 'this time is *no* different'. Nonetheless, it is worth asking whether some aspects of the current crisis in CEE might be different from the past emerging market crises. At least three developments deserve attention: first, the cases of parent bank financing from subsidiaries; second, the absence of a significant sudden stop of capital inflows for the region as a whole; and, third, the evidence of a stabilising influence of foreign bank ownership on cross-border and domestic credit flows in CEE.

As discussed above, one unusual feature of the crisis in CEE has been the apparent 'reverse flows' from subsidiaries in the region to parent banks in western Europe. More precisely, countries that experienced the sharpest reduction of cross-border bank inflows, such as the Czech Republic, Poland and Slovakia, were in fact those with the strongest fundamentals going into the crisis. And the reason for lower inflows was not the loss of confidence in these countries' policies or banking systems, but, apparently, the need of banks from certain advanced economies to maintain high levels of liquidity at home during the most acute phase of the crisis, or to reallocate the funds to subsidiaries in those CEE countries that were hit harder by the crisis. As banks in the Czech Republic, Poland and Slovakia had sufficient liquid funds at their disposal – partly because of low loan-to-deposit ratios, partly because credit demand had fallen (and, in the case of Slovakia, because these funds were in euros) – parent banks could sharply reduce cross-border loans to such banks or even take loans from them to boost liquidity at headquarters temporarily. This phenomenon was not observed during previous emerging market crises.

On the issue of sudden stops, as indicated in Table 2.4, the cumulative reduction of cross-border bank inflows to CEE during the current crisis was slightly higher, relative to the region's GDP, than during the Russian crisis of 1998, but smaller than during the Turkish crisis, especially when Slovakia is excluded as a special case. One could argue that the current crisis was not yet over and the impact on CEE could eventually be larger, especially considering that the cross-border flows decreased further in Q3:2009. But in view of the significant vulnerabilities in CEE before the crisis and the alarming warnings issued by some analysts (e.g., Sorsa et al., 2007), the relatively small reduction in cross-border inflows does come as a surprise.

On a narrower definition of sudden stops – that is, a reduction greater than two standard deviations of inflows observed over an extended period – there is no evidence that the CEE region as a whole experienced a sudden stop during 2008–9. Even at an individual country level there were only five instances of sudden stops in 2008–9, and the only one exceeding 1 per cent of GDP was the special case of Slovakia discussed above (Table 2.5).

The resilience of cross-border loans raises the question about the factors that may have mitigated some of the pronounced external vulnerabilities noted above and thus helped avoid the sudden stop. One likely factor is the presence of foreign-owned banks, especially in smaller CEE economies. When the BIS data discussed in section 2.3 are disaggregated, it turns out that cross-border loans have indeed been more stable in the smaller economies with a larger foreign bank presence, at least temporarily. In particular, there is a positive correlation between the share of foreign bank ownership and the ratio of cross-border loans to domestic private sector credit: a 10 percentage point higher share of foreign banks is associated with a 1.7 percentage point *increase* in the ratio of cross-border loans to domestic credit during the period Q3:2008–Q3:2009 (Figure 2.6).[5]

For instance, banks and the non-bank sector in SEE, where banking systems are almost fully foreign-owned, were significantly less affected by the decline in cross-border loans (Figure 2.6 and Tables 2A.1 and 2A.2). This is surprising because they had some of the largest

Table 2.4 Cross-border banking flows during recent emerging market crises

Period	Crisis	Cumulative reduction of inflows		Average reduction / qtr.
		USD billion	Per cent of GDP	
Emerging Asia				
1997:Q31999:Q4	Asian crisis	–167	–6.4	–0.6
2000:Q22001:Q1	Bursting of dot-com bubble	–35	–1.2	–0.3
2008:Q32009:Q2	Global crisis	–191	–2.4	–0.6
Latin America				
1998:Q31999:Q3	Contagion from Russian crisis	44	–2.4	–0.5
2001:Q32002:Q4	Argentine crisis	23	–1.4	–0.2
2008:Q32009:Q2	Global crisis	–27	–0.7	–0.2
CEE				
1998:Q4	Russian crisis	–1	–0.1	–0.1
2001:Q1-Q4	Turkish crisis	–8	–1.2	–0.3
2008:Q32009:Q2	Global crisis	–12	–0.6	–0.2
	Excluding Slovakia	–4	–0.2	–0.1

Source: BIS, locational banking statistics; IMF, WEO, October 2009, author's calculations.

Table 2.5 Sudden stops in cross-border bank flows, 2008–9

Country	Quarter	Size of sudden stop	
		USD billion	Per cent of GDP
Estonia	Q1:2009	–0.2	–0.8
Latvia	Q1:2009	–0.2	–0.5
Turkey	Q4:2008	–1.0	–0.1
Slovakia	Q1:2009	–6.4	–7.2
Slovenia	Q2:2009	–0.5	–0.9

Note: A sudden stop is defined as a decrease greater than two standard deviations of quarterly changes (exchange rate adjusted) in cross-border bank flows during the period Q1:1996–Q3:2009. Dollar amounts indicate the size of this 'excess' decrease in cross-border bank flows in a given quarter; GDP ratios are in terms of annual GDP.
Source: BIS, locational banking statistics; IMF, WEO, October 2009, author's calculations.

current account deficits and other external vulnerabilities in the region (Table 2.2). It is also surprising because, as discussed above, in February and March 2009 it became clear that the state of these economies was deteriorating much faster than had previously been expected. Although some of these countries (e.g., Estonia, Latvia, Romania and Serbia) did experience sharply lower cross-border inflows to banks in Q1:2009, this trend reversed in Q2–Q3:2009 (Table 2A.1).

Further evidence of potentially stabilising effects of foreign bank ownership is provided by the data on local currency loans made by foreign bank affiliates in CEE. These 'local-in-local' loans are of particular importance for financial stability because their funding base is expected to be more stable than the funding base of cross-border loans or foreign currency loans given by domestic banks in CEE. After expanding strongly for several years, the local currency loans of foreign bank affiliates slowed in Q4:2008 and Q1:2009. The decline probably reflected both weaker credit demand (as households and firms borrowed less, anticipating the spread of the crisis) and tighter credit supply, especially in countries hit by the crisis (e.g. the Baltic states), or those that had been experiencing very fast credit growth before the crisis (e.g. Romania and Serbia). However, as early as Q2:2009, foreign bank affiliates resumed local currency lending to CEE residents. With the exception of Hungary and Romania, this trend continued in Q3:2009.

One should also note that, after adjusting for exchange rate changes, the decline in local currency loans, with few exceptions, was relatively small, that is, up to 3 per cent of domestic private sector credit; whereas in many countries such loans *increased* by 3–4 per cent of domestic

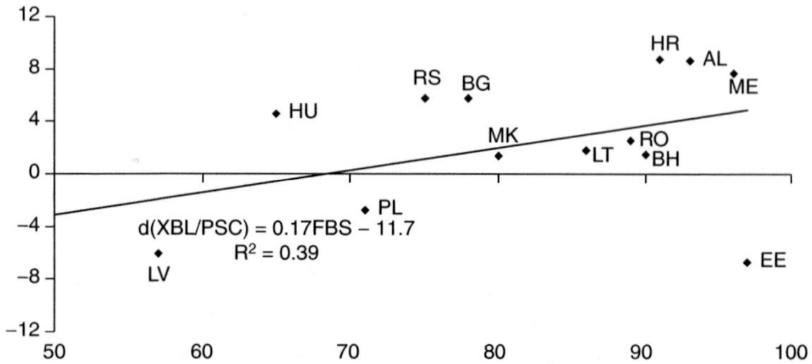

Figure 2.6 Cross-border loans and foreign bank ownership
Note: Horizontal axis: share of foreign-owned banks in total assets of the banking system in 2008, in percent. Vertical axis: change in cross-border loans from Q3:2008 through Q3:2009 (exchange-rate adjusted changes), as a share of domestic private sector credit, in percentage points.
Sources: IMF, BIS, author's calculations.

private sector credit or even higher during the period Q3:2008–Q3:2009 (Figure 2.7).[6] This indicates that, at least until Q3:2009, western European parent banks did not abandon their highly profitable subsidiaries in CEE, whose operations are generally seen as 'core' activities. Western European parent banks have also demonstrated this commitment over the past year through financial support in the form of subordinated debt and capital injections. Together with the maintenance of credit lines, these measures underline how closely the reputation of the parent banks has become aligned with that of its subsidiaries. Again, this pattern of behaviour on the part of international banks was not observed in previous emerging market crises.

Some aspects of the current crisis nevertheless have an air of déjà vu about them. As already noted, countries that have been more affected were the 'usual suspects' with pronounced external vulnerabilities (Table 2.2) and/or fiscal sustainability problems. It is interesting to note that the local bond markets – whose development was seen as a key to strengthening the resilience of emerging market financial systems after the Asian crisis – did not entirely help mitigate the crisis. Local currency bond markets were seriously disrupted by the crisis, with yields rising sharply in periods of distress, such as October 2008 and February–March 2009, when many foreign investors fled the market (Figure 2A.2). Moreover, unsuccessful domestic bond auctions were often key events that triggered the turmoil (e.g. in Hungary and

Latvia). But some insulation from more developed local bond markets was nonetheless provided: international bond markets were even more volatile (Figure 2.3). Moreover, those countries, such as Slovakia and Turkey, that reduced their exposure to international debt (both in absolute terms and relative to domestic debt markets) generally fared better in the crisis.

In summary, it would be premature to conclude that capital flows to CEE countries have become more stable because of the greater presence of foreign-owned banks and the alignment of CEE institutions, laws and governance practices with those of the EU. The old-fashioned external and domestic financial vulnerabilities still carry considerable weight – the crisis facing Greece in early 2010 is the most vivid example. Nevertheless, there seems to be some evidence supporting the view that the traditional sudden stops were not the main feature of the current crisis in CEE. How far this can be attributed to foreign bank ownership is an interesting subject for future research.

2.6 Looking ahead

As the dust raised by the financial turmoil in CEE is slowly settling, rough contours of some future changes in the pattern of capital flows to the region have started to emerge. This section takes a preliminary look at the two most important types of capital flow – international bank loans and foreign direct investment.

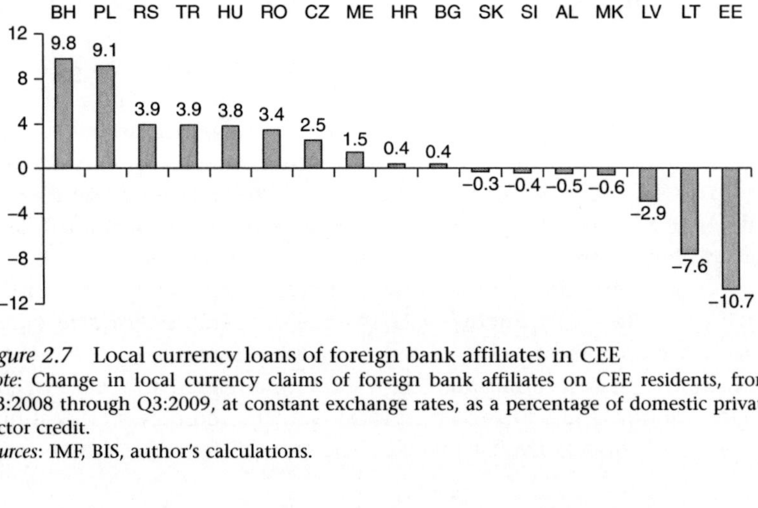

Figure 2.7 Local currency loans of foreign bank affiliates in CEE
Note: Change in local currency claims of foreign bank affiliates on CEE residents, from Q3:2008 through Q3:2009, at constant exchange rates, as a percentage of domestic private sector credit.
Sources: IMF, BIS, author's calculations.

Over the past decade, western European banks have greatly expanded their operations in CEE, with their market shares now ranging from 65 per cent to 98 per cent of total banking sector assets in individual countries. In the process, they have built up large exposures towards the region, ranging from 10 per cent to 25 per cent of GDP in Belgium, Greece, Italy, the Netherlands, Sweden and Switzerland, and up to 70 per cent in Austria at the end of 2007 (Table 2.6). In contrast to other emerging market regions, currency mismatches in CEE have increased. In addition, some foreign banks have relied heavily on international wholesale markets to finance their lending in CEE, so the proportion of aggregate debt denominated in foreign currency has risen to unusually high levels in many CEE countries. The combination of these factors can lead to considerable risks for both banks and host countries, and suggests that international banks are likely to adjust their funding strategies and liquidity management as a result of the crisis.

On the funding side, it is unclear at this stage whether the distinct adjustment patterns for the different components of foreign banks' claims on emerging markets – more subdued cross-border loans, on the one hand, and maintenance of local currency positions on the other – reflect a long-term change in international banks' business and funding strategies. Shifts in the patterns of bank lending and funding since the start of the crisis have led to a welcome decline in loan-to-deposit ratios. However, in the majority of CEE countries these ratios remain well above 1 – in the Baltic states they ranged from 1.9 to 2.8 in 2009. The reduction in loan-to-deposit ratios to safer levels prevailing in countries such as the Czech Republic and Turkey is not likely to take place over the medium term, given the structural deficit of saving over investment in most CEE countries.

On the other hand, it is also clear that international banks and their subsidiaries in CEE cannot go back to the 'business as usual' of financing rapid credit expansion in CEE, often in foreign currencies, with funds borrowed in international wholesale markets, or with 'excess' savings from western European home markets. Both of these sources have become much harder to tap since the crisis, and are not likely to spring back to previous flows any time soon. This raises the question as to how international banks might rebalance their operations in the region and how this might affect macroeconomic developments and financial stability.

Assuming that international banks decide to rely more extensively on local funding in CEE, and that local regulators impose tighter limits on maturity and currency mismatches, the self-funding strategies of

Table 2.6 Exposure of BIS reporting banks to CEE (as a percentage of GDP)

	2002	2007	Q3 2008	Q4 2008
Austria	6.8	71.6	66.8	64.3
Belgium	12.9	24.8	27.0	27.0
France	1.3	5.8	5.4	5.0
Greece	—	19.6	17.0	16.4
Germany	4.2	6.5	6.0	5.6
Italy	3.2	9.4	9.5	8.6
Netherlands	4.8	11.8	14.1	12.2
Sweden	3.1	20.6	22.0	21.6
Switzerland	2.7	13.3	11.9	10.0

Note: Consolidated foreign claims vis-à-vis developing Europe, on an immediate borrower basis.
Source: BIS; IMF.

subsidiaries will most probably take place via retail deposits. Greater access of subsidiaries to the wholesale funding obtained on the basis of their own credit ratings is hard to envisage at this stage. There are already some indications that competition for retail deposits in domestic markets has become more aggressive as a result. While this will raise funding costs, it will also make CEE banks less exposed to funding liquidity shocks when cross-border funding markets do not function normally. Greater reliance on domestic funding might also encourage more prudent lending by subsidiaries. On the other hand, as credit conditions become driven to a greater extent by the cost of local funding, gains from the free movement of capital across borders and the diversification advantage of those banks that rely on cross-border business activity would become eroded to some extent.

More importantly, fewer funds would be available to finance local credit expansion, given the structural imbalance between saving and investment in the region. In the run-up to the crisis, the key issue that preoccupied analysts and policymakers was whether credit supply in CEE had been 'excessive'. At present, the key concern seems to be that the ongoing slowdown, which is widely seen as having both demand and supply elements, could eventually turn into a credit crunch that would hurt the chances of a sustainable recovery. To illustrate this point, domestic bank credit to the private sector decreased in 16 CEE countries (excluding Poland) by a total of €12 billion in 2009 (1.8% of total loans outstanding), and external credit by a further €13 billion (1.9% of the total) (Table 2A.3).[7] If total credit supply decreased by almost 4 per cent on the back of huge efforts by the authorities, parent banks and international financial institutions to sustain credit flows during the crisis, one may wonder by how much it would have decreased without such support.

In summary, the activities of international banks in CEE are all likely to remain subdued in the next few years, while banks restructure their balance sheets and identify profitable new business opportunities. However, the long-term potential of the CEE banking industry remains for the most part untapped (UniCredit Group, 2009). Economic convergence in the region will continue, and the gap in terms of banking penetration will still hold for many years to come.

Appendix

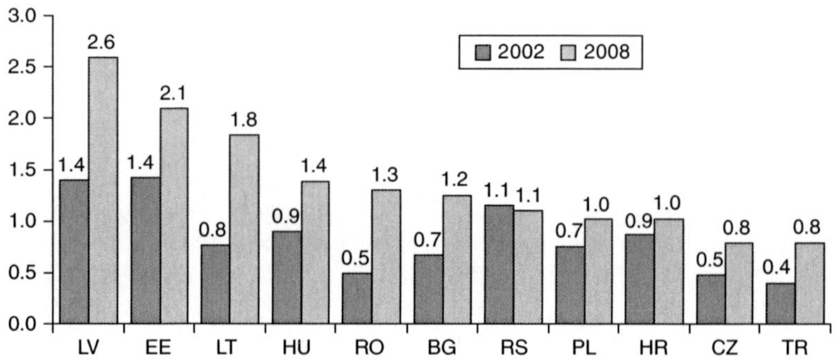

Figure 2A.1 Ratio of total loans to total deposits
Note: Private sector loans divided by total deposits in the domestic banking system (short- and long-term); end of period (for 2008, mostly August).
Source: IMF, International Financial Statistics.

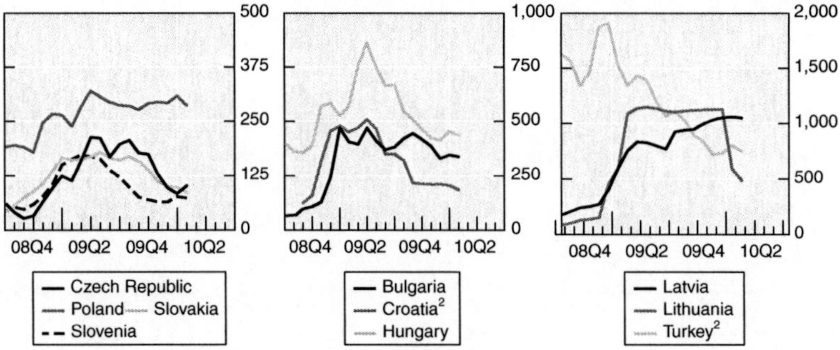

Figure 2A.2 Domestic currency bond spreads

Note: Spreads on domestic currency government bonds over 10-year German benchmark bonds, in basis points.

* For Croatia and Turkey, spread on 5-year domestic currency government bond over 5-year German federal public bond, in basis points.

Source: Bloomberg; Datastream, ECB.

Table 2A.1 Change in external loans vis-à-vis the *banks* in CEE (Estimated exchange rate adjusted changes)

	In millions of USD					As a percentage of GDP		
	2008		2009			2007	2008	2009*
	Q3	Q4	Q1	Q2	Q3			
Czech Republic	–1,672	–2,243	–2,507	107	–526	3.0	–0.2	–1.5
Hungary	–36	3,932	1,143	–2,384	–2,916	3.8	6.3	–3.3
Poland	–2,480	–4,460	–571	1784	–101	4.6	2.2	0.3
Slovakia	–421	975	–9,146	–513	1,961	6.5	3.3	–8.7
Slovenia	–943	–215	–1,147	–1,833	–613	10.1	2.7	–7.3
Estonia	11	494	–853	–400	–155	18.6	7.6	–7.8
Latvia	963	23	–1,587	–666	–363	16.5	8.2	–10.8
Lithuania	1,722	558	–213	27	–178	11.4	7.0	–1.0
Bulgaria	1,892	–100	–201	–574	–992	5.4	10.4	–3.9
Croatia	–1,855	1,883	541	674	821	–1.5	0.8	3.3
Romania	1,968	858	–2,484	–636	–100	7.5	4.4	–2.0
Turkey	8,301	–6,587	–2,711	2,844	–6,098	0.5	0.6	–1.0
Albania	–20	18	–21	–14	15	1.4	–1.2	–0.2
Bosnia-Herzegovina	–182	215	41	–102	–117	4.0	2.3	–1.0
Macedonia	–7	–36	3	8	12	0.4	–0.6	0.3
Serbia	109	434	–297	290	698	–2.9	1.0	1.6
Montenegro	95	32	–5	–20	–39	12.3	6.2	–1.4

Note: External loans of BIS reporting banks.
* Data up to 2009:Q3
Source: BIS, locational banking statistics.

Table 2A.2 Change in external loans vis-à-vis the *non-banks* in CEE (Estimated exchange rate adjusted changes)

	In millions of USD					**As a percentage of GDP**		
	2008		**2009**			**2007**	**2008**	**2009***
	Q3	**Q4**	**Q1**	**Q2**	**Q3**			
Czech Republic	–928	667	231	515	–631	1.3	1.0	0.1
Hungary	3,191	–1,213	343	1,106	1,454	4.1	6.2	2.3
Poland	1,989	–1,937	–349	–271	441	1.1	0.9	–0.0
Slovakia	1,473	–92	–585	237	–93	2.6	2.4	–0.5
Slovenia	79	985	166	–244	–344	4.6	3.5	–0.9
Estonia	–104	29	–169	6	–269	1.4	–0.0	–2.4
Latvia	–111	194	71	23	–236	7.8	1.3	–0.6
Lithuania	–111	–76	–372	–491	–251	3.1	2.4	–3.1
Bulgaria	552	789	–85	491	233	3.9	7.1	1.4
Croatia	768	1,085	–383	156	56	8.8	6.2	–0.3
Romania	1,835	1,831	1,164	–1,160	–1,066	3.4	3.9	–0.7
Turkey	3,558	–2,236	–3,983	–3,820	1,340	3.0	1.8	–1.1
Albania	47	280	–134	122	109	–0.2	4.1	0.8
Bosnia-Herzegovina	43	–1	295	–65	–1	1.8	1.3	1.4
Macedonia	42	41	–28	11	9	1.1	1.6	–0.1
Serbia	676	–240	–132	–171	–287	6.0	1.3	–1.4
Montenegro	39	25	9	11	139	4.9	5.1	3.6

Note: External loans of BIS reporting banks.
* Data up to 2009:Q3
Source: BIS, locational banking statistics.

Table 2A.3 Domestic and cross-border bank credit to the private sector, 2009 (in billions of euros)

	Domestic bank credit				Cross-border loans	
	Corporations		Households		Vis-à-vis the non-bank sector	
	2008	2009	2008	2009	2008	2009
Czech Republic	40.2	38.1	30.1	33.9	12.3	11.9
Hungary	40.1	36.7	27.4	27.4	19.3	20.4
Poland*	68.9	72.9	88.4	100.1	21.8	20.8
Slovakia	17.6	18.8	12.5	13.9	5.6	5.1
Slovenia	24.0	24.5	7.8	8.3	8.4	7.9
Estonia	7.9	7.7	7.7	7.5	2.1	1.8
Latvia	11.7	11.3	9.0	8.6	3.0	2.8
Lithuania	11.6	10.6	8.7	8.4	3.4	2.4
Bulgaria	16.1	15.9	9.3	9.8	7.4	7.6
Croatia	12.9	13.4	17.2	16.9	16.1	15.4
Romania	24.6	23.5	24.7	23.6	18.2	16.9
Turkey	90.9	90.0	53.2	57.7	67.2	57.7
Albania	2.0	1.9	1.1	1.1	0.4	0.5
Bosnia-Herzegovina	—	—	—	—	0.8	1.0
Macedonia	—	—	1.1	1.2	0.3	0.3
Total	368.5	365.3	298.2	318.4	186.3	172.5

Note: Amounts outstanding at end-period (or latest available for 2009).
External loans of BIS reporting banks (on locational basis).
* Corporate sector includes loans to financial institutions.
Source: IMF; BIS.

Notes

The author is Senior Economist, Bank for International Settlements (BIS), Basel (e-mail: dubravko.mihaljek@bis.org). The views expressed in this chapter are those of the author and do not necessarily represent those of the BIS. Earlier versions of this chapter were presented at the conference '20 Years of Transition in CEE: Money, Banking and Financial Markets' (London Metropolitan University, September 2009); the ECB Economic conference on emerging Europe (Frankfurt, October 2009); and seminars at the Federal Reserve Board, the IMF and the EBRD. Helpful comments from participants at these presentations are gratefully acknowledged. The author thanks Agne Subelyte for expert research assistance.

1. The Bank for International Settlements (BIS) collects and disseminates data on international banking transactions since 1964. The reports on transactions are submitted quarterly by banks from 41 advanced economies and cover over 90 per cent of total international banking transactions (see www.bis.org/statistics).
2. The authorities were at one point seeking ways to relieve the companies from these losses, arguing that the banks that sold the contracts did not fully explain the potential risks to their clients.
3. See, for example, http://www.cnb.cz/en/public/media_service/press_releases_cnb/2009/090224_statement_FT.html.
4. Some of the decrease in cross-border loans to banks in Slovakia in Q1:2009 may also reflect bank accounting and risk management changes associated with introduction of the euro to the country in January 2009.
5. During the critical phase of the crisis, from Q4:2008 to Q2:2009, the slope coefficient of the regression in Figure 2.6 is 0.14; the R^2 is 0.42
6. The exchange rate adjustment is necessary because parent banks report the value of local currency loans in US dollars, so these amounts have to be converted back to local currency values.
7. Poland was excluded from this calculation because data on corporate loans in Table 2A.3 include domestic credit to financial institutions.

References

European Bank for Reconstruction and Development (2009) *Transition Report 2009: Transition in Crisis?* London: EBRD.

Mihaljek, Dubravko (2008) 'The Financial Stability Implications of Increased Capital Flows for Emerging Market Economies', BIS Papers, No. 44, December 2008, pp. 11–44. www.bis.org.

Oesterreichische Nationalbank (OeNB) (2009a) Financial Stability Report No. 18, December. www.oenb.at.

Reinhart, Carmen and Rogoff, Kenneth (2009) *This Time is Different: Eight Centuries of Financial Folly*. Princeton: Princeton University Press.

Sorsa, Piritta, Bas Bakker, Christoph Duenwald, Andrea Maechler and Andrew Tiffin (2007) 'Vulnerabilities in Emerging Southeastern Europe: How Much Cause for Concern?' IMF Working Paper No. 07/236, October. www.imf.org.

UniCredit Group (2009) *Central and Eastern Europe Banking Outlook*. Vienna: UniCredit Bank Austria, November. www.bankaustria.at.

3

Are Product Market Structures Affected by Banking Concentration: Evidence from Transition Countries

Fabrizio Coricelli and Mojca Marc

3.1 Introduction

There is growing empirical literature on the relationship between concentration in product markets and concentration in the banking sector. Cetorelli (2001, 2004) and Cetorelli and Strahan (2006) found that countries or regions with more concentrated banking sectors tend also to have more concentrated product markets, thus suggesting that the causality goes from concentration in the banking sector to concentration in product markets. These results emphasise the negative effect of banking concentration on competition in product markets and hence on efficiency and even economic growth. Similarly, Pagano (1993) provides a theoretical model and empirical evidence of an adverse effect of banking market concentration on economic growth. However, such results do not appear robust, either at the theoretical level or at the empirical level. For instance, Petersen and Rajan (1995) build a theoretical model in which banks with market power are more willing to finance young firms. They also find empirical support for such an effect. Furthermore, Hellman and DaRin (2002) propose a theory and empirical evidence showing that more concentrated banking sectors promote the development of new sectors and thus act as catalysts for industrialisation. In this paper we investigate whether the differences in the results obtained in the literature may result from the focus on different country groupings and different periods of time. Specifically, we analyse whether the effects of bank concentration on product market concentration may depend on the different stages of development of countries. Indeed, bank concentration may have different effects on product market concentration depending on the level of development of financial markets because the latter is among the determinants of market structure and competition in the banking sector. Analysing a large set of European countries, we explicitly address the potential heterogeneity of effects of bank concentration. We focus on two country groups, contrasting old members of the European Union (EU) with so-called transition countries, many of them new members of the EU. The effect of bank concentration on product markets has powerful implications for banking regulation policy, especially regarding the number of banks allowed to operate in a particular territory, competition policy and the allowed mergers and acquisitions in banking markets. These effects should be taken into account also when considering the trade-off between financial stability and competition in banking markets.

In this chapter we verify the hypothesis of the differential effects of bank concentration on product market concentration depending on the level of development of countries. We focus on a set of European countries, which includes countries at significantly different stages of development. As in Cetorelli (2004), we focus on sectoral data and use the difference-in-difference approach of Rajan and Zingales (1998) to control for the difference in the financing needs of the sectors. Indeed, if market structure in the banking sector has an effect on industrial sectors, this effect should be stronger for sectors that have larger external financing needs.

The chapter is organised as follows. Section 3.2 illustrates the methodology and the econometric specification. Section 3.3 describes the data set used in the analysis. Section 3.4 contains the results of the empirical analysis. Section 3.5 contains some concluding remarks and discusses possible extensions of the analysis carried out in the chapter.

3.2 Methodology and econometric model

We use panel data to estimate empirically the sign and magnitude of the relationship between banking and product market structures. The econometric model is identified by exploiting sectoral differences, as in Cetorelli (2004), who in turn follows the seminal work by Rajan and Zingales (1998). The idea is that if banking market concentration has an effect on product market concentration, this effect should be larger for industrial sectors that are more dependent on external financing. Owing to the lack of proper data, concentration in product markets is proxied by average firm size. Larger average firm size indicates more concentrated industries and smaller average firm size indicates less concentrated industries. Banking market concentration is measured yearly for each country and an interaction term with external financial dependency of sectors is used to identify its effect.

Using the within (fixed effects) approach to estimate the econometric model, we control for time-, country- and sector-invariable characteristics that could produce biased estimates when OLS is used. Sectoral characteristics that might affect the average firm size are linked to technology and in particular to economies of scale. Typical country fixed effects might be related to country size, trade openness, tax regulation, conditions for the establishment of firms, and economic policies targeting small and medium companies. Time fixed effects capture general economic conditions that are invariant across industries. We include a group of developed (advanced) European countries as a control group to estimate the differences in the relationship between both market concentrations. We use dummies for both groups of countries and interact them with banking concentration terms. Dummy variable *TR* equals 1 for transition countries and 0 otherwise, whereas dummy variable *EU* equals 1 for advanced European countries.[1] Our econometric model is thus the following:

$$\begin{aligned} Average\ firm\ size_{ijt} = {} & \delta_{1jt} Dummy_{jt} + \delta_{2i} Dummy_i + \beta_{ijt} ShareVA_{ijt} + \\ & + \alpha_{1ijt} BankConc_{jt} \times EDI_i \times TR + \\ & + \alpha_{2ijt} BankConc_{jt} \times EDI_i \times EU + \varepsilon_{ijt} \end{aligned} \qquad (1)$$

Average firm size$_{ijt}$ is measured as the natural logarithm of the value added per firm in sector *i*, country *j* and year *t*. Firm size is measured in value-added terms in the benchmark model, but other specifications, using total revenues and employment, are also tested. $Dummy_{jt}$ is the country-time specific fixed effect, $Dummy_i$ is the sector specific fixed effect, and ε_{ijt} is the error term. $ShareVA_{ijt}$ represents the share of manufacturing sector *i* in total manufacturing value added. This variable controls for factors that influence the market structure of a particular sector in a particular country. Industry's life cycle theory predicts that a sector which has grown substantially should experience less new firm entry. A larger sector should therefore have larger average firm size and the coefficient β should be positive.

$BankConc_{jt} \times EDI_i$ is the interaction term between banking concentration for country *j* in year *t* and an indicator of external financial dependency for sector *i* (EDI_i). Banking concentration is alternatively measured by concentration ratios and Herfindahl's index (*HHI*). External financial dependency is measured as the fraction of capital expenditures not financed with cash flows from operations for mature US listed companies and it is taken from Cetorelli (2001), who in turn takes it from Rajan and Zingales (1998). The indicator *EDI* is equal to 1 for sectors that have an above-median level of dependency and equal to 0 for sectors with a below-median level of dependency. It is interacted with banking concentration and the coefficient on this interaction term (α) was found to be significantly positive and very robust in Cetorelli (2001, 2004) and Cetorelli and Strahan (2006).

A positive coefficient α implies that we should expect more concentrated product markets (i.e. larger average firm size in industries where mature firms are still in need of external finance) in countries with more concentrated banking markets. If the effect of banking concentration is negative (coefficient α negative), we should observe less concentrated product markets (i.e. smaller average firm size in industries where mature firms need external financing) in countries with more concentrated banking markets. Coefficients for the two groups of countries (α_1 and α_2) will show us whether banking concentration effect depends on the level of financial development.

3.3 Data description

We use EUROSTAT's industry level data over the period 1995–2004 for industry sectors for 26 European countries, 10 transition[2] and 16 advanced.[3] Industrial data include manufacturing sectors at 4-digit NACE Rev 1.1 level. EUROSTAT's data classified by NACE code were matched with ISIC 2 code to allow the use of data on the external financial dependency of industrial sectors. This procedure produced data for 34 manufacturing sectors.[4] EUROSTAT's database also provides information about the number of firms in individual sectors, which was used to calculate average firm size.

As a check, we construct a dataset from UNIDO's Industrial Statistics Database 2006, where we have data for 31 countries and 36 manufacturing sectors from 1987 to 2003.[5] Besides all the countries from our benchmark EUROSTAT dataset, we include in this dataset five additional transition countries for which data were available.[6] UNIDO's database provides information only about the number of establishments[7] in individual sectors and not about the number of firms, as EUROSTAT's database does. Since companies can have more establishments, there is some measurement error in the dependent variable when using these data. Cetorelli (2001) and Black and Strahan (2002) document a strong correlation between the number of establishments and the number of firms, and between the rate of creation of new businesses and the share of new establishments, respectively.

Data for banking markets concentration ratios are taken from BANKSCOPE September 2006 and October 2007 CDs; they range from 1997 to 2006.[8] Concentration ratios *CR3* and *CR5* are calculated as the share of the three or five largest banks' total assets. Herfindahl's index (*HHI*) is calculated as:

$$HHI = \sum_{t=1}^{n}\left(\frac{TA_i}{TA}\right)^2 \tag{2}$$

where:

n is the number of commercial, savings and cooperative banks in the country,

TA_i is total assets by individual bank i, and TA is the sum of n individual banks' total assets.

Savings and cooperative banks are included in the concentration measures because in several countries some of the top three (or five) largest banks are categorised in BANKSCOPE as savings and cooperative banks. In addition we use concentration ratios (*CR3*) from Cetorelli (2004),[9] who in turn uses data from Demirgüç-Kunt and Levine (2004), for the period between 1990 and 1997. The measure of external financial dependence is taken from Rajan and Zingales (1998). They observe that technological differences between industrial sectors generate different a need for external funds. Their external financial dependence measures the average share of capital expenditure that is not financed by cash from operations, for mature listed companies[10] in the US in the period 1980–90. Rajan and Zingales measure the need for external funds for US manufacturing sectors because the demand, rather than the supply, of funds is of interest and therefore it had to be estimated in a country with a well-developed financial market and small financial constraints.

We use the following institutional variables to control for general economic and financial markets' conditions: domestic credit provided by banking sector, domestic credit to private sector, market capitalisation of listed companies, gross domestic product per capita, and loans to non-banks provided by foreign banks. The data source for the last of these is Joint BIS-IMF-OECD-WB External Debt Hub (on www.jedh.org), whereas data for other variables come from the World Development Indicators database (World Bank). Table 3A.1 provides a summary of statistics for main variables whereas Table 3A.3 and Table 3A.4 provide data describing the pattern of industry structure and banking concentration both across countries and across sectors.

The dependent variable (*LNVA*) in the benchmark model is the logarithm of value added per enterprise. There are 6485 observations for this variable for 26 countries and 10 years (1995–2004). Average firm size is measured alternatively by average turnover and number of employees. Both variables are provided by EUROSTAT's database. Value added and turnover are deflated and converted into US dollars. When the UNIDO dataset is used, the dependent variable (*LNVAU*) is the logarithm of value added per establishment. In this case, we have 7495 observations for 31 countries and 17 years (1987–2003). Standard *t*-tests for mean equality show that the difference in means of average firm size in the two datasets is statistically insignificant.

On average, between 1987 and 2004, Estonia had the most concentrated banking market of all the countries included in the analysis. The average *CR3* and *CR5* were 98 per cent and 99 per cent, respectively. The least concentrated country in the same period was Luxembourg with an average *CR3* around 31 per cent of the market. The scatter plot of average concentration ratio *CR3* against average firm size for the EUROSTAT dataset shows Bulgaria having an extremely low average firm size and Estonia having an extremely high average banking concentration, indicating that these countries could be potential outliers. A possible additional outlier is also Slovakia with its extremely high average firm size for transition countries. *T*-tests for equality of means show that transition countries had on average more concentrated banking markets, regardless of the concentration measure used. In the UNIDO dataset there is a cluster of countries with a lower average firm size: Bulgaria, Romania, Croatia and Mongolia.

There is a small negative correlation (statistically significant at 1 per cent) between average firm size and every one of the three concentration measures in the EUROSTAT dataset (Table 3A.5). This suggests that on average countries with more concentrated banking markets have smaller firms. However, pairwise correlation coefficients for the UNIDO dataset show a positive, statistically significant correlation for *CR3* and a slightly stronger, negative, statistically significant correlation for *CR5* and *HHI* (Table 3A.6). This is a consequence of the fact that we have more observations for *CR3* than for the other two concentration measures. The additional *CR3* observations are for the period 1990–7 (taken from Cetorelli). Since the correlation between *CR3* and average firm size from the UNIDO dataset is negative and statistically significant for the period 1999–2004,[11] we can say that the positive overall correlation comes exclusively from the previous period, which is 1990–8.

The external financial dependency measure, taken from Rajan and Zingales (1998), is presented in Table 3A.2. The sector with mature companies least dependent on external finance is 323 (leather industry) and the one with the most dependent mature companies is 3832 (radio, TV and communication equipment). A scatter plot of external financial dependency against average firm size per sector shows there are three candidates for outliers: sectors 323, 324 (footwear), and 314 (tobacco) in both EUROSTAT and UNIDO datasets. All three sectors have extremely low external dependence with respect to their average firm size. Since we use an indicator variable for external dependency, these outliers do not affect our results. The median value of external financial dependency was 0.0812; the sectors that have larger values are classified as highly dependent on external funds and are indicated in Table 3A.2.

The control variable *SHVA* represents the fraction of value added in total manufacturing for individual sectors. There are 7116 observations for this variable. The control variable that measures the same in the UNIDO data set is called *SHVAU*. The mean of the fraction in the UNIDO dataset is statistically significantly higher than the mean in the EUROSTAT dataset; on average it is one percentage point higher in the UNIDO dataset. Pairwise correlation shows there is no statistically significant correlation between the fraction of value added in total manufacturing and concentration ratios, except for the case when *CR3* and the UNIDO dataset are used; there is a very small, but statistically significant negative correlation. This implies that our explanation variables can be considered as independent.

The variable *OECD* is a dummy variable equal to 1 for countries that are OECD members from the year they became members.

Additional control variables are included in the robustness check section. *T*-tests for mean equality formally confirm that advanced countries have more developed financial markets and economies. Pairwise correlation coefficients verify a moderate and statistically significant positive correlation between average firm size and all these institutional variables, which implies that more developed economies have on average larger firms.

Domestic credit (*Dom_cre*), domestic credit to private sector (*Priv_cre*) and market capitalisation of listed companies (*Mar_cap*) are measured as percentages of GDP in constant (year 2000) US dollars. The distribution of the last of these shows Luxembourg and Finland as outliers. The institutional variable measuring the amount of foreign loans in the economy (*Floans*) is calculated as the ratio of foreign loans to non-banking organisations to gross domestic product (in constant, year 2000 US dollars). The outlier with an extremely high ratio is Luxembourg. GDP per capita (*Gdp_pc*) is also measured in constant (year 2000) US dollars. The histogram of the variable shows an outlier with a very high GDP per capita (Luxembourg) and a three-modal distribution roughly marking the division of countries into three groups: advanced countries, transition countries that entered EU in 2004 and other transition countries.

Pairwise correlations between the share of value added in total manufacturing and institutional variables show mostly a small and statistically negative correlation, implying that in economically more developed countries manufacturing sectors on average represent smaller fractions of total manufacturing value added. *T*-tests confirm a statistically significant positive difference in mean fractions for transition countries. This could be either a consequence of a greater variety of manufacturing industries or of better data collecting methods in more developed countries. This problem potentially introduces measurement error in our explanatory variable.

3.4 Results

We first present the results of the benchmark model and then perform robustness checks in the next subsections.

3.4.1 The benchmark model

The benchmark model uses our EUROSTAT dataset for the period 1995–2004, whereas Cetorelli (2004) used UNIDO data for OECD countries in the period 1987–97. Product market structure (proxied by average firm size) is measured as the logarithm of value added per enterprise and banking market concentration is measured by *CR3*. The dummy variables for industry and country-time effects are included, but not reported since their purpose is only to purge the estimation of fixed effects and their own effects are not identified. Standard errors are heteroskedasticity robust. The panel is unbalanced because of missing values. Results are presented in Table 3A.7.

The estimation confirms a statistically and economically significant effect of the share of value added in total manufacturing on average firm size that was found also in Cetorelli (2001 and 2004), although it has a larger magnitude here. Sectors with larger shares have a larger average firm size. However, in contrast to Cetorelli (2001, 2004), our estimation shows a negative effect of banking market concentration on average firm size in sectors that are more dependent on external finance. Furthermore, this negative effect holds for both, transition and advanced countries, but it is statistically significant (at 5 per cent level) only in advanced countries. The average firm size in sectors where mature firms depend on external finance is thus smaller in advanced countries with more concentrated banking markets. This implies that more concentrated banking markets lead to less concentrated product market structures in advanced countries, while we cannot confirm such association for transition countries. The economic significance of the effect for advanced countries can be explained as follows: the country at the 75th percentile of banking concentration distribution is Belgium (high concentration), the country at the 25th percentile of distribution is Spain (low concentration); if we increase banking concentration from the 25th to the 75th percentile of the distribution, the average firm size in sectors where firms are highly dependent on external finance would decrease by 6 per cent.

Results seem robust to alternative measures for average firm size (logarithm of average number of employees per enterprise, logarithm of average turnover per enterprise) and banking concentration (*CR5* and *HHI*; see Table 3A.8). In four of the nine variations of the model, the negative effect for advanced countries is statistically significant, and in all nine variations the sign is negative. These results are in sharp contrast to Cetorelli's (2004) findings for European countries; he documents a positive, significant effect of banking concentration and a decrease of this effect after countries became members of the EU. Our results indicate that in the second half of the 1990s this positive relationship turned into a negative one. As our sample period extends well beyond Cetorelli's analysis and it covers a longer period of integration within the EU and a deepening of such integration, especially in terms of financial integration, we can conjecture that in a more integrated EU bank concentration reflects the exploitation of scale economies and thus greater efficiency. In other words, bank concentration is consistent with greater competition achieved through a closer integration of European financial sectors. Therefore, our analysis exposes the varying relationship between bank concentration and competition in the banking sector. In the end, what really matters for product market structure is the degree of competition in the banking sector, which is only weakly related to bank concentration.

Our results show that the effects of bank concentration differ between transition and advanced countries. Specifically, the negative effect is much more pronounced in the advanced countries. We believe this is related to the different level of financial development and the characteristics of financial integration achieved in these two groups of countries. In advanced countries (older members of the EU), financial integration within the EU induced concentration in the banking market that improved cost efficiency and competitiveness. Although transition countries also benefited from increased financial integration during and after the EU accession process, the degree and nature of integration was different. The financial integration of transition countries was less intense and characterised mainly by active penetration in credit markets by banks from advanced European countries. Other financial institutions – stock markets for example – are still predominantly locally oriented and not important as a source of financing; long-term finance comes mainly from foreign direct investment. After a huge increase in the number of banks in the early 1990s, there was extensive consolidation in the second half of the 1990s because many banks were not fit to survive in the market economy. At the same time, increased foreign bank presence (setting up subsidiaries, acquiring domestic banks and to a large extent also through cross-border loans) brought pressure on domestic competitiveness (Bonin et al., 2005; Fries et al., 2006). Since a large part of financial integration happened via cross-border loans, which do not affect domestic banking concentration, the link between integration, concentration and competition is broken and our model does not reveal a significant banking concentration effect for transition countries.

To verify the results of the previous subsection, we perform a number of additional robustness checks of the model. We first check whether the estimates are related to individual observations. Then, we check whether the results are showing the effects of the general economic and financial development of countries instead of the banking market concentration effect, as well as whether there are any cross-border loans and market size effects involved. Since the effect of banking concentration is likely to show with a lag, we check whether our estimates change substantially when we allow for a delayed effect of banking concentration. Given that our analysis differs from Cetorelli's in the dataset used (data source, countries, time-period), we finally check whether the results are different when the UNIDO database is used for estimation.

3.4.2 Outliers

Excluding countries with the lowest and highest banking concentration (Luxembourg and Estonia, respectively) does not change results substantially; in fact, the coefficients are slightly larger.[12] The same is true when Bulgaria and Germany, countries with the smallest and largest average firm size respectively, are dropped. Excluding three countries with the least and most concentrated banking markets (Luxembourg, Italy, France; and Estonia, Finland, Lithuania, respectively) and the top and bottom three countries in the average firm size ranking (Germany, Ireland, Austria; and Bulgaria, Lithuania, Latvia, respectively) still produces negative coefficients of the interaction terms that become considerably larger and statistically significant at 1 per cent level for both groups of countries. These estimates confirm a negative effect of banking concentration in advanced countries and suggest there might be a negative effect also in transition countries.

Next, we drop the two sectors that have the smallest and largest dependence on external funds (and also the top and bottom three sectors). The results again imply a negative, statistically significant relationship between industry market structure and banking market structure. The coefficients are much larger than in the benchmark model. We obtain similar results also when excluding two sectors with the smallest and largest average firm size, as well as when excluding the top and bottom three sectors. Regarding different economic development, Romania and Bulgaria are countries that stand out as outliers at the bottom end of the GDP per capita distribution, whereas Luxembourg stands out at the top end of the distribution. Dropping these three countries from estimation gives similar results as the benchmark model.

Overall, the model seems fairly robust to outliers. The negative effect of banking concentration is in most cases confirmed also for transition countries when we control for outliers.

3.4.3 Institutional variables

The identified relationship between average firm size and banking market concentration could be picking-up the effect of the general economic and financial development of the countries. Therefore we check this possibility by including interaction terms of external dependency and several measures of financial development. The estimates are presented in Table 3A.9.

When domestic credit (column 1) or private credit (column 2) is added to the model, the banking concentration effect for advanced countries increases, remains negative and even more statistically significant, whereas the effect for transition countries becomes positive, but statistically insignificant. We consider also the influence of stock market capitalisation on average firm size and banking concentration effect (column 3). As expected, the coefficients of the stock market capitalisation interaction terms are negative, but only the coefficient for advanced countries is statistically significant. The coefficients for banking concentration remain negative and of approximately the same magnitude; only the one for advanced countries is statistically significant. This shows that the fact that firms are able to get funds from a stock market is important only in advanced countries, whereas it has no effect on industry concentration, average firm size or banking concentration effect in transition countries. In advanced countries, though, the observed banking concentration effect on average firm size and industry concentration is in fact smaller because part of it was the result of stock market sources of external funds. The addition of GDP per capita (column 4) does not change the banking concentration effect in advanced countries much, whereas it decreases the effect for transition countries–both remain negative.

3.4.4 Cross-border loans

If firms are able to borrow abroad, there should be more entry into sectors that are highly dependent on external finance in countries that have more foreign loans in the economy. The expected coefficient on the interaction term between foreign loans and the external financial dependency indicator is therefore negative. Moreover, a significant effect of foreign banking loans on industry structure would imply that it is actually banking market competition and not banking market concentration that is affecting industry market structure. We base this conclusion on the assumption that domestic banks are behaving more competitively if firms are able to borrow abroad than if not. If this is true, borrowing abroad affects domestic banking market competition (or market contestability), but not domestic banking market concentration. If we could define relevant banking markets for sectors in each country more precisely than just as domestic (national) banking markets, there would be less difference between banking market concentration and competition in this respect.

It turns out that the interaction term with foreign loans for transition countries is indeed negative, statistically significant and large in comparison with banking concentration and other interaction effects so far included in the model (Table 3A.9, column 5). Also, its addition to the model turns the coefficient on banking concentration in transition countries to positive, but statistically not significant. The interaction term for advanced countries is, however, positive, small and statistically insignificant. The banking concentration effect in advanced countries is therefore slightly larger, still negative and statistically significant.

These results confirm that in transition countries the extent of cross-border borrowing affects industry market structure and average firm size more than banking concentration does. On the other hand, in advanced countries industry market structure is not affected by cross-border loans; instead it appears there is indeed a negative effect of banking concentration. This supports our claim that differences in financial integration are indeed the reason for observed differences in the banking concentration effect between advanced and transition countries.

3.4.5 Market size

Market size is one of the most important determinants of market structure; therefore it can also affect the relationship between product and banking market concentration (Marc, 2009). We check for differences related to different size effects by grouping observations into three groups – small, medium and large markets – and estimating separately the benchmark model. Variables *Dom_cre* and *Floans* proxy for banking market size, whereas GDP proxies for product market size. Observations in the first quartile of the relevant distribution are grouped into 'small', observations in the last quartile of the distribution into 'large', and the ones in the middle two quartiles of the distributions into 'medium'. Results (Table 3A.10) in general show that small banking and product markets are more likely to be characterised by a positive effect of the banking market concentration than are medium and large markets. Medium banking and product markets are strongly characterised by a negative banking concentration effect. Large banking markets in general show a negative, but not statistically significant effect, whereas large product markets show a statistically significant negative effect.

3.4.6 Delayed effects and correlation vs. causation

Rosen (2004) argues that using the same year for banking and industry concentration indicates only a correlation between the two concentrations, but not causation. In some cases, the correlation could be explained for example by merger waves. He suggests using the preceding three-year average concentration in banking markets as an explanation variable for the concentration in industry sectors in a particular year. We check the model with one-year lagged and preceding three-year average banking concentration (Table 3A.11). In both cases, the results do not change substantially. For advanced countries, there is still evidence of a statistically significant, negative banking concentration effect, which is even larger than in the benchmark model. Also, the banking concentration coefficient for transition countries is increased in comparison to the benchmark model, but it remains negative and statistically insignificant. This confirms our previous results and suggests there is indeed a causal relationship between banking concentration and industrial market concentration in advanced countries.

3.4.7 UNIDO dataset

Since our results differ substantially from Cetorelli's (2001 and 2004) and the deviation from his studies is in the dataset, we check our results also by using the UNIDO database as the source for value added sectoral data. The dataset is described in the previous section and we report here only the results of estimations (see Tables 3A.12 and 3A.13).

The benchmark model, estimated on UNIDO data for the same countries that we have in the EUROSTAT dataset, confirms a negative and statistically significant coefficient for the effect of banking concentration in advanced countries in the period 1990–2003 (column 1). Also, the coefficient for transition countries is negative, but not statistically significant. These coefficients have a similar magnitude as in the benchmark model estimated with the EUROSTAT dataset. Next we estimate the model on the UNIDO dataset in the same time period as in the benchmark model, that is, 1995–2003[13] (column 2). Both banking concentration coefficients remain negative, but they are not statistically significant. In the period before 1995, these coefficients are also not statistically significant, though the coefficient for transition countries is positive (column 2a).

In the next step, we change the measure of banking concentration to *CR5* and *HHI* and the period studied is therefore 1999–2003. With *CR5,* both banking concentration terms are negative and not statistically significant (column 3), whereas using *HHI* produces a small, positive and insignificant coefficient for advanced countries (column 4). Banking concentration measured with *CR3* has a negative, not statistically significant effect in both groups of countries in this period (column 5). Again, if we check the period before 1999, we find these coefficients are not statistically significant, though the coefficient for transition countries is positive (column 6).

Additional institutional variables that proxy for financial development in general have theoretically expected negative (statistically significant) coefficients and they render the banking concentration effects not significant. This shows that the negative banking concentration effect found in advanced countries in the UNIDO data is not very robust. The most interesting result is the effect of foreign loans. When foreign loans are added to the model, the banking concentration effect in both countries turns positive, but not statistically significant (column 11). The effect of foreign loans itself is quite large in comparison, and negative and statistically significant in both groups of countries. Not surprisingly, this effect is five times larger for transition countries. Similarly as in the EUROSTAT dataset, it seems there is no effect of banking concentration on industrial markets' concentration in transition countries. Besides, the results of this dataset imply there is no such effect even in advanced countries. Instead, there might exist a banking competition effect on average firm size as explained before, which is picked up by the ratio of foreign loans to GDP.

Overall, the estimates based on the UNIDO dataset again mostly imply there could be at best a negative effect of banking concentration for advanced countries and there seems to be no such effect (or it is much smaller) in transition countries. In any case, we find no evidence of a positive and statistically significant effect of banking concentration.

3.4.8 Structural break

The estimations imply there might be a structural break in the relationship between banking and industrial markets' concentration. We test for a structural break in control and explanation variables by constructing a dummy variable equal to 1 for the period after year t^*, and equal to 0 for the period before or equal t^*, where t^* denotes the year when the structural break happens. We interact this dummy variable (*DT*) with control and explanation variables and add these terms to the benchmark model where they will show the difference between periods before and after t^*.

We estimate nine models obtained by moving t^* from 1995 to 2003 on EUROSTAT's data. The results show a positive and statistically significant difference between periods when t^* is set to 1999 and 2000 for transition countries (results available upon request). This indicates that a structural break in the banking concentration effect happened around these two years in transition countries. The effect of banking concentration in transition countries was significantly negative before 2000 (2001) and even larger than in advanced countries, but it has since decreased considerably, whereas advanced countries did not experience this change. In fact, the banking concentration effect in advanced countries is remarkably stable in magnitude, negative and statistically significant in all models except in the one where t^* is 1995. Incidentally, 1999–2000 is the period when eight of ten analysed transition countries entered the EU (or were preparing to enter), so it is tempting simply to conclude that the financial integration brought by the accession process changed the way banking concentration affects concentration in product markets in these countries. Since most of the transition countries aspired to become members of the EU, they had to adopt banking regulation in line with the one prescribed for developed countries already in the EU. After the Second Banking Coordination Directive in 1993, there was a lot of activity in the area of banking regulation in all the transition countries that were aiming for EU membership. This certainly helped countries to focus better, advance the reform process and implement the regulation faster than would have been done otherwise, as demonstrated by slower processes in countries that joined EU more recently (Romania and Bulgaria) or are not yet EU members. Mamatzakis et al. (2005) investigate seven southeastern European countries in the period 1998–2002 (among them only Romania and Bulgaria are at present EU members) and find results that strongly support the view that structural reforms make banking more competitive. They believe potential accession to the EU is thus one of the conditions that may enhance market contestability. Although the accession process demanded changes in banking regulation that liberalised banking markets and also changed profoundly the nature of banking business, the structural break could be also a result of other events, for example merger waves, as pointed out by Rosen (2004); further research is therefore needed to confirm what the reason was for this structural break.

3.5 Conclusion

Our empirical analysis finds no evidence of a positive effect of banking market concentration on product market concentration, as argued by Cetorelli (2001, 2004) and Cetorelli and Strahan (2006). In fact, our results show, with some degree of robustness, that the effect is negative: countries with more concentrated banking markets have less concentrated real markets. The main source of our different results lies in the different samples analysed and the different time period.

Furthermore, we find that the relationship between market structures in banking and in industrial sectors is clearly different in transition countries. Overall, we find no significant effect for a subsample of countries, characterised by a lower degree of development of domestic financial sectors. Our results generally show a small and rarely significant negative effect for these countries. We demonstrate that one reason for such a lack of a significant relationship may lie in the crucial role of foreign loans in transition countries. Cross-border flows tend to break the link between domestic banking structure and industrial market structure. Finally, our results suggest that, rather than concentration per se, bank competition should be a better predictor of market structure in product markets. Indeed, this is the avenue that Marc (2009) has begun to research.

Appendix

Table 3A.1 Summary statistics of main variables

Variable	Obs	Mean	Std. Dev.	Min	Max	Source	Note
EUROSTAT							
LNVA	6485	−0.262	1.755	−7.396	6.730	EUROSTAT	1995–2004; 26 countries, 34 sectors
SHVA	7116	0.028	0.031	0.000	0.345	EUROSTAT	1995–2004; 26 countries, 34 sectors
TR	9104	0.374	0.484	0	1		
EU	9104	0.626	0.484	0	1		
OECD	9104	0.750	0.433	0	1		
UNIDO							
LNVAU	7495	−0.252	2.007	−10.184	7.793	UNIDO	1987–2003; 31 countries, 36 sectors
SHVAU	9453	0.037	0.043	0.000	0.607	UNIDO	1987–2003; 31 countries, 36 sectors
TR	18888	0.461	0.499	0	1		
EU	18888	0.539	0.499	0	1		
OECD	18888	0.599	0.490	0	1		
Other variables							
ED	17772	0.006	0.308	−1.330	0.394	Rajan & Zingales	1980–1990; US listed mature firms

(continued)

EDI	17772	0.500	0.500	0.000	1.000		
CR3	11304	0.620	0.186	0.205	1.000	Bankscope; N. Cetorelli	1999–2005; 1990–1997
CR5	6552	0.725	0.169	0.327	1.000	Bankscope	1999–2004
HHI	6552	0.183	0.120	0.036	0.670	Bankscope	1999–2004
Priv_cre	16452	61.150	37.600	1.679	158.653	WDI World Bank	1987–2004
Dom_cre	16776	77.300	40.026	5.477	170.623	WDI World Bank	1987–2004
Mar_cap	14832	43.281	48.257	0.004	479.743	WDI World Bank	1987–2004
Gdp_pc	18288	13175.4	10798.3	286.5	50536.7	WDI World Bank	1987–2004
Floans	10664	0.105	0.229	0.000	2.088	BIS–IMF–OECD–WB External Debt Hub	1995–2004

Table 3A.2 External financial dependency

ISIC rev. 2		External financial dependency
323	Leather	–1.33017
324	Footwear	–0.57282
314	Tobacco	–0.37546
3513	Synthetic resins	–0.22668
352	Other chemicals	–0.18361
313	Beverages	–0.14638
355	Rubber products	–0.12256
311	Food	–0.05206
390	Other manufacturing	–0.05130
353	Petroleum refineries*	–0.02171
322	Wearing apparel	–0.02010
3522	Drugs and medicines	0.02752
362	Glass and products	0.03103
3841	Shipbuilding and repairing	0.04087
381	Metal products	0.04370
372	Non-ferrous metals	0.07313
3511	Basic industrial chemicals	0.07534
371	Iron and steel	0.08709
341	Paper and products	0.10438
3843	Motor vehicles	0.10957
3411	Pulp, paper and board	0.12680
342	Printing and publishing	0.13582
321	Textiles	0.14100
369	Non-metallic products	0.15193
354	Petroleum and coal products	0.16202
384	Transport equipment	0.16324
361	Pottery, China etc.	0.16338
385	Professional goods	0.19365
382	Non-electrical machinery	0.21660
383	Electrical machinery	0.23002
331	Wood products	0.24919
3825	Office and computing machines	0.26072
332	Furniture and fixtures	0.32917
3832	Radio, TV and comm. equipment	0.39350
356	Plastic products	n.a.

Source: Rajan and Zingales (1998).
Note: *This sector was not included in the benchmark analysis, because it was not possible to accurately translate it from NACE.
Shaded sectors have above median external financial dependency.

Table 3A.3 Pattern of industry structure and banking concentration across countries

Country	Mean CR3	Mean LNVA	Mean number of banks	Mean number of firms
AT	48.56	0.70	177.67	26042.67
BE	77.00	0.52	56.50	29667.33
BG	49.00	–2.24	25.17	20605.33
CZ	64.75	–1.60	24.67	134914.30
DE	38.08	1.16	509.83	206569.50
DK	79.68	0.20	92.50	18847.67
EE	98.34	–1.35	5.33	3913.00
ES	49.96	–0.10	147.83	217909.00
FI	87.66	0.21	8.33	25114.67
FR	34.84	0.47	319.17	245777.50
HU	49.66	–0.90	25.33	49867.17
IE	61.56	1.28	31.67	3937.67
IT	29.27	–0.36	394.00	532855.30
LT	82.56	–1.88	9.00	7729.83
LU	23.72	0.32	108.33	784.50
LV	53.96	–1.78	21.33	6063.17
NL	81.15	0.12	41.83	44716.67
NO	65.42	0.71	51.17	11200.50
PL	43.66	–0.95	100.75	197445.00
PT	67.91	–0.44	41.83	73305.34
RO	59.99	–0.98	26.83	38462.00
SE	78.09	–0.30	68.83	43880.00
SI	59.84	–0.93	17.17	19761.67
SK	63.21	–0.24	15.50	4983.67
UK	39.47	0.70	144.33	156644.50
Transition	62.50	–1.29	27.11	48374.51
Advanced	57.49	0.35	146.26	109150.19

Note: CR3 is the concentration ratio of three largest banks in the banking market. It is measured as the market share of three largest banks in terms of total assets. The 'Mean CR3' refers to the average CR3 in the period 1999–2004. LNVA is the logarithm of value added per enterprise and the mean is calculated as the simple average LNVA in the period 1999–2004 by country. 'Mean number of banks' and 'Mean number of firms' denote the average number of banks and firms, respectively, in the period 1999–2004 by country.

Table 3A.4 Pattern of financial dependence and industry structure across sectors

ISIC 2		Mean ED	Mean LNVA
311	Food products	–0.0521	–0.7379
313	Beverages	–0.1464	0.5486
314	Tobacco	–0.3755	2.9109
321	Textile	0.1410	–0.8936
322	Apparel	–0.0201	–1.7898
323	Leather	–1.3302	–2.1445
324	Footwear	–0.5728	–1.1999
331	Wood products	0.2492	–1.6619
332	Furniture	0.3292	–1.5347
341	Paper and products	0.1044	–0.0058
342	Printing and publishing	0.1358	–1.1872
352	Other chemicals	–0.1836	0.0315
354	Petroleum and coal products	0.1620	2.8109
355	Rubber products	–0.1226	0.0903
361	Pottery	0.1634	–1.8129
362	Glass	0.0310	–0.1677
369	Non-metal products	0.1519	–0.5284
371	Iron and steel	0.0871	0.3029
372	Nonferrous material	0.0731	1.2573
381	Metal products	0.0437	–1.3529
382	Machinery	0.2166	–0.5371
383	Electric machinery	0.2300	–0.1442
384	Transportation equipment	0.1632	0.7313
385	Professional goods	0.1937	–0.9819
390	Other industries	–0.0513	–2.0775
3411	Pulp, paper	0.1268	1.6888
3511	Basic industrial chemicals, excluding fertilizers	0.0753	1.3728
3513	Synthetic resins	–0.2267	1.2632
3522	Drugs	0.0275	1.9947
3825	Office and computing	0.2607	–0.6641
3832	Radio	0.3935	–0.2945
3841	Ship	0.0409	–0.8775
3843	Motor vehicle	0.1096	0.7836

Note: 'Mean ED' is the average external financial dependency for American mature firms in the 1980s. The measure is taken from Rajan and Zingales (1998). LNVA is the logarithm of value added per enterprise and the mean is calculated as the simple average LNVA in the period 1999–2004 by sector.

Table 3A.5 Pairwise correlations EUROSTAT

	LNVA	SHVA	CR3	CR5	HHI	Dom_cre	Priv_cre	Mar_cap	Gdp_pc	Floans
LNVA	1									
SHVA	0.157*	1								
CR3	−0.044*	−0.004	1							
CR5	−0.079*	0.004	0.969*	1						
HHI	−0.065*	0.010	0.882*	0.806*	1					
Dom_cre	0.404*	−0.032*	−0.088*	−0.158*	−0.185*	1				
Priv_cre	0.389*	−0.038*	−0.114*	−0.177*	−0.192*	0.906*	1			
Mar_cap	0.283*	−0.024	−0.077*	−0.034*	0.012	0.429*	0.521*	1		
Gdp_pc	0.439*	−0.041*	−0.090*	−0.227*	−0.142*	0.630*	0.730*	0.584*	1	
Floans	0.154*	−0.039*	−0.290*	−0.318*	−0.193*	0.204*	0.297*	0.405*	0.537*	1

Note: *1 per cent significance level.

Table 3A.6 Pairwise correlations UNIDO

	LNVAU	SHVAU	CR3	CR5	HHI	Dom_cre	Priv_cre	Mar_cap	Gdp_pc	Floans
LNVAU	1									
SHVAU	0.1330*	1								
CR3	0.0902*	−0.0392	1							
CR5	−0.1114*	0.0089	0.9690*	1						
HHI	−0.1106*	−0.0928	0.8824*	0.8059*	1					
Dom_cre	0.4445*	−0.0230	−0.0875*	−0.1582*	−0.1851*	1				
Priv_cre	0.4624*	−0.0229	−0.1136*	−0.1768*	−0.1922*	0.9057*	1			
Mar_cap	0.2011*	0.0453*	−0.0772*	−0.0336*	0.0118	0.4289*	0.5209*	1		
Gdp_pc	0.5376*	−0.0012	−0.0897*	−0.2270*	−0.1419*	0.6298*	0.7303*	0.5839*	1	
Floans	0.3135*	0.0748*	−0.2901*	−0.3178*	−0.1932*	0.2042*	0.2996*	0.4049*	0.5373*	1

Note: *1 per cent significance level.

Table 3A.7 Benchmark results

Dependent variable = LNVA	
SHVA	17.124***
	(.581)
CR3*EDI*TR	−0.149
	(.117)
CR3*EDI*EU	−0.244**
	(.109)
R^2	0.6684
Number of observations	5394

Note: ***, **, * are 1, 5, and 10 per cent significance levels, respectively.

Table 3A.8 Estimation results for benchmark model (EUROSTAT dataset)

Dependent variable=Average firm size; measured in			
	Value added	**Turnover**	**Num. employees**
SHVA	17.124***	15.957***	11.056***
	(0.581)	(0.606)	(0.652)
CR3*TR*EDI	−0.149	−0.067	−0.066
	(0.117)	(0.123)	(0.104)
CR3*EU*EDI	−0.244**	−0.270**	−0.100
	(0.109)	(0.115)	(0.100)
Observations	5394	5391	5366
R^2	0.6684	0.9267	0.4206
SHVA	16.959***	15.637***	10.654***
	(0.638)	(0.668)	(0.715)
CR5*TR*EDI	−0.061	−0.001	0.035
	(0.137)	(0.145)	(0.121)
CR5*EU*EDI	−0.148	−0.182	−0.001
	(0.139)	(0.146)	(0.126)
Observations	4316	4313	4324
R^2	0.6855	0.936	0.444
SHVA	16.976***	15.662***	10.670***
	(0.638)	(0.667)	(0.716)
HHI*TR*EDI	0.050	0.077	0.092
	(0.212)	(0.225)	(0.184)
HHI*EU*EDI	−0.388**	−0.551***	−0.172
	(0.201)	(0.209)	(0.182)
Observations	4316	4313	4324
R^2	0.6856	0.936	0.4442

Note: ***, **, * are 1, 5, and 10 per cent significance levels, respectively
The benchmark model is indicated by the shaded area. The period analysed in the models with CR3 is 1995–2004, in all other models it is 1999–2004.

Table 3A.9 Estimations on EUROSTAT dataset – Institutional variables (1995–2004)

Variable	**(1)**	**(2)**	**(3)**	**(4)**	**(5)**
SHVA	17.184***	17.187***	17.145***	17.117***	17.156***
	(0.583)	(0.582)	(0.580)	(0.581)	(0.580)
CR3TR *EDI	0.274	0.232	−0.230	–0.063	0.104
	(0.193)	(0.177)	(0.165)	(0.166)	(0.168)
CR3EU *EDI	–0.327***	–0.334***	–0.189*	–0.220*	–0.286***
	(0.110)	(0.111)	(0.112)	(0.115)	(0.109)
Dom_cre *TR *EDI	–0.005**				
	(0.002)				
Dom_cre *EU *EDI	0.001				
	(0.001)				
Priv_cre *TR *EDI		–0.007***			
		(0.003)			
Priv_cre *EU *EDI		0.001			
		(0.001)			
Mar_cap *TR *EDI			0.000		
			(0.004)		
Mar_cap *EU *EDI			–0.001***		
			(0.000)		
Gdp_pc *TR *EDI				0.000***	
				(0.000)	
Gdp_pc *EU *EDI				0.000***	
				(0.000)	
Floans *TR *EDI					–3.734**
					(1.579)
Floans * EU *EDI					0.013
					(0.155)
R^2	0.669	0.669	0.669	0.670	0.669
Observations	5394	5394	5394	5394	5394

Note: ***, **, * are 1, 5, and 10 per cent significance levels, respectively.

Table 3A.10 Size effects (1995–2004)

		Size defined in terms of:		
		Dom_cre	**Floans**	**GDP**
Large	SHVA	17.839***	18.975***	17.868***
		(1.339)	(1.203)	(1.129)
	CR3TR*EDI		–0.243	
			(0.413)	
	CR3EU*EDI	–0.063	–0.227	–0.360*
		(0.183)	(0.219)	(0.190)
	R^2	0.4829	0.4626	0.4867
	Observations	2080	1563	1758
Medium	SHVA	16.683***	17.017***	17.413***
		(0.685)	(0.668)	(0.786)
	CR3TR*EDI	–0.470***	–0.260*	–0.784***
		(0.146)	(0.149)	(0.256)
	CR3EU*EDI	–0.528***	–0.284*	–0.591***
		(0.138)	(0.153)	(0.200)
	R^2	0.6131	0.6798	0.6252
	Observations	2272	2893	2980
Small	SHVA	18.327***	15.657***	16.869***
		(1.303)	(1.066)	(1.329)
	CR3TR*EDI	0.553*	0.563*	0.272
		(0.291)	(0.308)	(0.267)
	CR3EU*EDI	0.121	0.669*	0.202
		(0.447)	(0.379)	(0.910)
	R^2	0.5925	0.7240	0.6672
	Observations	1011	938	656

Note: ***, **, * are 1, 5, and 10 per cent significance levels, respectively

Table 3A.11 Lagged and average concentration measures

Variable	**(1)**	**(2)**	**(3)**	**(4)**	**(5)**	**(6)**
SHVA	17.296***	17.382***	16.935***	16.675***	16.957***	16.704***
	(0.616)	(0.779)	(0.708)	(0.962)	(0.708)	(0.963)
Lag CR3TR* EDI	–0.107					
	(0.120)					
Lag CR3EU* EDI	–0.259**					
	(0.113)					
Avg CR3TR* EDI		–0.196				
		(0.147)				
Avg CR3EU* EDI		–0.350***				
		(0.132)				
Lag CR5TR* EDI			0.001			
			(0.147)			
Lag CR5EU* EDI			–0.132			
			(0.152)			
Avg CR5TR* EDI				–0.003		
				(0.191)		
Avg CR5EU* EDI				–0.140		
				(0.198)		
Lag HHITR* EDI					0.175	
					(0.223)	
Lag HHIEU* EDI					–0.389*	
					(0.218)	
Avg HHITR* EDI						0.106
						(0.285)
Avg HHIEU* EDI						–0.427
						(0.272)
R^2	0.650	0.618	0.683	0.671	0.683	0.671
Observations	5149	3661	3634	2168	3634	2168

Note: ***, **, * are 1, 5, and 10 per cent significance levels, respectively
'Lag' denotes one-year lagged measures of banking concentration and 'Avg' denotes preceding three-year averages of banking concentration measures. The analysed period is 1995–2004 for CR3 models and 1999–2004 for CR5 and HHI models.

Table 3A.12 Estimations on UNIDO dataset

Variable	**(1)**	**(2)**	**(2a)**	**(3)**	**(4)**	**(5)**	**(6)**
	1990–2003	**1995–2003**	**1990–4**	**1999–2003**	**1999–2003**	**1999–2003**	**1990–8**
SHVA	11.635***	10.968***	12.137***	10.003***	9.883***	9.972***	13.882***
	0.834	1.109	0.684	1.158	1.181	1.166	0.720
CR3*TR*EDI	–0.156	–0.160	0.157			–0.239	0.174
	0.130	0.162	0.175			0.180	0.168
CR3*EU*EDI	–0.251**	–0.080	–0.092			–0.220	–0.033
	0.116	0.154	0.149			0.196	0.138
CR5*TR*EDI				–0.280			
				0.183			
CR5*EU*EDI				–0.276			
				0.193			
HHI*TR*EDI					–0.296		
					0.283		
HHI*EU*EDI					0.081		
					0.327		
R^2	0.714	0.688	0.719	0.693	0.693	0.693	0.709
Observations	4443	2835	1608	2050	2050	2050	2393

Note: ***, **, * are 1, 5, and 10 per cent significance levels, respectively.

Table 3A.13 Estimations on UNIDO dataset – institutional variables

Variable	**(7)**	**(8)**	**(9)**	**(10)**	**(11)**
SHVA	11.725***	11.800***	11.704***	11.795***	10.991***
	0.825	0.824	0.873	0.820	1.108
CR3*TR*EDI	–0.191	0.049	0.002	0.174	0.150
	0.212	0.203	0.158	0.209	0.229
CR3*EU*EDI	–0.164	–0.166	–0.280**	–0.147	0.015
	0.105	0.108	0.116	0.111	0.157
Dom_cre *TR * EDI	–0.004**				
	0.002				
Dom_cre *EU * EDI	–0.003***				
	0.001				
Priv_cre *TR * EDI		–0.015***			
		0.004			
Priv_cre *EU * EDI		–0.004***			
		0.001			

(continued)

Table 3A.13 Continued

Mar_cap *TR * EDI			–0.012***		
			0.004		
Mar_cap *EU * EDI			–0.001		
			0.000		
Gdp_pc *TR * EDI				0.000***	
				0.000	
Gdp_pc *EU * EDI				0.000***	
				0.000	
Floans *TR * EDI					–5.343**
					2.488
Floans *EU * EDI					–1.147**
					0.500
R^2	0.715	0.717	0.714	0.716	0.689
Observations	4430	4430	4331	4443	2835

Note: ***, **, * are 1, 5, and 10 per cent significance levels, respectively.

Notes

1. *EU* is equal to 1 for *all* analysed advanced countries, *not* only those that are EU members.
2. Bulgaria, Czech Republic, Estonia, Hungary, Lithuania, Latvia, Slovakia, Slovenia, Poland, and Romania (all have *TR*=1).
3. Austria, Belgium, Denmark, Finland, France, Germany, Greece, Ireland, Italy, Luxembourg, Netherlands, Norway, Portugal, Spain, Sweden, and UK (all have *EU*=1).
4. Sectors 353 (Petroleum Refineries) and 351 (Industrial chemicals) are not included in the dataset, because it was impossible to identify the necessary data in NACE 1.1 and translate it to ISIC 2.
5. For 28 manufacturing sectors we have data at 3-digit level and for 8 manufacturing sectors data at 4-digit level of ISIC code (Revision 2); downloaded from ESDS International website via Beyond 20/20 WDS.
6. Croatia, FYR Macedonia, Mongolia, Moldova, and Russia.
7. An establishment is defined as a plant or factory where production occurs.
8. Data for 1998 were excluded because of poor quality.
9. We would like to thank Nicola Cetorelli (Federal Reserve Bank of New York) for kindly providing his data.
10. Mature companies are companies that are present more than 10 years after listing.

11. The coefficient is –0.1314, significant at 5 per cent significance level.
12. Results of this subsection are available upon request.
13. EUROSTAT's data are for 1995–2004, but UNIDO's data stop at 2003.

References

Black, S. E. & Strahan, P. E., 2002. Entrepreneurship and Bank Credit Availability. *Journal of Finance*, 57(6), pp. 2807–33.

Bonin, J. P., I. Hasan & Wachtel, P., 2005. Bank Performance, Efficiency and Ownership in Transition Countries. *Journal of Banking and Finance*, 29(1), pp. 31–53.

Cetorelli, N., 2001. *Does Bank Concentration Lead to Concentration in Industrial Sectors?* Working paper, Federal Reserve Bank of Chicago.

Cetorelli, N., 2004. Real Effects of Bank Competition. *Journal of Money, Credit, and Banking*, 36(3), pp. 543–58.

Cetorelli, N. & Gambera, M., 2001. Banking Market Structure, Financial Dependence and Growth: International Evidence from Industry Data. *Journal of Finance*, 56(2), pp. 617–48.

Cetorelli, N. & Strahan, P. E., 2006. Finance As a Barrier to Entry: Bank Competition and Industry Structure. *Journal of Finance*, 61(1), pp. 437–61.

Demirgüç-Kunt, A. & Levine, R., 2004. *Financial Structure and Economic Growth: A Cross-Country Comparison of Banks, Markets, and Development*. Cambridge, MA: The MIT Press.

Fries, S., Neven, D., Seabright, P. & Taci, A., 2006. Market Entry, Privatization and Bank Performance in Transition. *Economics of Transition*, 14(4), p. 579–610.

Hellman, T. & Da Rin, M., 2002. Banks as Catalysts for Industrialization. *Journal of Financial Intermediation*, 11(4), pp. 366–97.

Mamatzakis, E., Staikouras, C. & Koutsomanoli-Fillipaki, N., 2005. Competition and Concentration in the Banking Sector of the South Eastern European Region. *Emerging Markets Review*, 6(2), pp. 192–209.

Marc, M., 2009. *Three Essays on Banking Market Effects on Product Market Structure*. PhD Dissertation, University of Siena.

Pagano, M., 1993. Financial Markets and Growth: An Overview. *European Economic Review* 37(2–3), pp. 613–22.

Petersen, M. A. & Rajan, R. G., 1995. The Effect of Credit Market Competition on Lending Relationships. *The Quarterly Journal of Economics*, 110(2), pp. 407–43.

Rajan, R. G. & Zingales, L., 1998. Financial Dependence and Growth. *American Economic Review*, 88(3), pp. 559–86.

Rosen, R. J., 2004. Comment on 'Real Effects of Bank Competition' by Nicola Cetorelli. *Journal of Money, Credit, and Banking*, 36(3), pp. 559–62.

4
Financing Constraints, Credit, Rationing, and Financing Obstacles: Evidence from Firm Level Data in South Eastern Europe

I. Hashi and V. Z. Toçi

4.1 Introduction

The transformation of the banking sector in transition economies has been one of the most dynamic and challenging aspects of the transition process. Reforms in South East European (SEE) countries were long delayed, especially in the first decade of transition. The banking sector was relatively inefficient, with a weak supervisory capacity, and old lending practices paved the way on many occasions for severe crisis and low levels of financial intermediation (Anderson and Kegels, 1998). In the second decade of transition, however, the banking sector in SEE underwent a fundamental restructuring and consolidation. Reforms of the macroeconomic environment and institutions of a market economy were undertaken, which promoted stability and the prospect of financial deepening. Notwithstanding the progress made, the level of banking sector credit to enterprises in transition economies in general and SEE in particular has not reached that of countries with comparable levels of economic development (EBRD, 2006). This is because banks have imposed credit rationing on creditworthy enterprises for a variety of reasons: inefficiencies in the banks themselves, information asymmetry between borrowers and banks, poorly functioning institutions such as the rule of law, and other institutional and market failures. These concepts are well grounded in the theoretical literature of the last three decades (Stiglitz and Weiss, 1981; Fazzari et al., 1988; and others). Credit rationing of creditworthy firms has important adverse implications for the growth of firms and the whole economy. Hence, it is important to investigate this phenomenon in the context of SEE countries, where the evidence to date is scarce.

In this chapter, the availability of finance is examined by bringing together two strands of the literature (credit rationing and financing constraints) into a single empirical framework, providing new evidence on credit rationing, financing constraints and financing obstacles faced by firms in SEE. The chapter focuses on the effects of this phenomenon on specific groups of firms such as SMEs, state-owned and foreign-owned firms, firms with good prospects, etc. Given that small firms are the most dynamic sector of the economy and critical to economic growth in SEE countries, the impact of market imperfections limiting their access to external finance, and therefore their potential growth, is also addressed in the paper. Other characteristics of firms such as ownership, past performance and financial disclosure, that may influence the degree of financing constraints are also explored. Other working hypotheses, such as the persistence of soft budget constraints for state-owned enterprises, whether credit rationing is a supply- or a demand-driven phenomenon, and the ability of banks to distinguish between 'good' and 'bad' borrowers, are also tested. Using a large survey of firms in Albania, Bosnia and Herzegovina, Bulgaria, Croatia, Macedonia, Romania and Serbia and Montenegro for 1999, 2002 and 2005, and extensive econometric modelling, the prevalence of financing constraints and credit rationing in the SEE region is confirmed, especially for the small business sector. However, during the period under review there has been a substantial decrease in financing constraints, especially in the category of small firms, implying a shift in the lending technology of banks towards the small business sector.

This chapter is organised as follows. In section 4.2, theories of credit rationing and financing constraints and some of the empirical work in the area are critically examined. While much of this literature was developed in the context of mature market economies, there have been a number of attempts to apply these concepts to the more developed transition economies. Sections 4.3 and 4.4 discuss the empirical work of this chapter – the data, models and results. Section 4.5 concludes.

4.2 Review of the Literature

4.2.1 Credit rationing and financing constraints: The theory

There is a well-established literature which argues that imperfections in the credit market stem from information asymmetries, transaction costs and agency issues. Such imperfections may give rise to credit rationing – a state in which information asymmetries between lenders and borrowers may result in the equilibrium interest rate not clearing the market. Instead, the demand for loans will exceed the supply and banks will deny credit to some borrowers who are observationally indistinguishable from those who receive loans despite their willingness to pay the prevailing interest rate. For example, if the borrower bears no cost when project returns are lower than the debt obligation, the moral hazard argument can lead to credit rationing because the borrower may divert the funds to riskier project *ex post* (Stiglitz and Weiss, 1981), engage in asset substitution (Schwartz, 1981), exert an inappropriate degree of effort on the project (Aghion and Bolton, 1997; Ghosh et al., 2001) or even falsely declare bankruptcy (Williamson, 1986). Banks cannot distinguish these borrowers from better-quality ones because of information asymmetries, hence they will ration their supply of credit.

The information asymmetry theories of credit rationing have often been criticised for assuming that banks are unable to distinguish between borrowers – given that banks are in the information processing business and have specialised expertise in analysing credit risk (Riley, 1987; Inderst and Muller, 2007).[1] For example, Riley (1987) criticises the work of Stiglitz and Weiss by arguing that as long as high risk and high return are positively correlated, the adverse effect of risk may be offset by a favourable effect of returns and, as the number of observationally distinct groups increases, credit rationing may not be an empirically important phenomenon. Milde and Riley (1988) develop the 'bank screening hypothesis' in which separating equilibria with no rationing is attained where banks screen their borrowers by offering larger loans to safer borrowers and by sorting out different risk classes. However, banks can separate small firms from large ones, firms in one sector from those in other sectors, etc. Since perfect screening is impossible, within each group some will receive loans while apparently identical firms will not and credit rationing will still occur.

The magnitude of credit rationing depends on the extent to which information asymmetries are more problematic for a specific group such as small firms, as opposed to other groups. If small firms have higher informational problems and are subject to credit rationing, it does not necessarily mean that they have 'bad' projects in hand. As Storey (1994) notes, if business proposals are turned down for reasons not connected to the viability of the project itself, for example, because firms lack a track record and collateral or are small, then credit rationing may be a problem in the credit market and may become the subject of government intervention. As Cressy (1996) notes, although the theoretical underpinnings of credit rationing theory may be challenged, its implications seem to have been accepted since in many countries substantial sums of public money have been spent on alleviating this problem.

It is important to recognise that if firms have access to external finance, they may still limit their investments to internally generated funds and underinvest because information and incentive problems may introduce a wedge between the costs of internal and external finance – as the financing constraints literature argues. 'Financing constraints' refer to the inability of firms to finance their desired level of investment that they would have undertaken in a perfect capital market. In perfect capital markets firms are indifferent about what sources they use (internal or external) to finance their investment. They would not find it difficult to raise external finance when profitable investment opportunities arise and, in this framework, internal and external funds are perfect substitutes. However, given market imperfections, reliance on internal funds may be higher since raising external finance is either more costly or impossible. The 'pecking order theory' (Myers and Majluf, 1984) or the 'hierarchy of finance hypothesis' (Fazzari et al., 1988) suggests that external finance will be more costly than internal funds for financing investment and that firms will not turn to external funds until internal sources are exhausted. This is due to a number of reasons, including monitoring costs (Townsend, 1979; Williamson, 1987), asymmetrical information entailing moral hazard and adverse selection (Jensen and Meckling, 1976; Stiglitz and Weiss, 1981), transaction costs in issuing bank debt, such as the costs of application, screening costs, bankruptcy costs, etc. Whereas the empirical literature, almost without exception, refutes the case of the perfect capital market, the work on credit rationing has produced ambiguous results. In order to assess the validity of the 'bank screening hypothesis' and credit rationing if it is an important problem, the dispute has to be resolved by testing the two hypotheses empirically. The present study finds that, in the context of transition economies, both theories may hold.

4.2.2 The empirical literature

The bulk of the empirical studies on credit rationing and financing constraints is based on the experience of firms in developed market economies. In more recent years there have been a number of attempts to apply the theory to the more advanced transition economies. However there has been almost no attempt to assess the nature or extent of credit rationing and financing constraints in the less advanced SEE countries.

The empirical literature on credit rationing and financing constraints has developed in two distinct frameworks. In terms of credit rationing, as Jaffee and Stiglitz (1990) note, the magnitude of this problem in the economy could be measured if the demand and supply for credit were known. However, what is observed is the quantity of credit that is transacted and not the excess demand for credit. Hence, credit rationing may be extremely difficult to identify, and so empirical tests are mainly indirect (Parker, 2002). One test for credit rationing is when the data allows the researcher to distinguish between firms that have applied for credit and those that have not (the demand effect) and also between firms that have been successful or unsuccessful in their application for credit (the supply effect). Using enterprise survey data from the Czech Republic, Hungary and Poland in the mid-1990s which allowed this distinction, Bratkowski et al. (2000) tried to determine how banks differentiate between different groups of firms and how they allocate credit: do they lend to firms with higher profitability; do they provide credit to firms with good prospects but weak track records; or do they treat collateral availability as the most important determinant of offering a loan? The authors found that banks were able to identify successful firms by lending to more profitable ones even without a track record but which were able to provide collateral. They also found that firms with less profit were less likely to apply for loans (e.g., no evidence of adverse selection). Based on these results, the authors conclude that credit rationing was not pervasive in the three countries in the early years of transition.

Studying the credit rationing problem in the housing loans market in the US, Jappelli (1990) explores the degree of rejection of applicants for bank loans as a measure of credit rationing. However, the author identified another group, those who did not apply for loans because they perceived that their application will be rejected by the bank. This group may be considered as credit rationed too since they cannot be treated as having had no demand for loans. The exclusion of this group may lead to biased results, because the self-selection of applicants may induce banks to adapt screening rules that differ from those that would prevail if this group of borrowers were also to apply.[2] Jappelli (1990) classifies this group as 'discouraged' borrowers and, together with the rejected group, considers them as 'credit constrained' borrowers to distinguish them from the strict definition of credit rationing. Similarly, Levenson and Willard (2000) adopt the definition of Jappelli (1990) for credit rationing and use survey data for investigating the small business sector in the US. The authors conclude that credit rationing was not a pervasive phenomenon in the US economy.[3]

The financing constraints literature, on the other hand, holds that if firms can easily obtain external funds without paying a premium, their investment decisions will be less sensitive to internally generated funds. In contrast, when the premium is high, firms use internally generated funds to fund their investment first and external funds are sought only after their internal resources have been exhausted. The empirical question in this line of an inquiry is to investigate whether a firm's investment decision is sensitive to changes in net worth, holding investment opportunities constant. In these models, investment is regressed on some proxies of net worth (e.g., cash flow or liquidity) and other firm characteristics. If the coefficient of cash flow is positive and significant, then it is said that firms face financing constraints. In this framework firms are classified *a priori* as more or less likely to face financing constraints based on the researchers' beliefs about the systematic differences between firms regarding their information opacity, riskiness, etc.

There are many *a priori* criteria on the basis of which firms may be considered to be more or less financially constrained. For example, Gilchrist and Zakrajsek (1995) use the size and age of firms as the criteria for financing constraints. As they point out, 'informational frictions' that add to the financing costs, and hence financing constraints, apply mainly to younger firms with a short track record and with a high degree of idiosyncratic risk and firms that are likely to be not well collateralised. Small firms in general are more likely to share these attributes and may be perceived as riskier. Also the screening and monitoring of small firms may be proportionately costlier to the lender. From a bank's point of view, fixed lending costs related to loan appraisals and monitoring make the costs per dollar lent relatively higher for small firms (Saito and Villanueva, 1981). Hence, they would be more financially constrained than larger and older firms. Also from the firm's perspective, the transaction costs of the application process are relatively higher for small firms. All these attributes may lead small and young firms to face higher financing constraints.

The ownership of firms (particularly state ownership and foreign ownership) have sometimes been used as the *a priori* criterion to distinguish between more and less financially constrained firms. In the transition context, one may expect that state-owned enterprises (SOEs) face fewer financing constraints because of the prevalence of soft budget constraints (SBCs) and the variety of government subsidies. Perotti and Carare (1996) and Konings et al. (2002) have shown that in Bulgaria and Romania SOEs did not exhibit financing constraints, due to the prevailing SBC regimes despite being highly indebted and having negative cash flows. Whereas in developed market economies this finding would be a sign of a perfect capital market, in the transition context it is seen as an indication of SBC. However, in the later years of transition subsidies to SOEs were cut, often following IMF recommendations, and budget constraints on SOEs hardened. In addition, after the entry of foreign banks access to finance for SOEs was reduced especially because of their delayed restructuring. On the other hand, foreign-owned firms, especially those originating from developed countries, may be expected to face lower financing constraints. This is because of their ability to access financial markets in their home countries, obtain financial resources through foreign direct investments, etc. The possible lower financing constraints faced by foreign firms may be explained by the fact that these firms also bring know-how and new technology, have better governance and may be more transparent to their lenders, and thus, may face fewer financing constraints from financial markets in their host countries. Perotti and Vesnaver (2004), for example, show that foreign-owned firms in Hungary face fewer financing constraints.

Another approach to the study of financing constraints has been recently developed by Beck et al. (2006). Unlike previous studies that inferred financing constraints from company financial statements, these authors maintain that firms' financing obstacles, which are indicative of financial constraints, can be identified directly by asking firms about these constraints. Using the survey data for 10,000 firms in 80 countries around the world in 1999, they test the severity of self-reported financial obstacles facing firms on the basis of firm and country characteristics. Given that the previous empirical work often relied on the balance sheet and income statement data of listed companies, the Beck et al. approach opened up the possibility of extending these investigations to the smaller transition economies of SEE. In these countries stock markets are either in their infancy or non-existent; they are also dominated by small firms which are not listed and more informationally opaque, or their financial statements are difficult or impossible to obtain. Hence, the survey data may be more appropriate for analysis of financing constraints facing the SME sector. The large-scale Business Environment and Enterprise Performance Surveys (BEEPS), conducted by the World Bank and EBRD, offer the possibility of using this approach for the SEE countries where the evidence on financing constraints, credit rationing and financing obstacles of firms is scarce.

4.3 Financing constraints, credit rationing and financing obstacles in SEE

4.3.1 The empirical framework

The empirical work in the remainder of this chapter utilises a survey-based approach to identify the determinants of firms' financing constraints. We use a database derived from three rounds of BEEPS in

1999, 2002 and 2005, focusing on the subset of firms in the SEE region. Following the approach employed by Beck et al. (2006), extending it in a number of ways, we investigate whether age, size and ownership have any influence on the various dimensions of firms' perceived financing constraints. The study differs from Beck et al. (2006) in many respects. First, the investigation is specific to transition countries in SEE. Second, the study extends the period of analysis using data from the 2002 and 2005 BEEPS. Third, using both logit and ordered logit models, several dimensions of firm's perceptions of financing constraints are considered: a general financing obstacle, specific obstacles such as high interest rates or high collateral requirements, access to long-term and short-term loans, etc. Fourth, more objective variables such as the share of investment that firms finance through internal funds and through bank loans are employed, bringing the estimation model closer to that of Fazzari et al. (1988). Fifth, additional control variables such as firms' performance measures (profitability and sales growth) and whether or not firms use accounting standards are introduced. Finally, the analysis contains more direct evidence of credit rationing by explicitly modelling the firm's decision to participate in the credit market and the lender's decision to reject or accept the firm's application for a loan. This is possible because the 2002 and 2005 BEEPS provide more detailed information on financing issues.

To assess the determinants of the likelihood of firms applying for a loan and being denied credit (i.e., direct credit rationing), we use the approach adopted by Bratkowski et al. (2000). However, unlike Bratkowski et al. (2000), who used a logit model to estimate two separate equations (the likelihood for of applying for a loan and the likelihood of being denied the loan), we use the Heckman model, which also enables us to deal with the possible selection bias. The model of 'discouraged' borrowers is also tested by employing a logit estimation procedure, following Jappelli's (1990) and Levenson and Willard's (2000) methodology. However, the model here differs from Jappelli's approach in the sense that here, borrowers are firms and not households; whereas the difference of this method from the Levenson and Willard (2000) approach is that they calculate the estimates for discouraged borrowers indirectly based on the parameter estimates of the regression of firms that apply for loans and are denied credit.[4] In addition, using logit and ordered logit models, the firms' self-reported difficulties in accessing short-term and long-term loans are assessed.[5] One of the reasons for employing several dimensions of financing constraints is that the firm's self-reported financing constraints are subjective by nature and may not represent the real importance of specific constraints. It is therefore useful to combine these with more objective indicators as explained above. This would also meet the need for the 'methodological cross-checking' advocated by Charnes et al. (1988).

4.3.2 Data and Models

The BEEPS is a joint World Bank/EBRD project designed to collect firm-level information on the impact of the business environment through detailed enterprise surveys at regular intervals. The surveys were conducted in transition economies in 1999, 2002 and 2005 and covered about 4000–9000 firms. The survey includes a broad range of questions aimed at evaluating the nature of obstacles faced by firms in important areas such as infrastructure, the judiciary, business regulation, crime, corruption, taxation and finance. The entrepreneurs were asked to assess and rank on a 1 to 4 scale how problematic a particular area (e.g. finance) is for the operation and growth of their firms.

The general model employed in the empirical framework utilising different specifications and estimation methods can be represented as follows:

$$Y_i = \alpha + \beta X_{1i} + \gamma X_{2i} + \varepsilon_i$$

where Y_i represents various measures of financing constraints; X_{1i} the vector of variables representing different firm characteristics; X_{2i} country and sector dummies; α, β, γ parameters to be estimated; and ε_i the random error. In the following section we use several versions of this model and a variety of econometric estimation methods.

A number of indicators have been used as measures of financing constraints (Y_i). In section 4.4.1 we use the proportion of a firm's investment expenditure financed by the firm's (i) internal funds and (ii) bank loans. Given the nature of the data (with both ratios varying between zero and 100 per cent and with many corner solution observations at both ends, the Tobit model ('censored regression model') is used for the purpose of estimation as the most appropriate model. This approach, as with Fazzari et al. (1988), posits that firms which rely more on internal funds, as opposed to external funds, to finance their investment are more financially constrained. In section 4.4.2 we focus on the probability of a firm's applying for a loan and the probability of a firm being denied the loan, and we assess the factors that influence these probabilities. We also assess the model of discouraged borrowers and the determinants of the difficulties of firms' access to short-term and long-term loans. In section 4.4.3 we assess the determinants of not only broad financing obstacles but also specific obstacles such as high interest rates and collateral requirements.

The characteristics of firms in all models include the firm's age (logged), size (measured by dummy variables indicating small and medium compared to the base category of large firms), ownership, performance (e.g. sales growth or profitability[6] as proxies for credit worthiness or future prospects), accounting method used (to signal transparency of financial reporting), sector and country of origin. It is expected that younger and smaller firms will be more financially constrained, for example, to finance a higher proportion of their investment through internal funds, and a smaller proportion through bank loans, compared to their older and larger counterparts. Majority foreign ownership is expected to be less financially constrained than that of private domestic companies. Firms with better performance and prospects may be better placed to use their own funds and also to apply for bank credit. Firms with better prospects may be in need of more external finance in order to exploit investment opportunities; hence they may be more likely to apply for external finance. To the extent that banks are able to identify this, they may be more willing to provide credit; thus, firms may be less constrained. At the same time, firms with low profitability may face liquidity problems and turn to banks for funds. This may be a sign of adverse selection allowing poorly performing firms to enter the loan market, worsening the pool of applicants which, in turn, may induce banks to limit credit availability. Profitability may decrease the likelihood of a firm's participating in the credit market, given the stringent requirements by banks and the high costs of external finance. Thus, profitable firms do not turn to banks for funding (the hierarchy of finance hypothesis). On the other hand, to the extent that a firm's profitability as an indicator of creditworthiness is observable to a bank, viable firms would find it easier to access external finance.

The three BEEP surveys differ from one another in a number of ways, particularly in terms of some questions. This means that the model run for each year, therefore, is slightly different from those run for other years because it may contain one or two different independent variables. But in addition to regressions for each year of the survey, the results also include a pooled regression which includes variables that have been covered in all three surveys. The pooled regressions contain year dummies which explain whether the financing constraints have been relaxed over time, given the dynamic changes in the banking sector in the SEE countries.

Table 4.1 summarises the descriptive statistics of the variables used in the models discussed in the next section. As Table 4.1 shows, most variables (except for Internal Funds, Bank Loans, Age and Sales Change, which are continuous) are either ordered or dummies. From the summary statistics it can be observed that, on average, firms rate high interest rates as a greater obstacle in the three rounds of BEEPS compared with other dimensions of financing obstacles. Different dimensions of financing obstacles are correlated, with the coefficients ranging from 0.29 to 0.66 in various years. Interestingly, firms' self-reported obstacles are not correlated with more objective measures such as Internal Funds and Bank Loans.[7]

4.4 Results

4.4.1 Financing constraints: reliance on Internal Funds and Bank Loans

The Tobit model is used to assess the determinants of the proportion of firms' investments financed through Internal Funds and Bank Loans (two separate specifications).[8] The Tobit estimates are presented in Table 4.2 (specifications 1–8). For each dependent variable, there are four specifications (one for each of the three years of the survey and one for the pooled data). The estimated coefficient on age is positive but insignificant in all but one specification. The exception is specification 4 with internal funds as the dependent variable, indicating that older firms finance a larger proportion of their investment through internal funds, that is, are more constrained, which is contrary to expectations and what is generally perceived in the literature.[9] However, age is insignificant in the regressions, with bank loans as the dependent variable. The change in the structure of the banking sector in the region (e.g., the entry of foreign banks and the closure of domestic banks) may also be an explanation for this outcome, in the sense that all firms were 'new' to foreign banks and the relationships had to be established from scratch.

The coefficients on size (especially small firms) are in most specifications highly significant and have the expected sign, indicating that SMEs may rely more on internal funds and less on bank loans to finance their investment needs, compared to larger firms – in few specifications the coefficients are insignificant at conventional levels. The estimated coefficient on state ownership is negative and significant in all the specifications for bank loans, indicating that the SOEs finance a smaller proportion of their investment through banks. This provides

Table 4.1 Descriptive statistics of variables

Variable	**Year**	**Obs**	**Mean**	**Std**	**Min**	**Max**
Dependent Variables						
Internal Funds	1999	820	62.17	39.10	0	100
	2002	1430	60.27	37.96	0	100
	2005	2000	61.47	36.25	0	100
Bank Loans	1999	820	8.72	21.18	0	100
	2002	1430	9.46	20.99	0	100
	2005	2000	13.02	23.66	0	100
Difficulty accessing short-term loans	1999	na	na	na	na	na
	2002	1293	2.72	2.13	1	5
	2005	na	na	na	na	na
Difficulty accessing long-term loans	1999	na	na	na	na	na
	2002	1260	3.07	2.14	1	5
	2005	na	na	na	na	na
Discouraged borrowers	1999	na	na	na	na	na
	2002	na	na	na	na	na
	2005	1426	0.32	0.47	0	1
Aplicants	1999	na	na	na	na	na
	2002	na	na	na	na	na
	2005	2039	0.52	0.50	0	1
Rejected borrowers	1999	na	na	na	na	na
	2002	na	na	na	na	na
	2005	1021	0.05	0.22	0	1
Financing obstacle	1999	855	3.09	1.10	1	4

(*continued*)

Table 4.1 Continued

Variable	**Year**	**Obs**	**Mean**	**Std**	**Min**	**Max**
	2002	1362	2.42	1.19	1	4
	2005	1949	2.35	1.14	1	4
High interest rate obstacle	1999	817	3.41	0.99	1	4
	2002	1410	2.67	1.12	1	4
	2005	1968	2.62	1.13	1	4
Collateral obstacle	1999	734	2.58	1.24	1	4
	2002	na	na	na	na	na
	2005	na	na	na	na	na
Access to long-term loan obstacle	1999	752	3.22	1.13	1	4
	2002	na	na	na	na	na
	2005	na	na	na	na	na
Explanatory Variables						
Age	1999	845	16.14	22.56	1	172
	2002	1464	16.28	19.73	3	202
	2005	2040	17.84	20.65	4	180
Small	1999	873	0.58	0.49	0	1
	2002	1464	0.66	0.48	0	1
	2005	2040	0.68	0.47	0	1
Medium	1999	873	0.22	0.41	0	1
	2002	1464	0.20	0.40	0	1
	2005	2040	0.22	0.41	0	1
Large	1999	873	0.21	0.41	0	1
	2002	1464	0.15	0.36	0	1
	2005	2040	0.11	0.31	0	1
State	1999	873	0.22	0.41	0	1
	2002	1349	0.14	0.36	0	1

	2005	2016	0.10	0.29	0	1
Private domestic	1999	873	0.71	0.45	0	1
	2002	1349	0.75	0.46	0	1
	2005	2016	0.80	0.40	0	1
Foreign	1999	873	0.08	0.26	0	1
	2002	1349	0.11	0.36	0	1
	2005	2016	0.11	0.31	0	1
Sales change	1999	812	12.61	59.32	−90	700
	2002	1360	18.31	58.22	−90	600
	2005	1968	10.63	36.92	−90	310
Profitability1	2002	1375	0.90	0.30	0	1
Profitability2	2005	1939	0.84	0.37	0	1
Accounting standards	1999	788	0.56	0.50	0	1
	2002	1294	0.49	0.50	0	1
	2005	1972	0.60	0.54	0	1

Note: a) Sector and country dummies not reported.

Table 4.2 Financing constraints of firms in SEE

	Internal Funds [Tobit model]				Bank Loans [Tobit model]			
	1999	2002	2005	Pooled	1999	2002	2005	Pooled
	(1)	(2)	(3)	(4)	(5)	(6)	(7)	(8)
Age	11.77	4.76	1.45	7.43*	0.06	10.10	2.82	4.64
	(7.95)	(6.71)	(5.31)	(4.10)	(8.81)	(7.77)	(5.40)	(4.31)
Small	37.78***	21.13***	7.25	19.98***	−52.04***	−40.17***	−18.18***	−32.33***
	(10.46)	(6.94)	(5.58)	(4.52)	(11.66)	(7.91)	(5.61)	(4.61)
Medium	21.67**	13.91**	4.55	9.82**	−9.14	−17.17**	−3.76	−8.76**
	(9.67)	(7.08)	(5.56)	(4.54)	(9.89)	(7.69)	(5.48)	(4.48)
State	6.37	0.52	−7.45	−1.63	−19.62*	−30.63***	−20.31***	−26.91***
	(9.60)	(6.73)	(5.68)	(4.53)	(10.25)	(8.21)	(6.09)	(4.91)
Foreign	3.21	−3.51	7.59	1.80	−16.15	2.13	−12.26**	−6.76
	(12.72)	(5.97)	(4.96)	(4.31)	(14.91)	(6.93)	(5.11)	(4.49)
Sales change	0.04	0.06	0.06	0.07***	−0.05	0.04	0.09**	0.02
	(0.05)	(0.04)	(0.04)	(0.02)	(0.07)	(0.04)	(0.039)	(0.02)
Profitability1		31.31***				9.25		
		(6.92)				(8.44)		
Profitability2							5.25	
	(4.42)							
Account. Standards	−13.64*	−0.94	−3.72	−0.25	2.32	8.53	7.90***	5.35*
	(7.62)	(4.36)	(3.08)	(2.92)	(9.11)	(5.17)	(3.04)	(3.04)
Year 1999				5.30				−13.77***
				(4.08)				(4.37)

Year 2002				−9.49***				−5.00
				(3.72)				(3.91)
Constant	6.41	−37.25**	58.46***	13.01	2.64	−6.65	−23.43	−11.43
	(32.62)	(17.09)	(13.32)	(11.52)	(35.47)	(20.37)	(14.50)	(12.72)
Obs.	674	1030	1845	2769	674	1030	1756	2769
Left Censored obs.	117	170	226	434	515	762	1135	1938
Uncensored obs.	306	536	1009	1436	143	249	596	778
Right censored obs.	251	324	610	899	16	19	25	53
Log Likelihood	−2069.87	−3381.39	−6311. 35	−9235.35	−1014.52	−1683.85	−3798.00	−5181.86
LR chi2	52.18***	201.44***	117.27***	182.99***	71.50***	143.52***	151.58***	279.94***
Pseudo R2	0.02	0.03	0.02	0.02	0.04	0.05	0.02	0.03

Notes: ***, **, * denote significance at 1%, 5% and 10%, respectively; standard errors in parentheses.

some evidence that the hardening of budget constraints, or even credit rationing, has become binding for SOEs. However, they do not seem to rely more on internal funds. This indicates that SOEs may still be receiving subsidies from the government, but not the 'soft' lending from the banks as in the early transition years.

The effect of foreign ownership is rather unclear. The variable is significant at five per cent level in only one specification, indicating that foreign firms rely less on bank loans than domestic firms to finance their investments. The evidence from the 'internal funds' specification suggests that these firms do not rely more on internal funds to finance their investment may support the view that foreign firms may turn to banks in their home countries or their parent banks for funds (presumably with better conditions). Regarding the performance variables, sales growth is estimated to have a positive effect, but is significant in only two specifications, providing some indication that firms with good prospects use both internal funds and bank loans more than firms with weak prospects. Profitability has a positive sign and is statistically significant at the one per cent level suggesting that more profitable firms finance a greater proportion of their investment through internal funds. However, this variable is not significant in the specification of Bank Funds. This may support the 'hierarchy of finance hypothesis' which suggests that because of the premium with external funds, firms finance their investments internally and do not turn to banks for finance until internally generated funds are exhausted.

The use of accounting standards has a statistically significant impact on the proportion of investment that firms finance through bank loans in two specifications. This suggests that firms with clearer financial reporting were able to rely more on banks to finance their investment. This variable has no effect on the use of internal funds (or only marginally as in one specification).

In terms of the year effect, the dummy for 2002 is negative and statistically significant at the five per cent level which indicates that firms in 2002 relied less on internal funds compared to 2005. On the other hand, in the specification for bank loans, the year dummy for 1999 is negative and statistically significant at the one per cent level which suggests that banks increased their role in supporting firms to finance their investment over the period. Overall, the estimates suggest that smaller firms and SOEs face the highest financing constraints. Profitable firms finance a larger proportion of their investment through internal funds, but not bank financing, which seems to be in line with the pecking order theory. It also seems that, over time, access to bank loans has improved for firms in SEE.[10]

4.4.2 Testing for credit rationing: rejected and discouraged applicants

Table 4.3 shows the results of the estimate aimed at assessing more directly whether firms in the SEE region experience credit rationing by considering three different indicators of credit rationing:

i. The likelihood of applying for a loan and being refused

The Heckman model is utilised to assess the determinants of the likelihood of applying for and being refused a loan (specifications 1 and 2). This model, with partial maximum likelihood estimation, is employed specifically to deal with the selection bias problem, given that those who apply may systematically differ from those who do not apply, and the latter group may be influenced by and reflect a response to credit denials. In other words, because applying may be systematically correlated with unobservables that affect the likelihood of being denied, using only those who apply may produce biased estimates in the equation of the likelihood of being denied. For example, firms, including non-applying firms, may anticipate the bank screening procedures and the acceptance criteria, a situation which will result in self-selection in applying for credit based on the perception of success and conditions of a loan offer. Hence, it is likely that the sample is subject to selection bias.

The first-stage equation includes the 'Financing Obstacle' variable as the part of selection since it may have an impact on the firm's decision to participate in the credit market but not have an impact on the bank decision to lend.[11] The coefficients in the first stage equation show which factors influence the firm's decision to apply for a loan whereas those in the second step show which factors influence the bank's decision to deny a loan, given that the firm has applied for a loan.

In the first specification estimating the likelihood of applying for a loan, the estimates show that small and medium-sized firms are significantly less likely to apply for bank loans than their larger counterparts. This may indicate self-selection in the market, that is, those with little collateral and/or who face high transaction costs that accompany the application process are less likely to enter the loan market. In terms of ownership, both SOEs and foreign firms seem less likely to apply for bank loans than private domestic firms. One explanation may be that SOEs do not apply because of the prospects of being denied; while foreign-owned firms do not apply because of the possibility of receiving funds from their home countries/parent companies. Sales growth is positive and statistically significant at the one per cent level, which suggests that firms with good prospects, that is, those in need of more investment,

Table 4.3 Tests for credit rationing of firms in SEE in 2005

	Heckman MLE model		The model of discouraged borrowers	Access to short-term and long-term loans	
	The likelihood of applying for a loan: 1=apply, 0=otherwise (Selection Model)	The likelihood of being rejected a loan: 1=rejected,0=otherwise (Second Stage Model)	The likelihood of being rejected and discouraged from applying for a loan=1; Otherwise=0 (Logit Model)	Imposible/very difficult Accessing Short-Term loans [Logit Model]	Imposible/very difficult Accessing Long-Term loans [Logit Model]
	(1)	(2)	(3)	(4)	(5)
Age	0.150	−0.020	−0.162	0.258	−0.005
	(0.120)	(0.028)	(0.260)	(0.268)	(0.245)
Small	−0.708***	0.050**	1.735***	1.056***	1.323***
	(0.131)	(0.022)	(0.326)	(0.295)	(0.270)
Medium	−0.213*	0.014	0.714**	0.043	0.313
	(0.130)	(0.018)	(0.326)	(0.315)	(0.280)
State	−0.570***	0.016	0.670**	0.208	0.346
	(0.132)	(0.030)	(0.289)	(0.262)	(0.242)
Foreign	−0.264**	−0.031*	−0.180	−0.389	−0.485**
	(0.109)	(0.016)	(0.268)	(0.254)	(0.227)
Sales change	0.002***	−0.0002*	−0.004**	−0.005***	−0.004**
	(0.000)	(0.0001)	(0.002)	(0.001)	(0.002)
Profitability1				−0.686**	−0.455*

				(0.269)	(0.248)
Profitability2	0.072	−0.054**	−0.673***		
	(0.094)	(0.026)	(0.182)		
Account. Standards	0.276***	−0.006	−0.452***	−0.008	0.074
	(0.068)	(0.011)	(0.147)	(0.170)	(0.155)
Financing Obstacle	0.148***				
	(0.030)				
Constant	−0.250	0.147*	−1.103	−2.216***	−1.706***
	(0.323)	(0.075)	(0.668)	(0.671)	(0.617)
Obs		1684	1265	963	947
Log Likelihood		−930.84	−682.07	−493.81	−565.37
LR chi2		244.00***	220.62***	147.47***	115.81***
Wald chi2		−0.031***			
Mill's λ					
Pseudo R2			0.139	0.13	0.10

Notes: ***, **, * denote significance at 1%, 5% and 10%, respectively; standard errors in parentheses.

seem to be more likely to apply for bank loans. This may indicate that adverse selection may not be a problem, since firms with poor prospects are less likely to participate in the credit market and worsen the pool of applicants. This may also be additional evidence of self-selection in the credit market in SEE. However, the profitability proxy is positive but insignificant. Firms employing accounting standards seem to be more likely to apply for a loan. The selection variable Financing Obstacle is positive and highly significant, indicating that firms reporting higher financing obstacles to their operation and growth are more likely to turn to banks for loans.

In the equation estimating the likelihood of being denied credit the dummy variable for small firms is statistically significant at the five per cent level. The results indicate that it is small firms which face the highest likelihood of being denied credit in the SEE. The dummy variable for foreign firms is negative and statistically significant (at the ten per cent level), indicating that foreign firms are less likely to be denied credit. The coefficients on Sales change and Profitability have an estimated negative effect and are statistically significant. Consistent with the 'bank screening hypothesis', this may be interpreted as banks being able to distinguish 'good' from 'bad' firms and firms with good prospects are less likely to be denied credit. It seems that banks do screen their applicants' creditworthiness and viable firms are more likely to receive loans. However, this should be interpreted with a caveat since, inter alia, keeping profitability, sales change and the use of some accounting standards constant, small firms are still less likely to participate in the credit market and are more likely to be denied a loan. This may indicate that some credit rationing is present in the market from both the demand side (which seems more prevalent) and the supply side, and that small firms face the highest constraints. Calculations from the BEEPS data reveal that 93.5 per cent of firms which applied obtained the loans they sought. As a result, credit rationing seems to work more through self-selection of firms on the demand side.

ii. A model of discouraged borrowers

As discussed previously, it is inappropriate to treat firms which do not apply for loans as having no demand for loans. Discouraged borrowers which do not apply for a loan for various reasons should be taken into account too (of all the firms in the SEE sample only 51.6 per cent applied for bank loans). The BEEPS 2005 dataset provides direct evidence of the reasons why firms may not apply for loans. Almost 60 per cent of non-applying firms did not apply because they had no need for loans;

the rest either considered interest rates too high (11.3 per cent), collateral requirements too high (2.8 per cent), the procedures for the application complicated (6.3 per cent), informal payments required (0.2 per cent), did not expect the loan would be approved (1.9 per cent), or a combination of above reasons (17.1 per cent), and others (2.2 per cent). Apart from firms that did not need loans and considered interest rates to be high, the rest (30.6 per cent of non-applying firms) may be considered as 'discouraged' borrowers, which jointly with the group of rejected applicants, constitute the sample of credit rationed firms as defined by Jappelli (1990). The data also show that from the sample of applicants 6.5 per cent were denied credit whereas the remaining 93.5 per cent received the loans they sought.[12]

In the SEE the rejection rate is higher for small firms – roughly one in ten small firms is denied credit, whereas the ratio for medium and large firms is one in 20. However, if the fact that some firms may not be creditworthy is taken into account, then the credit-rationed firms must account for a smaller proportion. Two performance measures were calculated for firms that were denied credit – the proportion of firms that were profitable and the proportion with growing sales. Around 67 per cent of rejected firms were profitable and 43 per cent had positive sales growth. Therefore, some creditworthy firms do appear to be denied credit, indicating that some credit rationing is present in the market. In the total sample of firms in the SEE, the rejected and discouraged firms, the upper bound of credit rationing constituted around 17 per cent, which is almost three times more than that calculated by Levenson and Willard (2000) for the US economy. Unfortunately, due to data unavailability, it was not possible to assess the share of these firms in total employment and sales of the sample.

In the model of discouraged borrowers, credit-rationed firms are identified by a dummy variable taking the value of one if the firm was refused a loan or if it was a 'discouraged borrower', and zero otherwise. Table 4.3 (specification 3) presents the logit estimates of the likelihood of a firm's being credit rationed. As in most previous models, age is insignificant. The results show that SMEs are significantly more likely to be credit rationed than their larger counterparts. In this specification the coefficient on foreign firms is negative but not significant, whereas that for SOEs is positive and statistically significant at the one per cent level, indicating that SOEs are more likely to be credit rationed. Firms' good prospects, as proxied by the change in firms' sales, have a negative and statistically significant effect on the likelihood of credit rationing. Profitability is also statistically significant at one per cent level, indicating that more profitable firms are less likely to be credit rationed. The 'use of accounting standards' enters with a negative sign and is statistically significant at the one per cent level, suggesting that if firms are able to provide proper information to their lenders, the likelihood of being credit rationed will be reduced. In all, the results broadly suggest that being large, performing well and using some accounting standards reduce the likelihood of being credit rationed.

iii. Difficulties of obtaining short-term and long-term loans

We consider the determinants of the likelihood of the firm reporting difficulties in obtaining short-term and long-term loans on a 1 to 5 scale, with 1 being very easy and 5 impossible, using both the logit and the ordered logit models. Some studies, for example, Hersch et al. (1997), transform the ordered dependent variable: 'how difficult is it to get a long-term loan from a bank?' ranking from 1, very easy, to 4, very difficult, into a dichotomous dummy variable (by amalgamating the top two rankings into 1 and the bottom two rankings into 0), and employ the logit model. Using BEEPS data from 2002, in this section the group of firms facing the highest difficulties in accessing loans is modelled using logit estimation. A dummy dependent variable is used, taking a value of one if the firm reports that it is impossible or very difficult to access short-term and long-term loans, and 0 otherwise (Table 4.3, specifications 4 and 5). In order to pick up all the variation in the data, an ordered logit model is also estimated for a dependent variable ranging from 1, very easy, to 5, impossible, indicating the difficulty experienced by firms in accessing loans. The results for an ordered logit model are largely consistent with logit estimates and are presented in Appendix.

As in most of previous specifications, age is insignificant. The reporting of greater difficulties in accessing either short- or long-term loans is statistically significant at the one per cent level for the group of small firms. However, the coefficient on medium-sized firms is insignificant. State-owned firms do not report significantly higher difficulties in accessing either long- or short-term loans, although the estimated coefficients have a positive sign. Being a foreign-owned firm decreases the likelihood of reporting difficulties in accessing long-term loans compared to private domestic firms, and the estimated effect of sales change and profitability are negative and statistically significant in both specifications. This indicates that firms with good prospects are less likely to be credit rationed. The results also suggest that the fact that firms use some accounting standards have no statistically significant effect on difficulties in accessing short- and long-term loans for the sample of firms in 2002. However, as shown previously, in later years (with 2005 data) these firms financed a greater proportion of their investment through bank funds and were less likely to be credit rationed, suggesting that the financing environment for firms with better information availability has improved.

4.4.3 The importance of financing obstacles for firms' operation and growth

In this section the dependent variables indicate a firm's perceived severity of several financing obstacles for the operation and growth of their business on a 1 to 4 scale: general financing obstacle (Financing Obstacle), high interest rates (High Interest Rates Obstacle), high collateral requirements (Collateral Obstacle) and access to long-term loans (Long-term Loan Obstacle). To better discriminate firms that report various dimensions of financing as a major obstacle, a logit model is employed for the dependent variable, taking 1 if a firm reports financing as a major obstacle and 0 otherwise. As previously, the ordered logit models are also employed so that all variation in the data is picked up. The estimates from the ordered logit models are broadly consistent with the logit estimates and are presented in Appendix.

i. General financing obstacle

In this section the determinants of the general financing obstacle are assessed, using the three rounds of BEEPS and a pooled regression. The results are presented in Table 4.4 (specifications 1–4). The estimates indicate that age generally does not have explanatory power for firms reporting financing as a higher obstacle. The estimated coefficient on small firms is positive and highly significant in all specifications, which indicates that small firms face greater financing obstacles compared to larger firms. The estimated effect of being a medium-sized firm is positive and significant in 1999 and in the model with pooled data. This provides some evidence that the medium-sized firms too face greater financing obstacles than their larger counterparts. Regarding firm ownership, the dummy variable for SOEs is not significant in any specification (except in specification 1 at 10 per cent level). This does not support the assertion that SOEs may have had access to 'soft' lending, and hence may report lower financing obstacles. The dummy variable for foreign-owned firms is negative and statistically significant in all specifications (except specification 2). This may support the previous claim that foreign firms may have lower financing constraints because they have better governance and banks are more willing to lend to this

Table 4.4 Financing obstacles of firms in SEE

	Financing Obstacle [Logit Model]				**Higest Interest Rates Obstacle [Logit Model]**				**Hign collateral requirements and access to long-term loans as an obstacle to firm operation and growth**	
	1999	**2002**	**20005**	**Pooled**	**1999**	**2002**	**2005**	**Pooled**	**Collateral Obstacle [Logit Model]**	**Access to Long-Term Loans Obstacle [Logit Model]**
	(1)	(2)	(3)	(4)	(5)	(6)	(7)	(8)	(9)	(10)
Age	−0.161	0.264	0.230	0.199	0.147	0.082	0.403*	0.411***	−0.066	−0.051
	(0.200)	(0.251)	(0.225)	(0.137)	(0.238)	(0.235)	(0.207)	(0.134)	(0.229)	(0.217)
Small	0.651**	0.584**	0.650***	0.620***	0.635**	0.360	0.637***	0.485***	1.191***	1.115***
	(0.267)	(0.272)	(0.256)	(0.162)	(0.312)	(0.243)	(0.233)	(0.152)	(0.311)	(0.283)
Medium	0.461*	0.015	0.296	0.371**	0.336	−0.170	0.262	0.192	0.515*	0.474*
	(0.248)	(0.286)	(0.253)	(0.162)	(0.294)	(0.259)	(0.232)	(0.154)	(0.287)	(0.258)
State	0.427*	−0.032	0.045	0.118	−0.356	−0.126	−0.801***	−0.438***	0.333	0.214
	(0.244)	(0.249)	(0.240)	(0.151)	(0.287)	(0.237)	(0.247)	(0.152)	(0.277)	(0.256)
Foreign	−0.573*	−0.222	−0.640***	−0.456***	−0.105	−0.198	−0.423**	−0.212	−0.263	−0.144
	(0.341)	(0.235)	(0.249)	(0.167)	(0.393)	(0.211)	(0.203)	(0.145)	(0.407)	(0.351)
Sales change	−0.002	−0.004**	−0.004**	−0.004***	0.001	0.001	0.000	−0.001	−0.002	0.001
	(0.002)	(0.002)	(0.002)	(0.001)	(0.001)	(0.001)	(0.001)	(0.001)	(0.002)	(0.001)

Profitability2			−0.540***				−0.509***			
			(0.163)				(0.153)			
Account.	−0.111	−0.007	0.144	−0.113	0.094	−0.167	0.106	−0.020	0.443*	0.393*
Standards	(0.191)	(0.164)	(0.128)	(0.103)	(0.228)	(0.218)	(0.119)	(0.098)	(0.228)	(0.211)
Year 1999				1.708***				2.132***		
				(0.141)				(0.139)		
Year 2002				0.505***				0.373***		
				(0.137)				(0.125)		
Constant	1.238	−1.534*	−2.029***	−2.127***	0.392	−1.868***	−2.978***	−2.446***	−2.713**	−1.177
	(1.116)	(0.627)	(0.592)	(0.404)	(1.011)	(0.605)	(0.575)	(0.398)	(1.175)	(0.975)
Obs	696	988	1713	2722	687	1021	1728	2729	601	619
Log Likelihood	−457.17	−521.55	−835.77	−1454.78	−305.79	−595.17	−969.11	−1581.58	−357.27	−391.82
LR chi2 Pseudo	50.52***	72.43**	116.11***	340.59***	130.61***	53.52***	147.93***	450.32***	65.71***	49.83***
R2	0.05	0.07	0.065	0.1048	0.176	0.07	0.071	0.1246	0.09	0.07

Notes: ***, **, * denote significance at 1%, 5% and 10%, respectively; standard errors in parentheses.

group, or that they may have access to finance from banks in their parent countries or foreign direct investments from their parent companies.

Regarding other explanatory variables, sales change is estimated to have a negative and statistically significant effect in nearly all specifications. This supports the previous finding that firms with good prospects may face lower financing obstacles. Profitability has an estimated negative sign and is statistically significant at the one per cent level in 2005, but in 2002 it is insignificant. It is important to note here that profitable firms may report lower financing obstacles either because this implies creditworthiness which may be identified by the lenders and have lower difficulties in accessing external finance, or because they may report lower obstacles because their profits suffice for the investments they used to undertake. As shown previously, profitable firms do not finance a higher proportion of investment through bank loans and are not more likely to apply for bank loans. However, the evidence also suggests that if they turn to banks for finance, they are less likely to be denied. The variable indicating that the firm uses some accounting standards is not significant in any of the specifications. In terms of the year effect, in the regression with pooled data, the coefficients for 1999 and 2002 are statistically significant and positive. This suggests that the financing obstacles seem to have decreased over time for the firms in SEE (more so in the 1999–2002 period than in the 2002–2005 period), which is in line with the deepening of the financial markets in these countries.

ii. High interest rates as an obstacle

Firms may have access to external financing, but this does not imply that they are not paying a risk premium associated with asymmetrical information and other credit market frictions. Using a similar approach, in this section the focus is on another dimension of the financing obstacle, namely the degree to which firms perceive high interest rates as an obstacle to the growth and operation of their businesses. The results are presented in Table 4.4 (specifications 5–8). As can be seen, age has an estimated positive sign and is statistically significant in two specifications. The coefficient on small firms is statistically significant and positive in all the specifications, except in specification 6, and the coefficient on medium-sized firms is not significant. This indicates that, apart from the general financing obstacle, belonging to the group of small firms increases the likelihood of reporting higher obstacles for operation and growth as a result of high interest rates. Being and SOE firm has an estimated negative and statistically significant effect on perceiving high interest rates as an obstacle, except in two specifications. An explanation may be that either SOEs receive cheaper credit or, if they are credit rationed, do not perceive high interest rates as an obstacle. As shown in the previous sections, the evidence suggests that SOEs are more likely to be credit rationed. The dummy variable for foreign firms is negative and statistically significant in the 2005 sample, giving some evidence that foreign firms may have access to cheaper loans than their domestic counterparts. The other explanatory variables, sales change and accounting standards, are not significant. As in the previous model, the estimated coefficient on profitability is negative and statistically significant at the one per cent level in 2005, but it is insignificant in 2002. In the pooled sample, the year dummies are positive and statistically significant, which suggests that in the earlier years firms perceived high interest rates as a greater obstacle for their operation and growth compared to 2005, broadly in line with the downward trend in lending rates in the SEE.

iii. Collateral requirements and access to long-term loans as an obstacle

In this section the determinants of firms' self-reported obstacles for their operation and growth due to high collateral requirements and access to long-term loans are explored and the data are available for the 1999 sample only. The estimates do not indicate a significant effect of age on firms perceiving collateral requirements and access to long-term loans as an impediment to their operation and growth (Table 4.4, specifications 9 and 10). Small and medium-sized firms report significantly higher obstacles compared to the base group of large firms. Neither SOEs nor foreign-owned firms are significantly different from private domestic firms in reporting these obstacles, although in all the specifications the state dummy is positive and the foreign dummy is negative. The coefficient on sales growth is insignificant in all specifications. The estimated coefficient on accounting standards is positive and significant at the 10 per cent level only, which suggests that firms which use an accounting standard are more likely to perceive access to short- and long-term loans as a major obstacle compared to firms which do not use any standards, that is, which consider themselves as better-quality borrowers.

To summarise, in terms of firms' self-reported financing obstacles, size appears to matter as a determinant of various dimensions of finance as an obstacle to firms' operation and growth. Small firms are more likely to face higher financing obstacles than large firms, whereas the evidence for medium-sized firms is weaker. The ownership effect also is an important determinant in various dimensions of financing obstacles. The regression results provide some evidence that foreign-owned firms are likely to face lower obstacles compared to their domestic counterparts. No evidence is found that state-owned firms are likely to face lower financing obstacles compared to private companies, indicating that a hardening of budget constraints may have been put in place in the SEE. In general, firms with better prospects and good performance seem to face fewer financing obstacles. The firm's age and whether the company uses accounting standards do not seem to have an impact on firm's reporting lower financing obstacles, these two variables being insignificant in most of the regressions.

4.5 Conclusions and policy implications

This chapter assesses the significance and determinants of financing constraints, credit rationing and financing obstacles faced by firms in the SEE region by using a wide range of indictors and a large data set from the three rounds of BEEPS. These indicators include the proportion of investment expenditure financed by internal funds and bank loans, the probability of applying for a loan and being rejected, the probability of being a discouraged borrower and the importance of financing as an obstacle to the growth of firms. The empirical results suggest that the cohort of small firms is relatively more constrained. Compared to the group of larger firms, small firms rely more on internal funds and less on bank loans to finance investment, are less likely to apply for a loan, are more likely to be refused a loan, are more likely to fall within the group of discouraged borrowers, and face greater difficulties in accessing both short- and long-term loans. Furthermore, financing, high interest rates and high collateral requirements pose a greater obstacle to the operation and growth of small firms than to larger firms.

In terms of ownership, the evidence indicates that foreign-owned firms face lower financing constraints compared to their domestic counterparts and SOEs. This may be explained by their ability to access financial sources from their parent companies and banks in their home countries. The estimates suggest that they do not rely much on the domestic banking sector – presumably because of better financing conditions in their home countries. SOEs, on the other hand, seem to face credit constraints from the financial sector, which suggests some hardening of budget constraints in the SEE region, at least in the bank–firm relationship.

There was some support for the 'bank screening hypothesis'. It was found that more profitable firms, those with better prospects and firms that implement some accounting standards face fewer constraints, which implies that banks do engage in screening their applicants to reduce information asymmetries and are able, to some extent, to distinguish 'good' from 'bad' borrowers. However, the bank screening hypothesis is not the only explanation. To the extent that screening is limited to observable characteristics of firms that make up each risk class, the unobserved heterogeneity remains within each class and credit rationing may still continue. There is also some evidence of self-selection in the credit market, since firms with poor prospects do not enter the market (i.e., the likelihood of adverse selection is less than expected). The evidence also suggests that there has been a substantial decrease in financing constraints in all firm categories. Importantly, the decrease in financing constraints is greater for small firms than for larger ones, indicating a shift in the lending policy of banks towards small business sector. This may be a natural evolution, given the dominance of this sector in the countries under investigation.

There is much room for government policies aimed at improving the position of small firms in the credit market. While loan guarantee schemes and other forms of subsidies to small firms may relax some of the financial constraints, these schemes also generate moral hazard and weaken the banks' incentive to screen the applicants effectively (Vogel and Adams, 1997). Given the importance of collateral as a major element of financing constraint, there may be some room for the government to improve the operation of the collateral system and, as argued by DeSoto (2000), activate the large volume of 'dead' capital in these countries. The collateral system can be improved by strengthening the protection of property rights, improving the functioning of courts and the rule of law, and establishing pledge registers for movable assets and land registers for immovable assets, and formalising land and other property titles that need to be integrated in a unified system of registration to facilitate the quick verification of property rights at low cost.

Credit rationing and financing constraints emanate from information asymmetries in the financial market. Government policies should aim to reduce the information asymmetry problem by devising regulations on financial reporting and disclosure and the use of appropriate accounting and auditing standards. Screening and monitoring by banks will be easier when firms become more transparent and the accounting information becomes more reliable and meaningful, enabling banks to adopt lending technologies based on 'hard' information. To the extent that weak transparency is an intrinsic feature of small firms, enhancing the availability of information through credit registers and other systems of notice will decrease the costs of screening loan applications.

Appendix

Table 4A.1 Various dimensions of financing obstacles, the ordered logit models

	Difficulty of Accessing Short-Term loans	Difficulty of Accessing Long-Term loans	Financing Obstacle				High Interest Rate Obstacle				Collateral Obstacle	Access to Long-Term Loans Obstacle
	(1)	(2)	(3)	(4)	(5)	(6)	(7)	(8)	(9)	(10)	(11)	(12)
Age	−0.036	0.145	−0.187	0.373**	0.117	0.229**	0.041	0.176	0.223	0.370***	−0.072	−0.107
	(0.196)	(0.200)	(0.193)	(0.190)	(0.166)	(0.110)	(0.222)	(0.199)	(0.159)	(0.114)	(0.200)	(0.221)
Small	0.944***	1.297***	0.810***	0.384*	0.326**	0.410***	0.465	0.219	0.376**	0.317***	1.044***	1.026***
	(0.208)	(0.214)	(0.257)	(0.204)	(0.159)	(0.123)	(0.305)	(0.201)	(0.161)	(0.123)	(0.280)	(0.266)
Medium	0.309	0.461**	0.655***	−0.011	0.200	0.359***	0.235	−0.018	0.280*	0.265**	0.459**	0.491**
	(0.209)	(0.206)	(0.226)	(0.204)	(0.163)	(0.121)	(0.268)	(0.192)	(0.199)	(0.116)	(0.228)	(0.230)
State	0.228	0.165	0.454**	−0.311	−0.131	−0.068	−0.353	−0.392*	−0.664***	−0.533***	0.152	0.185
	(0.212)	(0.217)	(0.232)	(0.209)	(0.183)	(0.125)	(0.277)	(0.207)	(0.169)	(0.124)	(0.243)	(0.243)
Foreign	−0.486***	−0.546***	−0.626**	−0.405**	−0.557***	−0.483***	0.076	−0.291*	−0.577***	−0.306***	−0.128	−0.266
	(0.184)	(0.183)	(0.271)	(0.174)	(0.151)	(0.117)	(0.326)	(0.165)	(0.161)	(0.113)	(0.276)	(0.322)
Sales change	−0.005***	−0.004***	−0.002	−0.003**	−0.002*	−0.003***	0.001	−0.001	−0.001	−0.001*	0.001	0.001
	(0.001)	(0.001)	(0.002)	(0.001)	(0.001)	(0.000)	(0.002)	(0.001)	(0.001)	(0.000)	(0.001)	(0.002)
Profitability1	−0.758***	−0.493**		0.067				0.202				
	(0.202)	(0.208)		(0.214)				(0.193)				
Profitability2					−0.517***				−0.431***			
					(0.127)				(0.129)			

Accounting Standards	0.061	0.076	−0.013	−0.015	0.105	−0.078	0.078	−0.128	0.013	0.008	0.515***	0.353*
	(0.135)	(0.133)	(0.177)	(0.123)	(0.089)	(0.077)	(0.228)	(0.123)	(0.056)	(0.008)	(0.189)	(0.202)
Year 1999						1.508***				1.989***		
						(0.110)				(0.123)		
Year 2002						0.1778***				0.361***		
						(0.061)				(0.096)		
Cut1	−1.299**	−1.147**	−1.467**	0.278	−0.374	0.320	−1.941**	−0.247	−0.090	0.346	1.046*	−0.271
	(0.517)	(0.496)	(0.609)	(0.519)	(0.435)	(0.317)	(0.904)	(0.515)	(0.420)	(0.315)	(0.693)	(0.849)
Cut2	0.445	0.463	−0.815	1.028**	0.557	1.148***	−1.411*	0.827	0.909**	1.309***	1.721***	0.119
	(0.517)	(0.399)	(0.606)	(0.521)	(0.435)	(0.318)	(0.904)	(0.513)	(0.423)	(0.316)	(0.688)	(0.849)
Cut3	1.761***	1.871***	0.403	2.157***	1.789***	2.349***	−0.309	2.041***	2.150***	2.446***	2.721**	1.041
	(0.519)	(0.500)	(0.601)	(0.528)	(0.436)	(0.320)	(0.901)	(0.515)	(0.425)	(0.318)	(0.693)	(0.848)
Cut4	3.742***	3.549***										
	(0.534)	(0.508)										
Obs	963	947	696	988	1713	2722	613	1021	1728	2729	601	619
Log Likelihood	−1337.76	−1361.53	−806.82	−1290.45	−2270.78	−3533.00	−487.75	−1368.5	−2294.57	−3442.07	−753.35	−637.47
LR chi^2	220.39***	163.92***	68.13***	95.73***	156.64***	384.05***	134.16***	61.7***	167.25***	445.93***	92.75***	58.93***
PseudoR^2	0.08	0.06	0.04	0.04	0.04	0.05	0.1209	0.04	0.04	0.07	0.06	0.05

Notes: ***,**, * denote significance at 1%, 5% and 10%, respectively; Robust standard errors in parentheses.

Notes

The views expressed in this chapter are those of the authors and do not reflect the views of the institutions that they represent. The authors would like to thank Professor Jean Mangan for useful comments.

1. Some authors refer to the advances in credit scoring as the evidence that banks can distinguish between customers of varying risk. However, credit scoring models used by commercial banks are statistical models based on borrowers' observable characteristics. Notwithstanding various estimation biases in the credit scoring models (see for example Greene, 1998; Parnitzke, 2005), the rating is made based on some *average* pattern of observationally distinct risk classes. Despite this, within each risk class, due to information asymmetries and the inability to sort borrowers perfectly, credit rationing may still emerge.
2. Besanko and Thakor (1987) point out that in some cases the bank's credit policy discourages borrowers from applying for credit by using non-price mechanisms, that is, collateral or application procedures, and that the bank need not explicitly reject borrowers to induce them to exit the market.
3. However, contrary to this, the bulk of other empirical studies have found that credit rationing is indeed binding – Perez (1998) for the US economy, Angelini and Generale (2005) for developing economies, and Rizov (2004) for a transition economy.
4. This is because their survey did not provide direct information on whether non-applicants expect to be denied, while the BEEPS provides direct information on the reasons why some firms did not apply for a loan, including firms' expectation of denial.
5. This method of measuring credit rationing is similar to Hersch et al. (1997) though the focus of their study was different – the previous business experience of firms' owners and whether they were members of the *nomenkatura*.
6. Because of the nature of the dataset and the fact that some questions have changed from one round of survey to another, two profitability variables are used in the estimations: Profitability1 for the 2002 survey, a dummy variable taking the value of 1 if the firm had positive gross profit to total sales ratio in 2001 and 0 otherwise; and Profitability2 for the 2005 survey, a dummy variable taking the value of 1 if the firm had reinvested some of its 2003 profits in 2004, and 0 otherwise.
7. The correlation matrix of variables is available upon request.
8. By comparing the results with a similar probit model, it can be shown that there is no misspecification in terms of heteroscedasticity and non-normality. The results are available upon request.
9. A specification replacing the age variable with a dummy taking the value of one if the firm is less than five years old and zero otherwise (not reported here), produces statistically insignificant results for all specifications.
10. There is no systematic difference among country and sector control variables in any of the models used in the analysis. Given that the focus of the study is on firm characteristics and in order to present more clearly the variables of interest, sector and country specific control variables are not reported, although they are included in all regressions.

11. To correct for the sample selection bias, there needs to be a variable that affects the selection equation without affecting the second. In the Heckman estimation, in the selection equation, the inverse Mill's ratio (λ) is estimated for each observation. In all the cases with this type of data, the two-stage estimation procedure is necessary to calculate the Mill's λ in order to infer whether the sample is subject to selection bias (see Heckman, 1979; Wooldridge, 2001 for the methodology). Mill's λ is statistically significant, which suggests that the sample is subject to selection bias. Therefore, the Heckman method is the appropriate technique for estimating the second-stage equation of the likelihood of the bank decision to deny a loan.
12. In a sample of small firms only, the corresponding figure for the US economy in 1988 was 2.14 percent (Levenson and Willard, 2000) and for Italy it was 2.7 percent during the economic boom in 1988 and 12.8 percent during the recession in 1993 (Guiso, 1998). In a more conservative approach, using only a sample of start-up firms in the UK, Cressy (1996) found that only six percent of business start-ups were denied a loan. The results may be very different in developing countries. Bigsten et al. (2000) find that more than half of the firms in the sample of six African countries had no demand for credit. Of those with a demand, only a quarter obtained a loan and small firms were constrained more.

References

Aghion, P. and P. Bolton (1997), 'A Theory of Trickle-Down Growth and Development', *Review of Economic Studies*, 64, 151–72.

Anderson, R. and C. Kegels (1998), *Transition Banking: Financial Development of Central and Eastern Europe*, London: Oxford University Press.

Angelini, P. and A. Generale (2005), 'Firm Size Distribution: Do Financial Constraints Explain it All? Evidence from Survey Data', Bank of Italy, Discussion Paper, No. 549.

Beck, T., A. Demirgüc-Kunt, L. Laeven and V. Maximovic (2006), 'The Determinants of Financing Obstacles', *Journal of International Money and Finance*, 25, 932–52.

Besanko, D. and A. Thakor (1987), 'Collateral and Rationing: Sorting Equilibria in Monopolistic and Competitive Credit Market', *International Economic Review*, 28, 671–89.

Bigsten, A., P. Collier, S. Dercon, M. Fafchamps, B. Gauthier, J. Gunning, A. Oduro, R. Oostendorp, C. Patillo, M. Soderbom, F. Teal and A. Zeufack (2000), 'Credit Constraints in Manufacturing Enterprises in Africa', ISA, Working Paper, No. 24.

Bratkowski, A., I. Grosfeld and J. Rostowski (2000), 'Investment and Finance in *de novo* Private Firms: Empirical Results from the Czech Republic, Hungary and Poland', *Economics of Transition*, 8, 101–16.

Charnes, A., W. Cooper and T. Sueyoshi (1988), 'A Goal Programming/ Constrained Regression Review of the Bell System Break-Up', *Management Science*, 34, 1–26.

Cressy, R. (1996), 'Are Business Start-Ups Debt-Rationed', *Economic Journal*, 106, 1253–70.

DeSoto, H. (2000), *The Mystery of Capital: Why Capitalism Triumphs in the West and Fails Everywhere Else*, New York: Basic Books.
European Bank for Reconstruction and Development (2006), *Transition Report*, London: EBRD.
Fazzari, S., R. Hubbard and B. Petersen (1988), 'Financing Constraints and Corporate Iinvestment', *Brooking Papers on Economic Activity*, 78, 141–95.
Ghosh, P., D. Mookherjee and D. Ray (2001), 'Credit Rationing in Developing Countries: An Overview of the Theory', in D. Mookherjee and D. Ray (eds),. *Readings in the Theory of Economic Development*, London: Blackwell Publishing.
Gilchrist, S. and E. Zakrajsek (1995), 'The Importance of Credit for Macroeconomic Activity: Identification through Heterogeneity', in L. Peek and E. Rosengren (eds), *Is Bank Lending Important for the Transmission of Monetary Policy*, Boston, MA: Federal Reserve Bank of Boston.
Greene, W. (1998), 'Sample Selection in Credit-Scoring Models', *Japan and the World Economy*, 10, 299–316.
Guiso, L. (1998), 'High-Tech Firms and Credit Rationing', *Journal of Economic Behavior and Organization*, 35, 39–59.
Heckman, J. (1979), 'Sample Selection Bias as a Specification Error', *Econometrica*, 47, 153–61.
Hersch, P., D. Kemme and J. Netter (1997), 'Access to Bank Loans in a Transition Economy: The Case of Hungary', *Journal of Comparative Economics*, 24, 79–89.
Inderst, R. and H. Muller (2007), 'A Lender-Based Theory of Collateral', *Journal of Financial Economics*, 84, 826–59.
Jaffee, D. and J. Stiglitz (1990), 'Credit Rationing', in B. Friedman and F. Hahn (eds) *Handbook of Monetary Economics, Volume II*, Amsterdam: North-Holland.
Jappelli, T. (1990), 'Who is Credit Constrained in the US Economy?' *Quarterly Journal of Economics*, 55, 219–34.
Jensen, M. and W. Meckling (1976), 'Theory of the Firm: Managerial Behaviour, Agency Costs and Ownership Structure', *Journal of Financial Economics*, 3, 305–60.
Konings, J., M. Rizov and H. Vandenbussche (2002), 'Investment and Credit Constraints in Transition Economies: Micro Evidence from Poland, the Czech Republic, Bulgaria and Romania', LICOS, Discussion Paper, No. 112.
Levenson, A. and K. Willard (2000), 'Do Firms Get the Financing They Want? Measuring Credit Rationing Experienced by Small Business in the US', *Small Business Economics*, 14, 83–94.
Milde, H. and J. G. Riley (1988), 'Signalling in Credit Markets', *Quarterly Journal of Economics*, 103, 101–29.
Myers, S. and N. Majluf (1984), 'Corporate Financing and Investment Decisions when Firms have Information that Investors Do Not Have', *Journal of Financial Economics*, 13, 187–221.
Parker, S. (2002), 'Do Banks Ration Credit to New Enterprises? And Should Governments Intervene?', *Scottish Journal of Political Economy*, 49, 162–93.
Parnitzke, T. (2005), 'Credit Scoring and the Sample Selection Bias', Institute of Insurance Economics, University of St. Gallen (mimeo).
Perez, S. (1998), 'Testing for Credit Rationing: An Application of Disequilibrium Econometrics', *Journal of Macroeconomics*, 20, 721–39.
Perotti, E. and L. Vesnaver (2004), 'Enterprise Finance and Investment in Listed Hungarian Firms', *Journal of Comparative Economics*, 32, 73–87.

Perotti, E. and O. Carare (1996), 'The Evolution of Bank Credit Quality in Transition: Theory and Evidence from Romania', CERT, Discussion Paper, No. 97/2.

Riley, J. (1987), 'Credit Rationing: A Further Remark', *American Economic Review*, 77, 224–7.

Rizov, M. (2004), 'Credit Constraints and Profitability', *Emerging Markets Finance and Trade*, 40, 63–83.

Saito, K. and D. Villanueva (1981), 'Transaction Costs of Credit to the Small-Scale Sector in the Philippines', *Economic Development and Cultural Change*, 29, 631–40.

Schwartz, A. (1981), 'Security Interests and Bankruptcy Priorities: A Review of Current Theories', *Journal of Legal Studies*, 10, 1–37.

Stiglitz, J. and A. Weiss (1981), 'Credit Rationing in Markets with Imperfect Information', *American Economic Review*, 71, 393–410.

Storey, D. (1994), *Understanding Small Business Sector*, London: Routledge Thomson Learning.

Townsend, R. (1979), 'Optimal Contracts and Competitive Markets with Costly State Verification', *Journal of Economic Theory*, 21, 265–93.

Vogel, R. and D. Adams (1997), 'Old and New Paradigms in Development Finance: Should Directed Credit be Resurrected?' CAER II, Discussion Paper, No. 2.

Williamson, S. (1986), 'Costly Monitoring, Financial Intermediation, and Equilibrium Credit Rationing', *Quarterly Journal of Economics*, 102, 135–45.

Williamson, S. (1987), 'Costly Monitoring, Loan Contracts, and Equilibrium Credit Rationing', *Journal of Monetary Economics*, 18, 159–79.

Wooldridge, J. (2001), *Econometric Analysis of Cross-Section and Panel Data*, Cambridge, MA: The MIT Press.

5
Efficiency, Persistence and Predictability of Central European Stock Markets

Ladislav Krištoufek

5.1 Introduction

The stock markets of the Czech Republic, Hungary, Poland and Slovakia have undergone important institutional changes since the fall of the communist regime, changes that are reflected in its increased transparency and liquidity. Such properties are necessary for the market to be efficient. Even though the efficiency of the markets is hard to test statistically, the test for long-range dependence in the evolution of the stock returns yields testable implications for the martingale hypothesis, which is used as a benchmark for market efficiency (McCauley et al., 2008; Mandelbrot, 1966).

The efficiency of the Central European stock indices has been tested by several authors. Worthington and Higgs (2003) researched weak efficiency, tested serial correlations, unit roots and variance ratios, and showed that out of all the Central European markets, only the Hungarian BUX is weakly efficient. Similarly, Hájek (2007) compares the Czech PX, Polish WIG and Hungarian BUX with corresponding variance ratios and Fischer factorial statistics and finds BUX to be the only weakly efficient one. Diviš & Teplý (2005) also use variance ratios and show that the Central European markets converge to higher efficiency. Egert and Kočenda (2005) find short-term spillover effects between the Central European indices, which also reject the weak efficiency. Finally, Jagric, Podobnik and Kolanovic (2005) examine the indices with the wavelet transform long-range dependence test and show that the markets have undergone interesting dynamics, with periods of high inefficiency but also with a trend towards efficiency.

Long-range dependence was found in a wide portfolio of indices (Di Matteo, 2007; Di Matteo et al., 2005; Matos et al., 2008) and is used as a measure of market efficiency as its presence in time series enhances predictability (Cajueiro & Tabak, 2005; Da Silva et al., 2007) and can show optimal investment horizons (Lo, 1991). As the estimators of long-range dependence are not restricted to specific distributions, they provide quite a robust measure. We apply a time-dependent Hurst exponent (Grech & Mazur, 2004, 2005) to uncover the possible inefficiency together with its evolution.

The chapter is organised as follows. In the section 5.2, the basic notion of long-range dependence is presented. In the section 5.3, the Hurst exponent, which is crucial to the detection of long-range dependence, and its connection to market efficiency are introduced. Section 5.4 briefly describes the data set. Section 5.5 presents the results of global and local (time-dependent) long-range dependence and furthermore focuses on predictability and its changes with a changing Hurst exponent. We show that WIG and BUX are the most efficient of the group of share markets, PX remains very close to significant long-range dependent behaviour. SAX is shown to lack sufficient liquidity to be described correctly by the Hurst exponent.

5.2 Long-range dependence

Long-range dependence is present in stationary time series if the autocorrelation function of the process decays as $\rho(\mathrm{k}) \approx CK^{2H-2}$ for lag k approaching infinity. The parameter $0 < H < 1$ is called the 'Hurst exponent' after water engineer Harold Edwin Hurst, who used the exponent to describe river flow behaviour (Hurst, 1951; Mandelbrot & van Ness, 1968).

The critical value of the Hurst exponent is 0.5; it suggests two possible processes. H being equal to 0.5 implies either an independent process (Beran, 1994) or a short-term dependent process (Lillo & Farmer, 2004). An independent process has zero auto-covariances at all non-zero lags. On the other hand, the short-term dependent process shows non-zero auto-covariances at low lags, exponentially decaying to zero correlations at high lags. However, the two following cases are more important for the notion of market efficiency.

If $H>0.5$, the auto-covariances of the process are positive at all lags and the process is called long-range dependent with positive correlations (Embrechts & Maejima, 2002) or persistent (Mandelbrot & van Ness, 1968). The auto-covariances are hyperbolically decaying and non-summable, so that $\Sigma_{k=0}^{\infty} \gamma(k) = \infty$ (Beran, 1994). On the other hand, if $H<0.5$, the auto-covariances are significantly negative at all lags and the process is said to be long-range dependent with negative correlations (Embrechts & Maejima, 2002) or anti-persistent (Mandelbrot & van Ness, 1968). Similarly to the previous case, the auto-covariances are hyperbolically decaying but summable, so that $0<\Sigma_{k=0}^{\infty}\gamma(k)<\infty$ (Embrechts & Maejima, 2002). The persistent process implies that a positive movement is statistically more likely to be followed by another positive movement, or vice versa. On the other hand, the anti-persistent process implies that it is more statistically probable that a positive movement will be followed by a negative movement, and vice versa (Vandewalle, Ausloos & Boveroux, 1997).

Mandelbrot (1963) showed that long-range dependent processes are closely connected to stable distributions through an α parameter while $\alpha = 1/H$ (Panas, 2001). Note that this implication is valid only from long-range dependence to stable distribution and not vice versa. Parameter α is crucial to the existence of variance. For $1<\alpha<2$, the distribution has an infinite or undefined second moment and thus variance (Peters, 1994).

5.3 Hurst exponent estimation and market efficiency

This chapter uses the two most common methods of the Hurst exponent estimation – the rescaled range analysis (R/S) of Hurst (1951) and the detrended fluctuation analysis (DFA) of Peng et al. (1994). The crucial difference between the methods is that DFA is constructed for non-stationary time series and therefore works well with trends in the process that are, on the other hand, a deficiency of R/S. Both methods are biased by the presence of short-range dependence in the underlying process. To deal with the problem, the modified rescaled range analysis (M-R/S) of Lo (1991) is used as well. As we show in this section, the Hurst exponent is estimated and therefore the true exponent of the underlying process need not be estimated correctly. Therefore, we also present the expected values and confidence intervals for hypothesis testing based on Monte Carlo simulations.

5.3.1 Classical and modified rescaled range analyses

Rescaled range analysis is the oldest Hurst exponent estimation method and was proposed by Harold E. Hurst while working as an engineer in Egypt (Hurst, 1951) and further adjusted by Mandelbrot & Wallis (1969). In the procedure, one divides the time series of T continuous returns into N adjacent sub-periods of length υ so that $N*\upsilon = T$. For each sub-period, the rescaled range of the profile (cumulative deviations from the mean) is calculated as R_i/S_i, where R_i is a range of the corresponding profile and S_i is a standard deviation of corresponding returns. The same procedure is applied to each sub-period of given length and the average rescaled range is calculated. Rescaled ranges then scale as $(R/S)_\upsilon \approx c * \upsilon^H$ with varying υ, where c is a constant (Taqqu, Teverovsky & Willinger, 1995; Di Matteo, 2007). The linear relationship in a double-logarithmic scale indicates the power scaling (Weron, 2002). To uncover the scaling law, an ordinary least squares regression on logarithms on each side of the equation is applied and H is estimated.

The *V statistic*, which is used for cycle detection, stability testing of the Hurst exponent or a change in scaling behaviour (crossover) detection, is defined as $V_v = (R/S)_v / \sqrt{\upsilon}$ and converges in the distribution defined as $F_V(x) = 1 + 2\sum_{k=1}^{\infty}(1 - 4k^2x^2)e^{-2(kx)^2}$ (Lo, 1991; Hurst, 1951, Peters; 1994). The statistic is constant, increasing and decreasing with increasing scale for no long-range dependence, persistence and anti-persistence, respectively.

The length υ is usually set as a divisor of T, which yields a number of different lengths υ equal to the number of divisors (Peters, 1994). However, we use the procedure used in, for example, Weron (2002) so that we use the length υ equal to the power of a set integer value. Thus, we set a basis b and a minimum and a maximum power *pmin* and *pmax*, respectively, so that we get sub-periods of length $\upsilon = b^{p\min}, b^{p\min+1}, \ldots, b^{p\max}$.

As the R/S analysis presented above (usually called 'classical') as well as detrended fluctuation analysis described in the next section is biased by the presence of short-range dependence (e.g., autoregressive processes), Lo (1991) proposed a modified rescaled range analysis which differs from the classical analysis by the use of modified standard deviation defined with a use of auto-covariance γ of the selected sub-interval up to lag ξ as

$$S_{I_n}^M = \sqrt{S_{I_n}^2 + 2\sum_{j=1}^{\xi}\gamma_j\left(1 - j/(\xi+1)\right)}\cdot$$

Thus, R/S turns into a special case of M-R/S with $\xi = 0$. The choice of the correct lag ξ is critical to the estimation of modified rescaled ranges (Wang et al., 2006; Teverovsky, Taqqu & Willinger, 1999). Lo (1991) suggested an optimal lag based on the first-order autocorrelation coefficient of returns $\hat{\rho}(1)$ defined as (where [] is the nearest lower integer operator):

$$\xi^* = \left[\left(\frac{3\upsilon}{2}\right)^{\frac{1}{3}}\left(\frac{2\hat{\rho}(1)}{1-(\hat{\rho}(1))^2}\right)^{\frac{2}{3}}\right].$$

One then derives estimates of modified rescaled ranges for different scales υ, constructs the *V statistics* and compares them to critical values of the distribution shown with null hypothesis of no long-range dependence. The Hurst exponent is not usually estimated as modified rescaled ranges for low scales and can be complex as a result of the inefficient estimation of modified standard deviation.

5.3.2 Detrended fluctuation analysis

Detrended fluctuation analysis (DFA) was first proposed by Peng et al. (1994) while examining series of DNA nucleotides. Compared to the R/S analysis, the DFA focuses on fluctuations in trends rather than a range of signals. Therefore, DFA can be used for non-stationary time series that are contrary to R/S.

The first steps in the procedure are the same as those of R/S analysis as the whole series is divided into non-overlapping periods of length υ, which is again set on the same basis as in the abovementioned procedure. Then a polynomial fit $X_{\upsilon,l}$ of the profile for each sub-period is constructed. The choice of order l of the polynomial is rather a rule of thumb but is usually set as the first or the second order polynomial trend as higher orders do not add any significant information (Vandewalle, Ausloos & Boveroux, 1997). We adhere to linear trend filtering and thus use DFA-1 in this chapter. A detrended signal $Y_{\upsilon,l}$ is constructed as $Y_{\upsilon,l}(t) = X(t) - X_{\upsilon,l}(t)$ and a fluctuation $F_{DFA}(\upsilon,l)$ calculated as $F_{DFA}(\upsilon,l) = \sqrt{1/T \sum_{t=1}^{T} Y_{\upsilon,l}^2(t)}$.

F_{DFA} then scales as $F_{DFA}(\upsilon,l) \approx c * \upsilon^{H(l)}$, where again c is a constant independent of υ (Weron, 2002). An ordinary least squares regression on the logarithms is applied and the Hurst exponent $H(l)$ for a set l-degree of polynomial trend is estimated in the same way as for R/S (Grech & Mazur, 2005).

5.3.3 Hurst exponent and market efficiency

The efficient markets hypothesis (EMH) is a well-known theory which was simultaneously developed by Eugene Fama (Fama, 1965a; Fama, 1965b; Fama, 1970) and Paul Samuelson (Samuelson, 1965) during the 1960s. An efficient market is described as one reflecting all available information. We adhere to the martingale definition of EMH (Samuelson, 1965), which is more general than the random walk definition (Fama, 1970) and allows for dependence in the series (McCauley et al., 2008; Los, 2003). A weakly efficient market is then defined as that which follows martingale.

The martingale process is defined as a random process $(X(t), \Phi_t : t = 1,2,...)$ with $E\{|X(t)|\} < \infty$ and $E\{X(t)|\Phi_s\} = X(s)$ for $s < t$, where Φ_s is an information set at time s and E is an expected value operator (Fama, 1970; Neftci, 2000; LeRoy, 1989). As the martingale process is connected with the existence of variance, the Hurst exponent becomes crucial to testing weak martingale efficiency.

If H is equal to 0.5, an independent or a short-range dependent process is implied (Karytinos, Andreou & Pavlides, 2000; Rose, 1996). A persistent process is linked to the Hurst exponent significantly higher than 0.5 and implies rejection of independence which in turn rejects random walk model (Embrechts & Maejima, 2002). However, the value of $1/2 < H < 1$ implies $1 < \alpha < 2$, which in turn indicates undefined or infinite variance. Such a result also implies that the square root of the variance is infinite or undefined and so the martingale hypothesis is rejected, which eventually leads to the rejection of weak market efficiency (Cajueiro & Tabak, 2005; Da Silva et al., 2007). On the other hand, an anti-persistent process only rejects the random walk, but the martingale model cannot be rejected as the process has defined variance (Der & Lee, 2006; Da Silva et al., 2005; Embrechts & Maejima, 2002). Therefore, only a Hurst exponent value significantly higher than 0.5 leads to rejection of the hypothesis of martingale efficient market.

Moreover, Hurst exponent significantly different from 0.5 implies either a persistent or an anti-persistent process, which in turn implies the increased predictability of the time series. The market is therefore not efficient, as the use of historical data can yield significantly above-average profits. To check for improved predictability, we provide a statistical test in section 5.5.

5.4 Data

We examine the daily logarithmic returns of the Hungarian BUX, Czech PX, Slovakian SAX and Polish WIG. The basic descriptive statistics are summarised in Table 5.1; the evolution of rescaled index values is shown in Figure 5.1. A comparison of the index values shows that BUX experienced the most rapid growth followed by PX and WIG. Nevertheless, the three indices follow a very similar path of evolution. However, SAX shows completely different progress as it reached its peak almost three years earlier than the others.

From the table, we can see that all four indices are negatively skewed and leptokurtic. Such results are consistent with the stylised facts of fatter tails whereas the left tail is longer (Cont, 2001). The deviation

Table 5.1 Descriptive statistics

	BUX	PX	SAX	WIG
Mean	0.000438	0.0002	0.00247	0.00016
Min.	–0.12649	–0.16185	–0.11484	–0.08443
Max.	0.13178	0.12364	0.11880	0.08155
SD	0.01682	0.01535	0.01368	0.01688
Skewness	–0.22025	–0.48709	–0.27216	–0.2773
Excessive kurtosis	7.14249	12.27884	9.467	2.7021
Jarque-Bera statistic	4160.749	18863.73	10509.38	465.702
– p-value	0.0000	0.0000	0.0000	0.0000
KPSS	0.3996	0.2240	0.5246	0.4677
– 10% critical value				0.347
– 5% critical value				0.463
– 1% critical value				0.739
Observations	1950	2984	2805	1469
Start date	26.7.2001	1.7.1997	1.7.1997	1.10.2003
End date	30.6.2009	30.6.2009	30.6.2009	30.6.2009

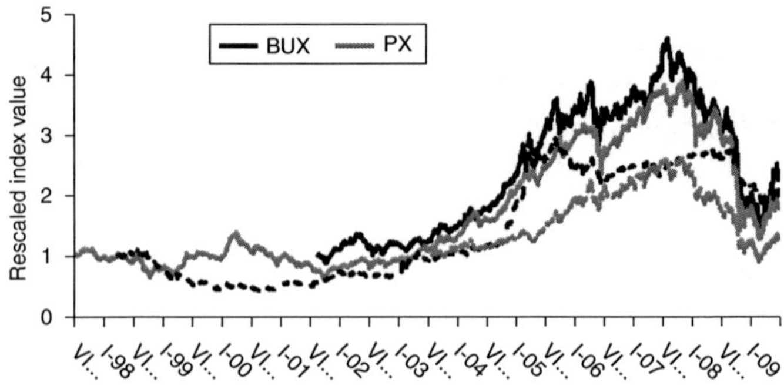

Figure 5.1 Comparison of index values
Note: Index values are rescaled by dividing by the first observation of the time series. Comparison shows that BUX experienced the most rapid growth followed by PX and WIG. Nevertheless the three indices follow very similar path of evolution. However, SAX shows completely different progress as it reached its peak almost three years earlier compared to the others. Note that each series starts at a different date so that the comparison is not straightforward.

from the normal distribution is supported by the Jarque-Bera statistic (Jarque & Bera, 1981). All of the time series are stationary based on the KPSS test at a 1 per cent significance level (Kwiatkowski et al., 1992), which is quite important, as non-stationarity would be sufficient to reject the random walk hypothesis.

5.5 Results

In this section we present the results of both the global and the local long-range dependence tests. For global dependence, the global Hurst exponent method is used together with an examination of individual rescaled ranges, DFA fluctuations and corresponding *V statistics*. In the case of local (time-varying) dependence, we use the time-dependent Hurst exponent to show the evolution of dynamics and to uncover potential changes of the dynamics.

5.5.1 Global dependence

The global Hurst exponent shows potential long-range dependence in the process for the period ending on 30.6.2009. Rescaled ranges, DFA fluctuations and corresponding *V statistics* for both methods are shown in Figure 5.2. Quite interestingly, each index shows different behaviour when compared with the others. BUX shows a crossover at a scale of 128 trading days, PX at 256 trading days, SAX at 512 trading days, and WIG does not show significant crossover on one specific scale but between 64 and 128 trading days. However, none of the values of the statistics at crossover scale exceed critical levels for forming optimal investment horizons as presented by Lo (1991). *V statistics* based on both R/S and DFA-1 are similar to the exception of PX, where the crossover is cleared for the DFA-1 *V statistic* so that the potential non-stationarity or trending can be present in the process. Therefore, the estimates of R/S and DFA-1, mainly for the time-dependent Hurst exponent, might be different for PX and potential trending must be taken into consideration. On the other hand, BUX, SAX and WIG seem free of such bias based on the global long-range properties.

The estimates of Hurst exponents together with regression standard errors for each index are summarised in Table 5.2. For the estimation, only scales from 16 trading days to a quarter of chosen time series lengths are used, as proposed by other authors (Peters, 1994; Grech & Mazur, 2004; Matos et al., 2008; Alvarez-Ramirez, Rodriguez & Echeverria, 2005; Einstein, Wu & Gil, 2001). The results are consistent with crossover detection as standard errors of the regression increase when the scales higher than the crossover scale are included in the estimation. Moreover, the estimates of R/S are higher than those of DFA-1 discussed in the next section. Estimates of the Hurst exponent for both methods are decreasing with increasing time series length for BUX, PX and WIG. The trend is reversed for SAX, which indicates potential changes in dynamics as the estimated Hurst exponent is

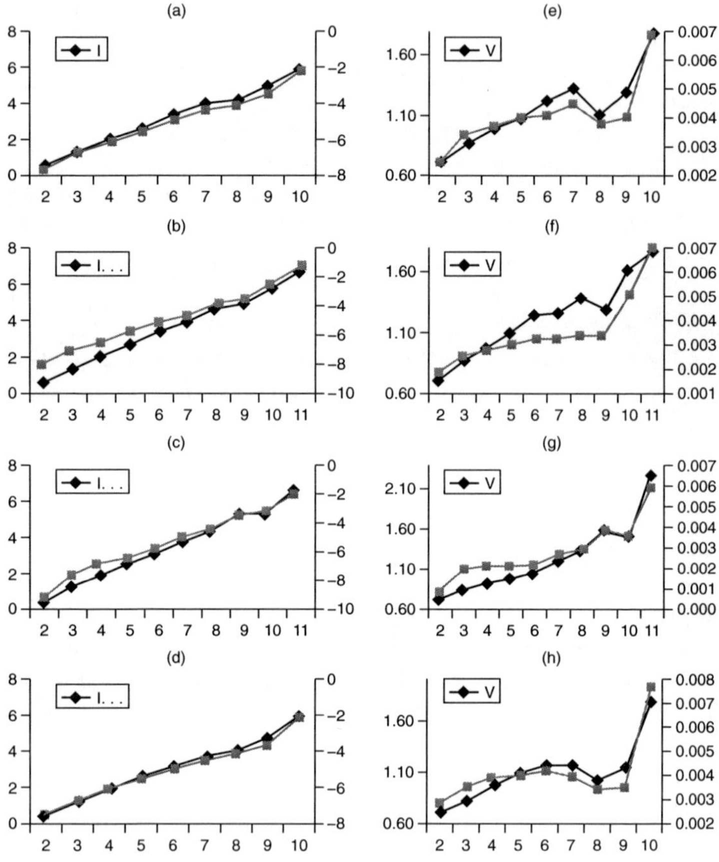

Figure 5.2 Global properties of BUX, PX, SAX and WIG

expected to converge to the asymptotic limit of 0.5 with increasing time series length (Weron, 2002; Grech & Mazur, 2005; Couillard & Davison, 2005). The changes in dynamics are further discussed in the following sections, which deal with the local (time-dependent) properties of the time series.

5.5.2 Monte Carlo simulations

Testing the null hypothesis of no long-range dependence based on the comparison of estimates of the Hurst exponent with a value of 0.5 has already shown it to be not correct. Finite sample properties of the presented methods showed that the estimates can vary significantly and

Table 5.2 Global Hurst exponent estimates

	Time series length	R/S estimate	Standard error	DFA-1 estimate	Standard error
BUX	512	0,6358	0,0287	0,5871	0,0198
	1024	0,5604	0,1395	0,5264	0,1121
PX	512	0,6314	0,0474	0,5771	0,0541
	1024	0,6241	0,0410	0,5681	0,0471
	2048	0,5894	0,0909	0,5575	0,0483
SAX	512	0,6191	0,0562	0,6137	0,0846
	1024	0,6319	0,0515	0,6288	0,0743
	2048	0,6519	0,0657	0,6697	0,1180
WIG	512	0,5745	0,0571	0,5129	0,0487
	1024	0,5153	0,1177	0,4660	0,0944

0.5 is only an asymptotic limit for an infinite number of observations (Couillard & Davison, 2005; Weron, 2002). Therefore, we present the results of 10 000 Monte Carlo simulations of the Hurst exponent for standardised normal distribution *N(0,1)*. We set the crucial parameters according to the suggestion presented by other authors and the results of global dependence in the previous section. We estimated Hurst exponents for both methods on the time series of 512 observations as the lowest detected crossover was present at a scale of 128 trading days (for BUX) and the suggested ratio between the maximum scale and the time series length is one to four. The lowest crossover was chosen because, for the higher scale, the estimates can be biased as the scaling behaviour changes for BUX, though the estimates for other indices remain reliable. As for the choice of scales, we use a minimum scale of 16 days and a maximum scale of 128. The results of the simulations are presented in Figure 5.3.

We can see that the estimates of the Hurst exponent can be really far from the asymptotic limit of 0.5. Moreover, the estimates of R/S are biased upwards, which agrees with previous results (Peters, 1994; Couillard & Davison, 2005; Weron, 2002). Therefore, we need to construct confidence intervals to be able to test the null hypothesis of no long-range dependence of the time series. As the simulated Hurst exponents are not normally distributed according to the Jarque-Bera test, we use 2.5 per cent and 97.5 per cent percentiles rather than standard deviations for the confidence intervals at a 5 per cent significance level.

5.5.3 Time-varying dependence

For the description of potential changes in the dynamics and in long-range dependence properties we use a time-dependent Hurst exponent

(a)

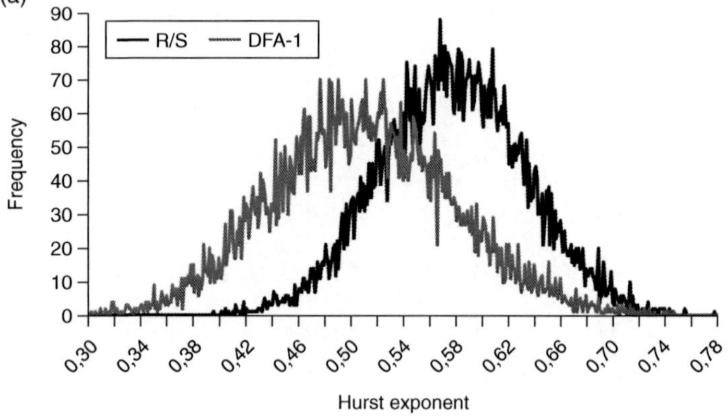

(b)

	R/S	DFA-1
mean	0.5763	0.5079
SD	0.0551	0.0687
skewness	0.0104	0.1189
excess kurtosis	–0.1316	–0.0205
JB	7.4569	23.7407
JB p-value	0.0240	0.0000
$P_{2.5\%}$	0.4693	0.3773
$P_{97.5\%}$	0.6848	0.6479

Figure 5.3 Results of Monte Carlo simulations
Note: (a) Histrograms of Monte Carlo simulations based on 1000 realizations for R/S and DFA-1 (b) Descriptive statistics for Monte Carlo simulations. SD, JB, $P_{2.5\%}$ and $P_{97.5\%}$ stand for standard devition, Iarque-Bera statistics, 2.5% Percentile and 97.5% percentile, respectively

(Grech & Mazur, 2004, 2005; Czarnecki, Grech & Pamula, 2008) with an estimation period of 512 days and a sliding step of a single trading day. Figure 5.4 shows the results for both R/S and DFA-1.

The estimates of the Hurst exponent are very similar for both methods after rescaling and thus the potential non-stationarity did not bias the results. Comparison of the histograms of the Hurst exponents show an expected difference between R/S and DFA-1 for BUX, PX and WIG, direct comparison of estimates is shown in Figure 5.4 The estimates for SAX show an interesting feature as the estimates of both methods are almost equal, contradicting the findings of the Monte Carlo simulations, which clearly show that R/S overestimates the Hurst exponent when

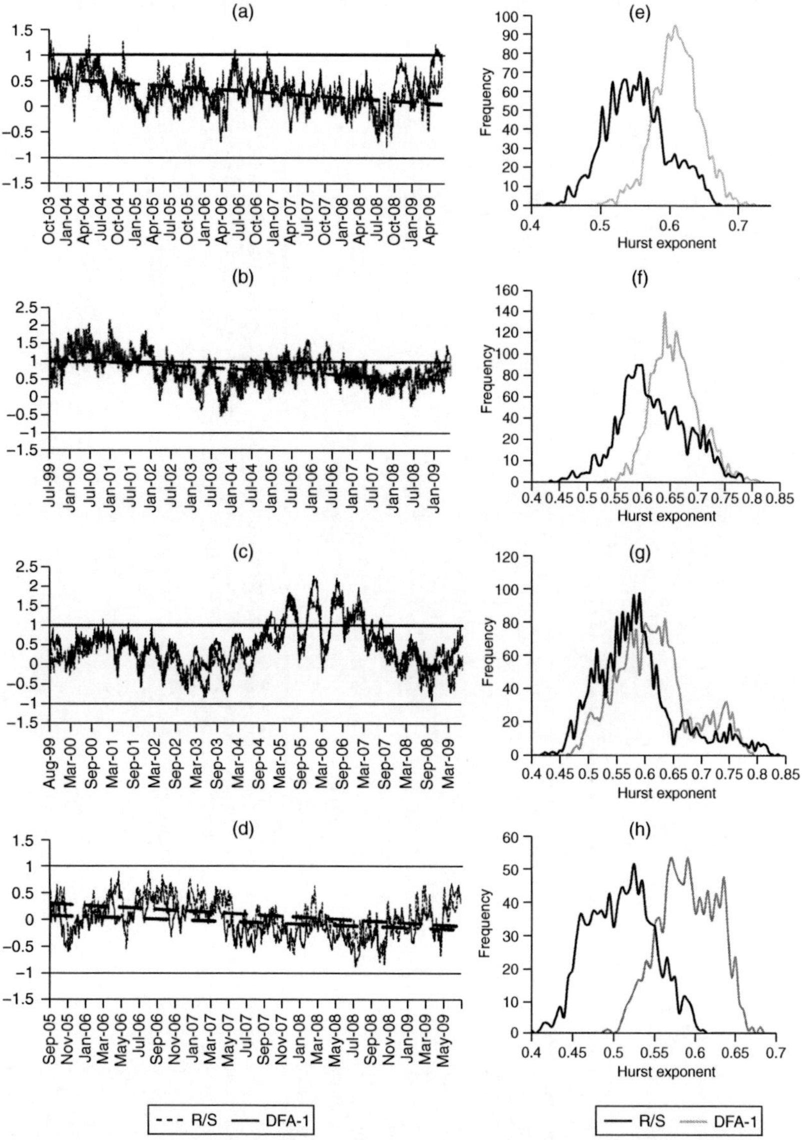

Figure 5.4 Time-dependent Hurst exponents for BUX, PX, SAX and WIG
Note: (a)-(b) Estimates of Hurt exponents for R/S (dashed) and DFA-1 (solid) are rescaled so that upper and lower confidence intervals for both methods are of value 1 and -1, respectively, for BUX, PX, SAX and WIG, respectively. Linear time trends are represented by bold dashed line. (e)-(h) Histrograms of time-dependent Hurst expenent for R/S (gray) and DFA-1 (black) for BUX, PX, SAX, and WIG, respectively.

Table 5.3 Time trends of Hurst exponent

	BUX		PX		SAX		WIG	
	R/S	DFA-1	R/S	DFA-1	R/S	DFA-1	R/S	DFA-1
Constant	0.6562	0.5798	0.7124	0.6769	0.6044	0.5525	0.6352	0.5435
Trend	$-3.72*10^{-5}$	$-2.25*10^{-5}$	$-3.17*10^{-5}$	$-3.46*10^{-5}$	$5.5*10^{-6}$	$1.95*10^{-5}$	$-4.74*10^{-5}$	$-3.69*10^{-5}$
SE	$1.9*10^{-6}$	$2.8*10^{-6}$	$1.1*10^{-6}$	$1.6*10^{-6}$	$2.1*10^{-6}$	$2.3*10^{-6}$	$3.9*10^{-6}$	$4.4*10^{-6}$
T-stat	−19.8802	−7.9488	−29.3448	−21.3566	2.6104	8.4246	−12.2955	−8.3044
P-value	0.0000	0.0000	0.0000	0.0000	0.0091	0.0000	0.0000	0.0000
F-stat	395.2231	63.1832	861.1153	456.1031	6.8144	70.9743	151.1805	68.9626
P-value	0.0000	0.0000	0.0000	0.0000	0.0091	0.0000	0.0000	0.0000
R^2 adj.	0.2152	0.0415	0.2581	0.1555	0.0025	0.0296	0.1356	0.0663

Note: 'Constant' and 'trend' stand for a respective regression coefficient with the Hurst exponent as an explanatory variable and time *t* as the explaining variable. SE, T-stat and P-value, F-stat and P-value represent the standard error of trend coefficient, the corresponding T-statistic and P-value, F-statistic and P-value testing the null hypothesis of zero trend coefficient. 'R^2 adj.' stands for adjusted squared R.

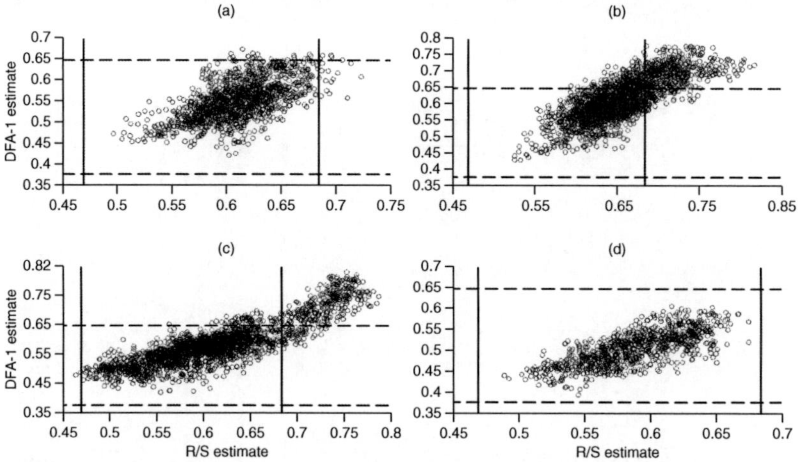

Figure 5.5 Comparison of time-dependent Hurst exponents for R/S and DFA-1
Note: Charts show Hurst exponent estimates for R/S and DFA-1 for BUX, PX, SAX and WIG, respectively. Solid lines show 95% confidence intervals for R/S and dashed lines show 95% confidence intervals for DFA-1. Upper right and lower left sections represent rejection of "no long-range dependence" hypothesis.

compared to DFA. Moreover, the distribution of estimates for SAX is skewed, with a longer right tail. Both of the results might be caused by the low liquidity of the Slovakian index, which can be shown by the frequency of the non-trading days (i.e., zero return days for stock index). The frequency of such days is 6 out of 1950 (0.31%), 10 out of 2984 (0.34%), 373 out of 2805 (13.30%) and 30 out of 1469 (2.04%) for BUX, PX, SAX and WIG, respectively.

Figure 5.4 also presents the linear time trends of the Hurst exponent. The estimates and the descriptive statistics for the trends are summarised in Table 5.3. All of the trends are significantly different from zero – negative for BUX, PX and WIG, and positive for SAX. Therefore, we can state that the Czech, Hungarian and Polish stock indices are becoming more efficient in our broad sense, whereas the Slovakian index is losing its efficiency in time. It is, however, necessary to say that such strong statements must be based on further statistical analysis of time-dependent Hurst exponents that is beyond the scope of this chapter and is a focus for future research.

WIG shows no single period with persistent or anti-persistent behaviour for both methods. BUX follows with only several persistent periods whereas PX and SAX show a high number of persistent periods. Figure 5.5 presents a comparison of estimates for both R/S and DFA and

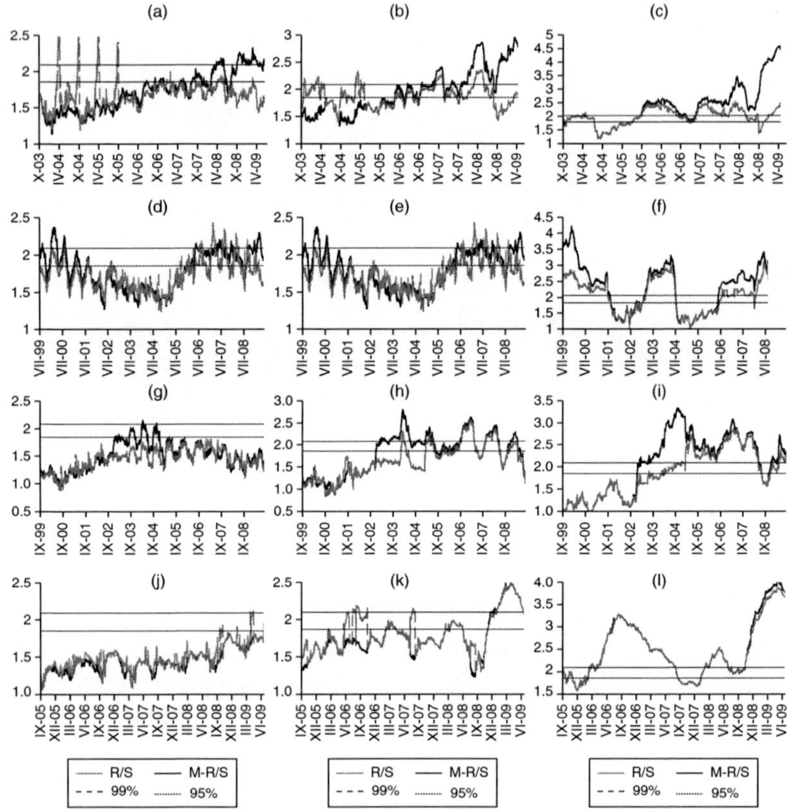

Figure 5.6 Comparison of classical and modified rescaled range

Notes: Comparison of rescaled ranges for classical and modified methods for (a)–(c) BUX, (d)–(f) PX, (g)–(i) SAX, (j)–(l) WIG. The upper straight line represents the 99% confidence interval for null hypothesis of no longer range dependence. The lower straight line represents the 95% confidence interval for the same null hypothesis. The time series length is set at 512 trading days with scale of 128, 256 and 512 for the first, the second and the third column, representatively.

clearly distinguishes (by dividing the figure into nine parts) between estimates that show long-range dependence based on either R/S or DFA or both or no long-range dependence at all.

To check for potential short-range dependence bias, we use a modified rescaled range with scales of 128, 256 and 512 trading days with a time series length of 512 trading days. We use the sliding window method, similar to a time-dependent Hurst exponent, to uncover the changes in behaviour of the time series. Figure 5.6 summarises the results for all the examined indices. For PX and SAX, the two indices with long persistent periods, there is no significant difference between the classical rescaled ranges and the modified rescaled ranges, which corresponds to the results of the time-dependent Hurst exponent, for any tested scale, and thus significant long-range dependence is not caused by short-range dependence bias.

5.5.4 Predictability test

As persistence is connected to market efficiency, we support the connection by using a predictability test. Since there are only a few or no persistent periods for BUX and WIG, we perform the test on PX and SAX only. The data set is divided into several groups according to the separation in Table 5.4 so that we get six groups – R/S persistent, DFA persistent, R/S and DFA persistent, R/S or DFA persistent, R/S and/or DFA persistent, neither of the aforementioned. For the test statistic, we construct a variable which is equal to 1 if the sign of return of the next period is the same as the one of this period and 0 otherwise – a hit rate. Such a statistic is well connected to the definition of the long-range dependent process. Groups of persistent periods are expected to yield a significantly higher hit rate, whereas the independent periods are expected to yield a hit rate of 0.5. The results are based on two-sample T-tests for equal mean and unknown variance and are summarised in Table 5.4.

PX meets the expectations as it shows a significantly higher hit rate for persistent periods when compared to the periods of no long-range dependence. The difference between the prediction power of R/S and DFA is insignificant. The results are not clear for SAX as the testing statistic is hard to use with so many non-trading periods. Such results support the need of liquid market for the correct estimation of the Hurst exponent (Peters, 1994).

The result can be used for a simple trading rule when we buy if the return today is positive and the Hurst exponent indicates significant persistence, and short-sell if the return today is negative and the Hurst exponent again shows significant persistence. If such a strategy, based on significant persistence for both methods, is compared to a buy-and-hold strategy, the average return is 0.26 per cent and 0.02 per cent, respectively. More importantly, the difference between the return for the whole period is 61.79 per cent for a buy-and-hold strategy and 125.12 per cent for the Hurst exponent-based strategy. If buy or short-sell signals are practised when at least one method indicates significant persistence, the whole period return increases to 190.71 per cent. However, such strategies require very active trading, with 483 and 869 days of buying or short-selling, which means 966 and 1738 market operations

Table 5.4 Predictability test

	A		b	a			b			T-statistic	P-value
				mean	variance	#	mean	variance	#		
PX	R/S and/or DFA persistent	against	non-persistent	0.5788	0.2441	869	0.5165	0.2499	1603	2.9808	0.0029***
	R/S or DFA persistent			0.5699	0.2457	386				1.8974	0.0583*
	R/S and DFA persistent			0.5859	0.2431	483				2.7026	0.0070***
			R/S or DFA persistent				0.5699	0.2457	386	0.4731	0.6363
	R/S persistent		DFA persistent	0.5825	0.2436	594	0.5805	0.2438	758	0.0745	0.9406
SAX	R/S and/or DFA persistent		non-persistent	0.5152	0.2504	394	0.4746	0.2495	1553	1.4411	0.1501
	R/S or DFA persistent			0.6220	0.2370	127				3.2761	0.0013***
	R/S and DFA persistent			0.4644	0.2497	267				0.3065	0.7594
			R/S or DFA persistent				0.6220	0.2370	127	2.9784	0.0032***
	R/S persistent		DFA persistent	0.4954	0.2507	329	0.4940	0.2507	332	0.0376	0.9700

for two abovementioned strategies, respectively. With so many market operations being transacted, transaction costs can become a significant barrier to such strategies. Break-even transaction costs for the two strategies to have the same final cumulative return as buy-and-hold strategy are 0.066 per cent and 0.074 per cent for one transaction, respectively. However, such low transaction costs are not realistic for PX so that both strategies remain statistically significant but are not significant on an economic basis.

5.6 Conclusion

We have shown that the stock markets of the Central European countries have undergone an interesting evolution in their efficiency. However, the whole group is very heterogeneous. The Polish WIG is the most efficient market according to a long-range dependence test, as it shows no significant cycles and no significant persistent periods. The Hungarian BUX is the second most efficient market, with several persistent periods and a potential cycle of a half-year. The Czech PX shows a significant trend towards efficiency while remaining very close to the confidence interval separating independent and long-range dependent behaviour. The Slovakian SAX as a very shallow and illiquid market yields unreliable results and shows the need of liquidity only for Hurst exponent estimation.

None of the estimates was significantly biased by a presence of short-range dependent processes in the time series. Moreover, profitable trading rules are very likely to be based on the Hurst exponent as we have shown on PX. Even though the rule is only statistically significant, it opens the field for more complicated rules as the proposed one is rather simple.

Notes

Support from the Czech Science Foundation under grant 402/09/H045 and the Grant Foundation of the Charles University under grant 118310, and institutional support from the Department of Education MSMT 0021620841, are gratefully acknowledged.

References

Alvarez-Ramirez, J., Rodriguez, E. & Echeverria, J. 'Detrending Fluctuation Analysis Based on Moving Average Filtering', *Physica A*, Vol. 354 (2005): 199–219.

Beran, J. *Statistics for Long-Memory Processes, Monographs on Statistics and Applied Probability 61*, New York: Chapman & Hall (1994).
Cajueiro, D. & Tabak, B. 'Possible Causes of Long-Range Dependence in the Brazilian Stock Market', *Physica A*, Vol. 345 (2005): 635–45.
Cont, R. 'Empirical Properties of Asset Returns: Stylized Facts and Statistical Issues', *Quantitative Finance*, Vol. 1, No. 2 (2001): 223–36.
Couillard, M. & Davison, M. 'A Comment on Measuring the Hurst Exponent of Financial Time Series', *Physica A*, Vol. 348 (2005): 404–18.
Czarnecki, L., Grech, D. & Pamula, G. 'Comparison Study of Global and Local Approaches Describing Critical Phenomena on the Polish Stock Exchange Market', *Physica A*, Vol. 387 (2008): 6801–11.
Da Silva, S., Matsushita, R., Gleria & I. Figueiredo, A. 'Hurst Exponents, Power Laws, and Efficiency in the Brazilian Foreign Exchange Market', *Economics Bulletin*, Vol. 7, No. 1 (2007): 1–11.
Da Silva, S., Matsushita, R., Gleria, I. Figueiredo, A. & Rathie, P. 'International Finance, Lévy Distributions, and the Econophysics of Exchange Rates', *Communications in Nonlinear Science and Numerical Simulation*, Vol. 10, No. 4 (2005): 365–93.
Der, R. & Lee, D. 'Beyond Gaussian Processes: On the Distributions of Infinite Networks', *Advances in Neural Information Processing Systems*, No. 18 (2006): 275–82.
Di Matteo, T., Aste, T. & Dacorogna, M. 'Long-Term Memories of Developed and Emerging Markets: Using the Scaling Analysis to Characterize their Stage of Development', *Journal of Banking & Finance*, No. 29 (2005): 827–51.
Di Matteo, T. 'Multi-Scaling in Finance', *Quantitative Finance*, Vol. 7, No. 1 (2007): 21–36.
Diviš, K. & Teplý, P. 'Information Efficiency of Central Europe Stock Exchanges', *Finance a úvěr – Czech Journal of Economics and Finance*, Vol. 55, No. 9–10 (2005): 471–82.
Egert, B. & Kočenda, E. 'Contagion Across and Integration of Central and Eastern European Stock Markets: Evidence from Intraday Data', William Davidson Institute Working Paper No. 798, University of Michigan, Michigan, USA (2005): 1–30.
Einstein, A., Wu, H.-S. & Gil, J. 'Detrended Fluctuation Analysis of Chromatin Texture for Diagnosis in Breast Cytology', *Fractals*, Vol. 9, No. 4 (2001).
Embrechts, P. & Maejima, M. *Selfsimilar Processes*, Princeton, USA: Princeton University Press (2002).
Fama, E. 'Efficient Capital Markets: A Review of Theory and Empirical Work', *Journal of Finance*, Vol. 25 (1970): 383–417.
Fama, E. 'Random Walks in Stock Market Prices', *Financial Analysts Journal*, Vol. 21 (1965a): 55–9.
Fama, E. 'The Behavior of Stock Market Prices', *Journal of Business*, Vol. 38 (1965b): 34–105.
Grech, D. & Mazur, Z. 'Can one Make any Crash Prediction in Finance Using the Local Hurst Exponent Idea?' *Physica A*, Vol. 336 (2004): 133–45.
Grech, D. & Mazur, Z. 'Statistical Properties of Old and New Techniques in Detrended Analysis of Time Series', *Acta Physica Polonica B*, Vol. 36, No. 8 (2005): 2403–13.

Hájek, J. 'Weak-Form Efficiency Test in the Central European Capital Markets', *Politická Ekonomie*, Vol. 6 (2007): 773–91.

Hurst, H. E. 'Long Term Storage Capacity of Reservoirs', *Transactions of the American Society of Engineers*, Vol. 116 (1951): 770–99.

Jagric, T., Podobnik, B. & Kolanovic, M. 'Does the Efficient Market Hypothesis Hold? Evidence from Six Transition Economics', *Eastern European Economics*, Vol. 43, No. 4 (2005): 79–103.

Jarque, C. & Bera, A. 'Efficient Tests for Normality, Homoscedasticity and Serial Independence of Regression Residuals: Monte Carlo Evidence', *Economics Letters*, Vol. 7, No. 4 (1981): 313–18.

Karytinos, A., Andreou, A. & Pavlides, G. 'Long-Term Dependence in Exchange Rates', *Discrete Dynamics in Nature and Society*, Vol. 4 (2000): 1–20.

Kwiatkowski, D., Phillips, P., Schmidt, P. & Shin, Y. 'Testing the Null of Stationarity Against the Alternative of a Unit Root: How Sure are we that the Economic Time Series have a Unit Root?' *Journal of Econometrics*, Vol. 54 (1992).

LeRoy, S. 'Efficient Capital Markets and Martingales', *Journal of Economic Literature*, Vol. 27, No. 4 (1989): 1583–621.

Lillo, F. & Farmer, J. 'The Long Memory of the Efficient Market', *Studies in Nonlinear Dynamics & Econometrics*, Vol. 8, No. 3 (2004).

Lo, A. 'Long-Term Memory in Stock Market Prices', *Econometrica*, Vol. 59, No. 5 (1991).

Los, C. *Financial Market Risk: Measurement and Analysis*, London: Routledge (2003).

Mandelbrot, B. & van Ness, J. 'Fractional Brownian Motions, Fractional Noises and Applications', *SIAM Review*, Vol. 10 (1968): 422–37.

Mandelbrot, B. & Wallis, R. 'Robustness of the Rescaled Range R/S in the Measurement of Noncyclic Long-Run Statistical Dependence', *Water Resources Research*, Vol. 5 (1969): 967–88.

Mandelbrot, B. 'Forecasts of Future Prices, Unbiased Markets and "Martingale" Models', *Journal of Business*, Vol. 39 (1966): 242–55.

Matos, J., Gama, S., Ruskin, H., Sharkasi, A. & Crane, M. 'Time and Scale Hurst Exponent Analysis for Financial Markets', *Physica A*, Vol. 387, No. 15 (2008): 3910–15.

McCauley, J., Bassler, K. & Gunaratne, G. 'Martingales, Detrending Data, and the Efficient Market Hypothesis', *Physica A*, Vol. 387, No. 1 (2008): 202–16.

Neftci, S. *An Introduction to the Mathematics of Financial Derivatives*, 2nd edition, New York, USA: Academic Press (2000).

Panas, E. 'Estimating Fractal Dimension using Stable Distributions and Exploring Long Memory through ARFIMA Models in Athens Stock Exchange', *Applied Financial Economics*, Vol. 11 (2001): 395–408.

Peng, C., Buldyrev, S., Havlin, S., Simons, M., Stanley, H. & Goldberger, A. 'Mosaic Organization of DNA Nucleotides', *Physical Review E*, Vol. 49, No. 2 (1994): 1685–9.

Peters, E. *Fractal Market Analysis – Applying Chaos Theory to Investment and Analysis*, New York: John Wiley & Sons (1994).

Rose, O. 'Estimation of the Hurst Parameter of Long-Range Dependent Time Series', Report No. 137, Research Report Series, Institute of Computer Science, Würzburg, Germany: University of Würzburg (1996).

Samuelson, P. 'Proof that Properly Anticipated Prices Fluctuate Randomly', *Industrial Management Review*, Vol. 6 (1965): 41–9.

Taqqu, M., Teverosky, W. & Willinger, W. 'Estimators for Long-Range Dependence: An Empirical Study', *Fractals*, Vol. 3, No. 4 (1995): 785–8.

Teverovsky, V., Taqqu, M. & Willinger, W. 'A Critical Look at Lo's Modified R/S Statistic', *Journal of Statistical Planning and Inference*, Vol. 80, No. 1–2 (1999).

Vandewalle, N., Ausloos, M. & Boveroux, Ph. 'Detrended Fluctuation Analysis of the Foreign Exchange Market', *Econophysic Workshop*, Budapest, Hungary (1997).

Wang, W., Van Gelder, P., Vrijling, J. & Chen, X. 'Detecting Long-Memory: Monte Carlo Simulations and Application to Daily Streamflow Processess', *Hydrology and Earth System Sciences Discussions*, Vol. 3 (2006).

Weron, R. 'Estimating Long-Range Dependence: Finite Sample Properties and Confidence Intervals', *Physica A*, Vol. 312 (2002): 285–99.

Worthington, A. & Higgs, H. 'Weak-Form Market Efficiency in European Emerging and Developed Stock Markets', Queensland University of Technology Discussion Paper No. 159, Brisbane, Australia (2003).

6

Non-Linear Stock Market Co-Movement in Central and East European Countries

Barry Harrison and Winston Moore

6.1 Introduction

As a result of financial globalisation, interest has grown in the extent of stock market integration between different countries. Stock markets can be considered integrated if their prices have a tendency to move together, or if one market leads another. The results of such investigations have important implications for portfolio diversification along international lines. In particular, significant co-movement of international stock markets increases the exposure of domestic investors to foreign shocks and therefore offers very limited scope for gains from international diversification. Also, an understanding of the determinants of stock market co-movement might aid understanding of the home country bias that investors exhibit (Lewis 1999), that is, the preference of investors for domestic investments over foreign investments.

A great number of studies have investigated possible linkages between the world's developed markets and in particular major US and European stock markets or major US and Japanese stock markets (see e.g. Koch and Koch 1991; Kasa, 1992; Georgoustsos and Kouretas, 2001; Aggarwal, Lucey, and Muckley, 2003; Bessler and Yang, 2003; Fraser and Oyefeso, 2005). There have been fewer investigations into stock market linkages among emerging, economies with most focusing on Asia and Latin America (Ghosh et al., 1999; Koutmos and Booth, 1995; Chen, Firth, and Rui, 2002; Johnson and Soenen, 2002; Manning, 2002; Ng, 2002; Fujii, 2005).

Since the collapse of communism at the end of the 1980s and the beginning of the 1990s, the economies of Central and Eastern Europe (CEE) have established functioning stock markets as part of the transition process. For those economies admitted to the EU (Bulgaria, the

Czech Republic, Estonia, Hungary, Poland, Latvia, Lithuania, Romania, Slovakia, Slovenia) these stock markets have been modelled along similar lines to those in developed market economies. These countries have also attempted to put in place adequate corporate governance structures that require as part of this, internationally accepted standards of disclosure. Their markets have also been opened up to overseas investors and rights of ownership have been established. Investigations of stock market efficiency in CEE countries admitted to the EU overwhelmingly confirm that at the very least they exhibit a weak form of efficiency (Bohl et al. 2006; Rockinger and Urga 2001; and Harrison and Paton 2005). Given these developments, as well as political and economic stability and impressive rates of growth, these economies potentially offer investors attractive opportunities for portfolio diversification.

Linne (1998) was the first to investigate long-run linkages between East European markets (Czech and Slovak Republics, Hungary, Poland and Russia) with the developed economies of France, Germany, Italy, Japan, Switzerland, the US and the UK. For investors seeking to diversify their portfolios, this early study provided encouraging results finding that only the Slovakian stock market exhibited co-movement with all of the developed markets. Similarly, Gilmore and McManus (2003) found only weak short-run correlations and no long-run correlations between the Czech Republic, Hungary and Poland with US stock markets. These results are supported by Egert and Kocenda (2007), who report no robust co-integrating relationship between the relatively new markets of the Czech Republic, Hungary and Poland and the developed markets of Frankfurt, London and Paris.

A problem with these studies is that their standard methodology is static co-integration developed by Johansen (1988) and Johansen and Juselius (1990), and consequently they give very little information about processes that are time varying. Phylaktis and Ravazzolo (2002) have shown that for Pacific Basin countries financial integration is accompanied by economic integration at both real and financial levels. This has important implications for financial integration for countries admitted to the European Union. Furthermore, in the case of our target countries there are good reasons for believing that stock markets in CEE might be increasingly integrated with the developed stock markets of western Europe. As full members of the EU, these CEE countries are establishing stronger economic ties with other EU Members through trade, cross-border investments and policy coordination. The Maastricht Criteria establish rules for entry into EMU which are designed to promote economic convergence. Studies by Asprem (1989), Bodurtha et al.

(1989) and Canonova and De Nicoló (1995) have shown the relevance of common factors in international stock market linkages. Nasseh and Strauss (2000) demonstrate that stock prices in European countries are determined by domestic economic variables and by German economic variables for the period 1962–95. Fratzscher (2002) has shown that increasing integration in European equity markets in the 1990s was due mainly to the drive towards EMU.

More recently, Phengpis et al. (2004) have investigated the impact of economic convergence on stock market returns in four stock markets in the EMU (France, Germany, Italy and the Netherlands) and one stock market in the EU (the UK). They find that economic convergence is an important factor contributing to returns in the countries investigated, with the exception of Germany, which implies that Germany plays some role as policy leader in relation to the other countries. Phengpis and Apilado (2004) further demonstrate that stock market returns of a group of five non-EMU countries are driven by their own unique stochastic trends and are not co-integrated with each other or with any EMU, UK or US stock market. They further showed that stock market returns for a group of five EMU member countries were strongly co-integrated, suggesting that economic interdependence encourages stock market co-movement. Kim et al. (2005) find that the introduction of the euro caused a regime switch among participating country stock markets and deepened stock market linkages both within the EU and between the EU and Japan and the US. This finding is contradicted by Syriopoulos (2007), who detects no impact due to EMU. He suggests that this might be because macroeconomic policies have already been adjusted to support convergence with the EU. Importantly for our purposes, he demonstrates the existence of major linkages between the stock markets of Poland, the Czech Republic, Hungary and Slovakia with Germany and the US. Aggarwal and Kyaw (2005) investigate the impact of the formation of the NAFTA on stock markets within member countries and find that after the formation of NAFTA, stock markets in the NAFTA region became more integrated.

It is now widely acknowledged that a wide range of tests is needed to assess the complex nature of financial integration, especially since this process might be time varying (Kearney and Lucey (2004). An important paper by Gilmore, Lucey and McManus (2008) applies various static and dynamic methodologies to examine the co-movements of the major CEE equity markets (Hungary, the Czech Republic and Poland) with those of London and Frankfurt for the period 1995–2005. The authors also investigate the time varying properties of co-movement using a rolling-window approach. The results of this investigation provide encouraging news for investors seeking to diversify their portfolios along international lines. Static co-integration tests find no evidence of any long-run relationship between the CEE markets investigated and Frankfurt or London. Dynamic tests do reveal periods of co-integration as well as instances where short-run behaviour overpowers the long-run equilibrium relationship, but the authors conclude that any relationship is episodic and on the whole there is little evidence of any steady increase in co-movement among the markets investigated.

In this paper we extend the work of Gilmore, Lucey and Mcmanus (2008) by providing a time-varying assessment of non-linear co-movement using an enhanced database of CEE countries. The non-linear tests for time-varying co-movement employed in this study, unlike the traditional approaches to testing for co-integration, encompass a number of alternative forms of non-linearity. In addition, because sample dependency can distort results when a series is converging, we test whether our results are robust compared to data gathered at different frequencies. Our data set includes the 10 CEE countries that have become full EU Members since, as indicated above, there is increasing evidence that economic integration might promote stock market co-movement. Investigating this group of countries is timely because one country (Slovenia) adopted the euro on 1 January 2007 and Estonia will adopt the euro on January 1st 2011. The remainder are committed to adopting the euro when the necessary conditions are fulfilled. Indeed, three of our target countries (Latvia, Lithuania and Slovakia) participate in the Exchange Rate Mechanism of the EU and all of these countries remain committed to the Maastricht Criteria. To this extent they share certain macroeconomic aims and common goals.

The remainder of this chapter is structured as follows. Section 6.2 analyses the observations on stock market returns for CEE countries and section 6.3 outlines the three approaches employed to evaluate stock market co-movement. In section 6.4 we detail our empirical results and section 6.5 provides a summary and conclusions.

6.2 Data and summary statistics

The study uses data on the stock market indices for 10 CEE countries (Slovenia, Slovak Republic, Estonia, Latvia, Lithuania, Bulgaria, Czech Republic, Romania, Hungary and Poland) and two European stock exchanges (Frankfurt and London). We express stock price indices in their national currencies since this restricts any change in index values exclusively to stock price movements and so avoids the distortions resulting from the numerous currency devaluations that have taken place in CEE countries (Voronkova, 2003). The data were obtained from Datastream. Following Voronkova (2004) and Lagoarde-Segot and Lucey (2007), we use daily data to incorporate the information on market interactions contained in high-frequency series; Table 6.1 provides summary statistics for daily returns between 1994 and 2006. Daily returns are calculated as $r^i_{t,d}=ln(p^i_{t,d}/p^i_{t,d-1})*100$, where $p^i_{t,d}$ is the stock market index of *i-th* country, in year *t* on trading day *d*. The highest mean returns were in Bulgaria (0.159 per cent) and Latvia (0.104 per cent). In addition, mean daily returns are generally higher across the stock exchanges for the CEE countries than for either the DAX or the FTSE; the average daily returns for CEE countries is 0.073 per cent compared to 0.036 per cent and 0.016 per cent for the DAX and the FTSE, respectively.

Despite the larger daily returns available on CEE exchanges, volatility was also significantly higher on these equity markets relative to those in London and Frankfurt. The average volatility across the CEE countries (measured by the standard deviation of daily returns) is 1.446 compared to 1.478 for the DAX and 1.123 for the FTSE. Of the CEE countries investigated, the Czech Republic, Lithuania and Slovenia are the least volatile.

Table 6.1 Summary statistics of daily returns of CEE and European stock exchanges

	Mean	**Median**	**Std. Dev.**	**Skew**	**Kurt.**	**Jarque-Bera**
Germany (dax)	0.036	0.055	1.478	–0.167	5.943	1144.093
United Kingdom (ftse)	0.016	0.003	1.123	–0.143	5.559	719.681
Slovenia (slex)	0.046	0.000	1.094	0.818	46.409	246096.900
Slovak Republic (slvx)	0.032	0.000	1.283	–0.411	10.470	7056.424
Estonia (esx)	0.076	0.000	1.746	–1.313	27.164	67916.250
Latvia (latx)	0.104	0.029	1.558	–1.236	24.265	34851.770
Lithuania (litx)	0.087	0.033	0.910	–0.214	18.807	19013.440
Bulgaria (bulx)	0.159	0.028	1.843	–0.417	39.829	91319.210
Czech Republic (czehx)	0.027	0.000	1.158	–0.285	6.090	1287.294
Romania (romx)	0.073	0.000	1.680	–0.159	9.544	4328.895
Hungary (hunx)	0.079	0.000	1.669	–0.963	17.946	29615.620
Poland (polx)	0.050	0.000	1.521	–0.168	7.071	2176.203

Note: All Jarque-Bera statistics are significant at normal levels of testing.

In addition to the relatively higher level of volatility in CEE countries, as expected, the distribution of returns also seems to be non-normal. With the exception of equity markets in Slovenia, Estonia and Hungary, most of the returns (including the DAX and the FTSE) are negatively skewed. The measure of excess kurtosis for all the exchanges deviates significantly from that expected from returns drawn from a normal distribution. In particular, Slovenia, Estonia, Latvia, Lithuania and Bulgaria all had measured excess kurtosis significantly above 3. The non-normality is confirmed by the significance of the Jarque-Bera statistic.

6.3 Econometric approach

Let P_t represent the stock market index in a given CEE country and P_t^* the stock market index of the benchmark exchange, in this case London (FTSE) or Frankfurt (DAX). If the two series are integrated of order one, $I(1)$, then in the model:

$$P_t = \mathrm{P}_t^* + u_t \tag{1}$$

where u_t is normally assumed to be $I(1)$. If $u_t \sim I(0)$, however, there exists a bivariate co-integrating relationship between the variables and therefore some linkage between the CEE country index and benchmark index.

Tests for a linear co-integrating relationship of the type given in Equation (1) have been developed by Johansen and Juselius (1990). The maximum eigenvalue statistic tests the null hypothesis that there exists at most r co-integrating vectors. The test statistic is computed as:

$$LR_{\max}(r_0) = -T\log(1-\lambda_{r_0+1})$$

for $r = 0,1,\ldots,k-1$ where λ are the eigenvalue statistics and asymptotic critical values can be found in Johansen and Juselius (1990).

In fact, the relationship between the two series may not always be linear. Li (2006) shows that the co-integrating relationship between two exchanges may be log-linear and deterministic, log-linear and stochastic or non-linear in the price indices, depending on whether the risk premium is a linear or non-linear function of domestic and foreign risks. Equation (1) may therefore be rewritten as:

$$g(P_t) = f(P_t^*) + e_t \tag{2}$$

where $g(.)$ and $f(.)$ are monotonically increasing functions. If $e_t \sim I(0)$, then there exists a non-linear co-integrating relationship between the two exchanges.

The functions $g(.)$ and $f(.)$ are not observed, but Breitung (2001) has developed tests of non-linear co-integration based on the ranks of the observed series, $R_T[g(P_t)]=R_T(P_t)$ and $R_T[f(P_t^*)]=R_T(P_t^*)$. Breitung (2001) computes two test statistics:

$$\kappa_T = T^{-1}\sup_t |d_t| \tag{3}$$

and

$$\varepsilon_t = T^{-3}\sum_{i=1}^{T} d_t^2 \tag{4}$$

where $d_t = R_T(P_t) - R_T(P_t^*)$ and $\sup_t |d_t|$ is the maximum value of $|d_t|$ over $t = 1,2,...,T$. The null hypothesis tested is that of no (non-linear) co-integration and is rejected if the test statistics are too small. Breitung (2001) provides critical values for the test statistics in Table 6.1 of the chapter. One of the main advantages of Breitung's (2001) tests is that they encompass a number of other alternative forms of non-linearity. Therefore, rather than testing one type of non-linearity, which might not necessarily be the correct form, the statistics are able to evaluate whether or not there exists some long-run association between two or more variables.

Because co-integration tests are usually sample dependent (Stephon and Larsen, 1991) the authors employ time-varying co-integration tests with a rolling window. To obtain time-varying measures of the co-integration statistics, the step size, k, is set at 20, 4 and 1 for daily weekly and monthly series respectively. Rolling three-year sub-samples are therefore generated using $3D+k$ observations, where D is the number of trading periods. The test statistics in each case are then scaled by the critical values at the 5 per cent level. To overcome the problem of non-synchronous trading days, some authors employ weekly or monthly data, which sidesteps the problem but at the expense of lost information (see Miller, Muthuswamy and Whaley, 1994). Testing for co-integration at each frequency of observation allows the authors to investigate the possible implications this might have on stock market integration.

Breitung's (2001) test, although able to detect the presence of co-integration, does not indicate whether the relationship is linear or non-linear. Using the following equation:

$$P_t=\gamma_0+\gamma_1 P_t^*+f^*(P_t^*)+v_t \tag{5}$$

the null hypothesis of linearity $f^*(P_t^*)=0$ for all t and $v_t \sim I(0)$ can be tested. Since $f^*(P_t^*)$ is unknown, a multiple of the rank transformation is used instead, that is, $f^*(P_t^*) = \Theta R_T(P_t^*)$. Breitung notes that if P_t^* is exogenous and $v_t \sim N(0,\sigma^2)$, a score statistic TR^2 from the least squares regression:

$$\hat{v}_t = \lambda_0 + \lambda_1 P_t^* + \lambda_3 f^*(P_t^*) + \xi_t \quad (6)$$

where $\hat{v}_t$ are the residuals under the null hypothesis. The test statistic is distributed as χ^2 with one degree of freedom.

6.4 Empirical results

6.4.1 Full sample

Before testing for cointegration, unit root tests are done for all the stock market indices expressed in level terms and the results are given in Table 6.2. The tests were done with and without a trend as recommended by Engle and Granger (1987) and Breitung and Gouriéroux (1997). The tests suggest the null hypothesis of a unit root in the level series cannot be rejected in all cases.[1] In contrast, the null hypothesis of a unit root in the differenced series is rejected in all cases. The stock market price indices for CEE countries as well as the DAX and FTSE are $I(1)$; stationarity is achieved after first differencing the level series. As a preliminary investigation of stock market linkages in Europe, bivariate tests for co-integration are provided in Table 6.3. These tests are done using daily observations for the full sample period.

Given that the variables are $I(1)$, the study then employed the Johansen and Juselius (1990) maximum eigenvalue statistic to test for linear co-integration between each CEE country exchange and the DAX and FTSE. The results are given in Table 6.3 and are done both with and without a trend. Looking first at the results for the DAX, the null hypothesis of no co-integration is rejected only in three out of the 10 countries studied: Slovenia, Lithuania and Bulgaria. However, these results should be treated with caution due to the lower predictive power of the full-sample maximum eigenvalue statistic when there are structural breaks in the sample period (Andrade, Bruneu and Gregoire, 2005). Moore and Wang (2007), in investigating the volatility of stock exchanges in new EU member states between 1994 and 2005 using a Markov switching model, find that in the early stage of transition stock returns were usually in the high-volatility regime. The authors note that

Table 6.2 ADF and Breitung tests for unit roots (daily)

Series tested	ADF		Breitung	
	Without trend	**With trend**	**Without trend**	**With trend**
Levels				
dax	–1.028	–1.609	0.057	0.012
ftse	–1.652	–1.726	0.018	0.011
slex	1.484	–0.474	0.084	0.020
slvx	0.008	–1.112	0.048	0.021
esx	0.764	–0.568	0.061	0.020
latx	0.483	–1.792	0.090	0.019
litx	0.755	–1.757	0.086	0.019
bulx	1.663	–1.957	0.097	0.014
czehx	–0.560	–1.361	0.042	0.018
romx	1.346	–1.378	0.079	0.022
hunx	1.209	–0.952	0.077	0.011
polx	0.936	–0.655	0.069	0.008
Differences				
dax	–10.177**	–10.177**	0.000**	0.000**
ftse	–22.333**	–23.333**	0.000**	0.000**
slex	–10.670**	–10.837**	0.000**	0.000**
slvx	–11.462**	–11.567**	0.000**	0.000**
esx	–7.675**	–7.825**	0.000**	0.000**
latx	–10.074**	–10.148**	0.000**	0.000**
litx	–8.061**	–8.252**	0.001**	0.000**
bulx	–12.656**	–12.863**	0.001**	0.000**
czehx	–7.866**	–7.941**	0.000**	0.000**
romx	–9.300**	–9.611**	0.000**	0.000**
hunx	–15.077**	–15.197**	0.000**	0.000**
polx	–18.222**	–18.284**	0.000**	0.000**

Note: ** indicates significance at the 1 per cent level of testing.

this volatility was primarily due to the spillover effects from crises in Asia and Russia.

These results may also be due to non-linearity in stock price data owing to diversity in agents' beliefs, heterogeneity in investors' objectives, herd behaviour and endowment switches between high and low economic growth (Sarantis, 2001). Table 6.4 therefore provides Breitung's non-linear test for co-integration using the full sample of data. Similar to Johansen co-integration tests, there is no evidence of co-integration between stock exchanges in CEE countries and the DAX and FTSE. These results are similar to those obtained by Égert and Kocenda (2007) who analyse co-movement among three stock markets in CEE and their interdependence with western Europe. The authors find no

Table 6.3 Johansen's tests for co-integration (full sample)

	H_0:rank = p	Without trend	With trend
DAX			
slex	$p = 0$	20.594*	7.112
	$p = 1$	2.425	2.037
slvx	$p = 0$	9.995	5.827
	$p = 1$	0.343	0.006
esx	$p = 0$	15.907	8.045
	$p = 1$	1.123	0.580
latx	$p = 0$	9.941	4.624
	$p = 1$	4.430	0.057
litx	$p = 0$	20.241*	11.008
	$p = 1$	3.758	0.506
bulx	$p = 0$	29.907**	15.396
	$p = 1$	7.556	0.310
czehx	$p = 0$	7.781	3.782
	$p = 1$	0.680	0.008
romx	$p = 0$	14.168	6.918
	$p = 1$	0.925	0.160
hunx	$p = 0$	11.698	6.161
	$p = 1$	11.171	0.372
polx	$p = 0$	13.312	7.356
	$p = 1$	1.260	0.210
FTSE			
slex	$p = 0$	21.415*	6.939
	$p = 1$	3.470	3.291
slvx	$p = 0$	11.713	8.522
	$p = 1$	0.393	0.084
esx	$p = 0$	14.947	8.811
	$p = 1$	1.490	0.847
latx	$p = 0$	12.404	6.924
	$p = 1$	5.450	0.016
litx	$p = 0$	21.613*	12.138
	$p = 1$	4.999	0.047
bulx	$p = 0$	29.325**	14.811
	$p = 1$	7.869	0.831
czehx	$p = 0$	10.617	6.604
	$p = 1$	1.005	0.260
romx	$p = 0$	14.227	7.211
	$p = 1$	1.365	0.321
hunx	$p = 0$	8.162	4.188
	$p = 1$	1.403	0.062
polx	$p = 0$	11.428	6.942
	$p = 1$	3.125	2.628

Note: ** and * indicate significance at the 1 and 5 per cent levels of testing, respectively.

Table 6.4 Breitung's tests for co-integration (full sample)

	κ_T	ξ_T
DAX		
slex	0.670	0.093
slvx	0.958	0.210
esx	0.761	0.175
latx	1.097	0.253
litx	0.998	0.235
bulx	1.135	0.245
czehx	0.860	0.169
romx	0.855	0.211
hunx	0.555	0.058
polx	0.648	0.050
FTSE		
slex	0.710	0.148
slvx	0.778	0.157
esx	0.810	0.165
latx	0.963	0.184
litx	0.896	0.159
bulx	0.973	0.169
czehx	0.805	0.164
romx	0.792	0.164
hunx	0.753	0.125
polx	0.634	0.104

Note: ** and * indicates significance at the 1 and 5 percent level of testing, respectively.

robust co-integration for any of the stock index pairs or for any of the extended specifications. Similarly, Chelley-Steeley (2005), using smooth transition analysis, notes that during the recent history of the CEE countries, their markets were heavily segmented. This segmentation has, however, declined significantly over time. These findings suggest that testing for stock market co-movement over the entire sample of data could provide misleading results, since the exchanges may have been in the process of converging.

As further evidence of the need to take into account the time-varying properties of stock exchanges in CEE countries, Figure 6.1 plots the scaled tests for non-linearity recommended by Breitung (2001). As a result, values above the unit line indicate that the null hypothesis of no non-linearity could not be accepted at normal levels of testing. The figure suggests that there are periods where linear models of stock

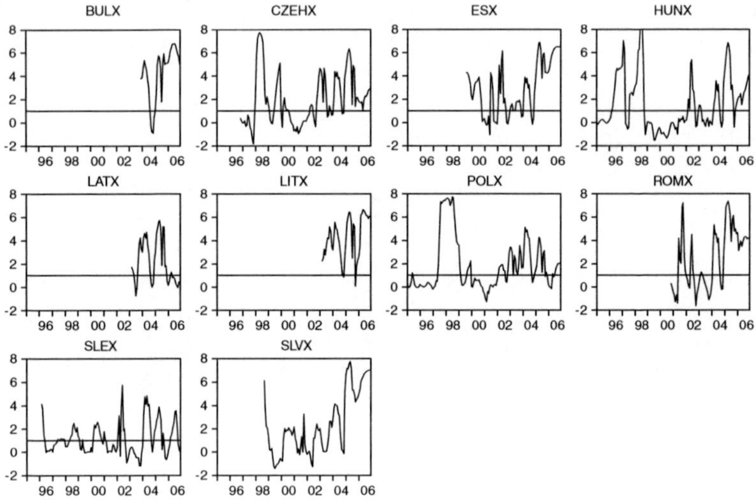

Figure 6.1 Tests for non-linearity

market co-movement are unlikely to represent the dynamics in CEE countries adequately. The findings presented in this section are therefore instructive and suggest that co-movement in Europe is likely to be non-linear and time-varying. As a result, the following section addresses both of these issues.

6.4.2 Time-varying results

Given that the evidence so far suggests that stock markets in CEE countries are to a large extent segmented from those in the rest of Europe, the authors employ time-varying co-integration techniques to investigate whether this hypothesis holds for various sub-periods. The three co-integration test statistics ($LR_{\max}$ denoted by EIG, κ_T denoted by KAPR, and ε_t denoted by XI) are calculated using rolling three-year sub-samples and the step size is set so that the test statistics are obtained for each month in the sample period. The acronyms for each of the test statistics are affixed at the front of each figure to denote which test is used. In addition, 'D', 'W' and 'M' appended to each chart title represent daily, weekly and monthly observations, respectively.

Figure 6.2 presents the results from using the DAX as the benchmark index and therefore tests the null of no co-integration between the given CEE exchange and the DAX. Since the scaled test statistics are plotted, all values above 1 (the horizontal straight line) indicate that the null hypothesis is rejected at normal levels of testing.

The results indicate that co-movement between stock exchanges in CEE countries and those in western Europe is heterogeneous. In the

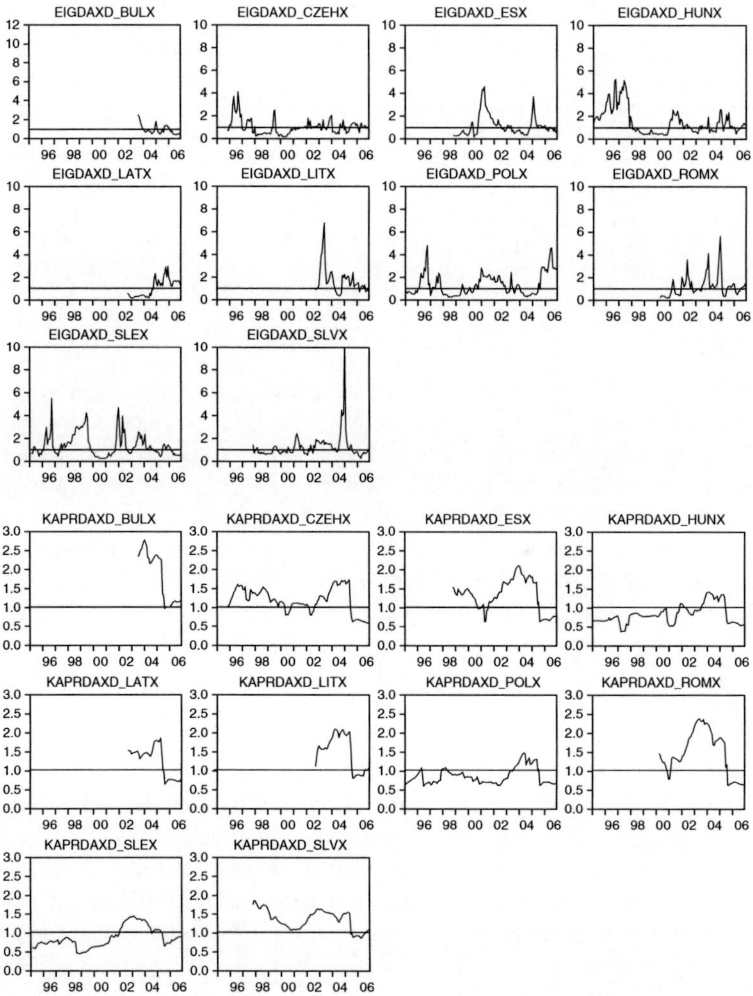

Figure 6.2 Time varying linear and non-linear tests for co-integration between the DAX and CEE countries' exchanges

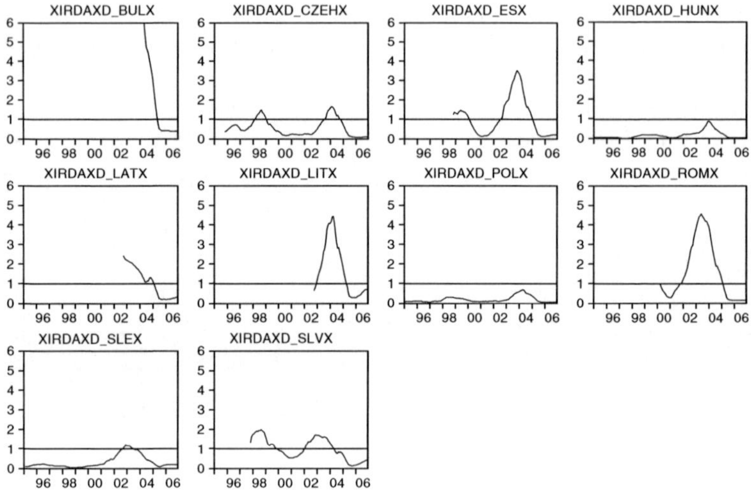

Figure 6.2 Continued

case of Slovenia, the non-linear co-integration statistics suggest that the null hypothesis of no co-integration could not be rejected for most of the sample period. After 2001, however, the null hypothesis of no co-integration is rejected up until 2006, when there is a slight dip in the co-integration statistics. The increased capital market integration probably reflects the removal of foreign investment restrictions following the enactment of the country's Foreign Exchange Act. This has enhanced portfolio diversity by incorporating foreign securities (Andritzky, 2007). In contrast, the slight dip in the statistic for 2006 could reflect growing investor risk aversion towards emerging markets during the year.

In the Slovak Republic, test statistics suggest that there exists a relationship between the domestic stock exchange and those in Europe. This result is somewhat surprising, since trading activity is mainly done as pre-negotiated trades and the market is fairly small and illiquid. However, Herrmann and Jochem (2003) note that money markets in the Slovak Republic display a high degree of international integration in the euro area. In addition, this association has strengthened since 1999. The findings for Estonia are quite similar, but with a pronounced upward shift in the co-integration test statistics in 2002, 2003 and 2004. Egger and Pfaffermayr (2004) note that the Eastern enlargement was characterised by a substantial, positive anticipation effect in the period prior to the announcement and the formal establishment of each of the integration steps. This anticipation effect could explain the significant jump in the statistics observed between 2002 and 2004.

Given that stock exchanges in Latvia, Lithuania, and Bulgaria were only recently re-established relative to other CEE countries, the co-integration statistics for these nations are available only from 2002 onwards. The results for the three exchanges are quite similar. The Johansen maximum eigenvalue statistic suggests that the linear co-movement between the stock exchanges in these countries and those in western Europe was, at best, episodic. However, Breitung's non-linear co-integration statistics suggest that there was some degree of co-movement between stock exchanges in these countries and those in the rest of Europe after 2002. These results suggest that, despite their relatively late start, market returns in these countries are fairly integrated (although non-linearly) with the rest of Europe. Encouragingly, our results are in line with those reported by Mateus (2004). Set in an unconditional asset-pricing framework, Mateus attempts to measure the impact that global risk factors have on excess returns in emerging countries. The author finds that global risk factors have high predictive power for Bulgaria, Estonia, Lithuania, Romania and Hungary, whereas local risk factors were more important in the Czech Republic, Latvia, Poland and Slovenia.

The co-integration statistics suggest that co-movement between the stock markets in the Czech Republic and Romania and those in western Europe seems to be rising over time. These results are similar to those obtained by Schotman and Zalewska (2006), Chelley-Steeley (2005) and Mateus (2004) and seem to be driven by greater financial integration in the Czech Republic (Herrmann and Jochem, 2003). In the case of Hungary and Poland, the co-integration test statistics have been rising over time. However, for most of the sample period until 2002, the null hypothesis of no co-integration could not be rejected. This result could be due to the insignificance of global risk factors on excess returns in Poland (Mateus, 2004) and the greater influence of Mediterranean countries on Hungary relative to western Europe (Brüggerman and Trenkler, 2007).

To evaluate the robustness of the results obtained earlier, the exercise is also conducted using the FTSE as the benchmark index.[2] Given the high degree of stock market integration within Europe, however, the results were very similar, (see Yang and Bessler, 2004).

As noted earlier, another objective of this study is to evaluate the impact that data frequency has on testing for market integration. To facilitate this, we calculate the time-varying co-integration test statistics using monthly and weekly data, to evaluate the robustness of the results already provided using daily observations. In general, data frequency has little or no impact on the results obtained from the non-linear co-integration statistics. However, Johansen's co-integration test statistic can vary quite significantly with data frequency. In most countries, somewhat different findings are obtained if monthly, weekly or daily data are employed in the analysis. These results are robust to changes in the benchmark index employed.

The results presented in this section suggest that the Johansen co-integration test statistic can provide misleading inferences if there is non-linearity in the relationship between the variables. Breitung's co-integration test statistic suggests that there is some co-movement between stock exchanges in CEE countries and those in western Europe.

6.5 Conclusions

In this chapter, we explored the possible co-movement of CEE stock markets with those of the UK and Germany by testing for the existence of a co-integrating relation between a pair of stock market indices. Using the full-sample data, the standard co-integration test by Johansen revealed very little evidence of co-integration between either the FTSE or the DAX and a CEE stock market index. Testing for the possibility of a non-linear co-integrating relationship using Breitung's (2001) test revealed even less evidence of co-integration.

Mindful of the fact that the CEE stock markets are highly volatile relative to those of the UK and Germany, and that the Johansen test is sensitive to data volatility as well as the sample period considered, we proceeded to test for co-integration by using a rolling window approach. Our results suggest that co-movement between CEE and developed European exchanges is heterogeneous. In general, we find evidence of co-movement with western exchanges in Slovenia and the Slovak Republic. Using linear co-integration techniques, we find limited evidence of co-movement between the stock markets in Latvia, Lithuania and Bulgaria with those of western Europe. However, we find stronger evidence of co-movement between these exchanges and Western Europe using Breitung's non-linear co-integration statistic. We also find evidence that while co-movement between the Czech Republic, Hungary Poland and Romania with western Europe is limited, it seems to be increasing over time.

In summary, we find that Johansen's co-integration test statistic can provide misleading inferences if there is non-linearity in the relationship between the relevant stock market indices. Breitung's co-integration test statistic provides more reliable results and suggests that there is some co-movement between stock exchanges in CEE countries and those in western Europe. We find no evidence that the frequency of observations has any effect on our results.

Notes

1. Lag lengths were chosen using the Schwarz Bayesian criterion.
2. Results available from authors upon request.

References

Aggarwal, R. and Kyaw, N. A. (2005) 'Equity Market Integration in the NAFTA Region: Evidence from Unit Root and Cointegration Tests', *International Review of Financial Analysis*, 14, 393–406.

Aggarwal, R., Lucey, B. and Muckley, C. (2003) 'Dynamics of Equity Market Integration in Europe: Evidence of Changes Over Time and with Events', IIIS Discussion Paper 19, Dublin, Ireland.

Andrade, P., Bruneau, C. and Gregoire, S. (2005) 'Testing for the Cointegration Rank when Some Cointegrating Directions are Changing', *Journal of Econometrics*, 124: 269–310.

Andritzky, J. R. (2007) 'Capital Market Development in a Small Country: The Case of Slovenia', IMF Working Paper WP/07/229, Washington, DC.

Asprem, M. (1989) 'Stock Prices, Asset Portfolios and Macroeconomic Variables in Ten European Countries', *Journal of Banking and Finance*, 13: 589–612.

Bessler, D. A. and Yang, J. (2003) 'The Structure of Independence in International Stock Markets', *Journal of International Finance and Money*, 22: 261–87.

Bodurtha, J. N., Cho, D. C. and Senbet, L. W. (1989) 'Economic Forces in the Stock Market', *Global Finance Journal*, 1: 21–46.

Bohl, M. T., Gootschalk, K., and Pál, R., (2006) 'Institutional Investors and Stock Market Efficiency: The Case of the January Anomaly', MPRA Paper No 677.

Breitung, J. (2001) 'Rank Tests for Non-Linear Cointegration', *Journal of Business and Economic Statistics*, 19: 331–40.

Breitung, J. and Gouriéroux, C. (1997) 'Rank Tests for Unit Roots', *Journal of Econometrics*, 81: 7–27.

Brüggerman, R. and Trenkler, C. (2007) 'Are Eastern European Countries Catching Up? Time Series Evidence for Czech Republic, Hungary and Poland', *Applied Economics Letters* 14: 245–9.

Canova, F. and De Nicoló, G. (1995) 'Stock Returns and Real Activity: A Structural Approach', *European Economic Review*, 39: 981–1015.

Chelley-Steeley, P. L. (2005) 'Modelling Equity Market Integration using Smooth Transition Analysis: A Study of Eastern European Stock Markets', *Journal of International Money and Finance*, Vol. 24(5): 818–31.

Chen, G-M., Frith, M. and Rui, O. M. (2002) 'Stock Market Linkages: Evidence from Latin America', *Journal of Banking and Finance*, 26: 1113–41.

Égert, B. and Kocenda, E. (2007) 'Interdependence between Eastern and Western European Stock Markets: Evidence from Intraday Day', *Economic Systems*, 31: 184–203.

Egger, P. and Pfaffermayr, M. (2004) 'Foreign Direct Investment and European Integration in the 1990s', *World Economy*, 27: 99–110.

Engle, R. F. and Granger, C. W. J. (1987) 'Cointegration and Error Correction: Representation, Testing and Estimation', *Econometrica*, 55: 251–76.

Fraser, P. and Oyefeso, O., (2005) 'US, UK and European Stock Market Integration', *Journal of Business, Finance and Accounting*, 32: 161–81.

Fratzscher, M. (2002) 'Financial Market Integration in Europe: On the Effects of EMU on Stock Markets', *International Journal of Finance and Economics*, 7: 165–93.

Fujii, E., (2005) 'Intra and Inter-Regional Causal Linkages of Emerging Stock Markets: Evidence from Asia and Latin America In and Out of Crises', *Journal of International Financial Markets, Institutions and Money*, 15: 315–42.

Georgoustsos, D. A. and Kouretas, G. P. (2001) 'Common Stochastic Trends in International Stock Markets: Testing in an Integrated Framework', University of Crete Working Paper (http://wwwdbase-soc-uoc.gr/ewp/papers/cst.pdf).

Ghosh, A., Saidi, R. and Johnson, K. (1999) 'Who Moves the Asia-Pacific Stock Markets – US or Japan? Empirical Evidence Based on the Theory of Cointegration', *Financial Review*, 34: 159–70.

Gilmore, C. G. and McManus, G. M. (2003) 'Bilateral and Multilateral Properties between the German and Central European Equity Markets', *Studies in Economics and Finance*, 21: 40–53.

Gilmore, C. G., Lucey, B. M. and McManus, G. M. (2008) 'The Dynamics of Central European Equity Market Comovements', *Quarterly Review of Economics and Finance*, 48: 605–22.

Harrison, B. and Paton, D. (2005) 'Transition, the Evolution of Stock Market Efficiency and Entry into EU: The Case of Romania', *Economics of Planning*, 37: 203–23.

Herrmann, S. and Jochem, A. (2003) 'The International Integration of Money Markets in the Central and East European Accession Countries: Deviations from Covered Interest Parity, Capital Controls and Inefficiencies in the Financial Sector', Discussion paper 08/03, Economic Research Centre, Deutsche Bundesbank, Frankfurt, Germany.

Johansen, S. (1988) 'Statistical Analysis of Cointegrating Vectors', *Journal of Economic Dynamics and Control* 12: 231–54.

Johansen, S. and Juselius, K. (1990) 'Maximum Likelihood Estimation and Inference on Cointegration with Applications to the Demand for Money', *Oxford Bulletin of Economics and Statistics*, 52: 169–210.

Johnson, R., and Soenen, L., (2002) 'Asian Economic Integration and Stock Market Comovement', *Journal of Financial Research*, 25: 141–57.

Kasa, K. (1992) 'Common Stochastic in International Stock Markets', *Journal of Monetary Economics*, 29: 95–124.

Kearney, C. and Lucey, B. M. (2004) 'International Equity Market Integration: Theory, Evidence and Implications', *International Review of Financial Analysis*, 13: 571–83.

Kim, S. J., Moshirian, F. and Wu, E. (2005) 'Dynamic Stock Market Integration Driven by the European Monetary Union: An Empirical Analysis', *Journal of Banking and Finance*, 29: 2475–502.

Koch, P. and Koch, T. (1991) 'Evolution in Dynamic Linkages across Daily National Stock Indexes', *Journal of International Money and Finance*, 10: 231–51.

Koutmos, G. and Booth, G. G., (1995) 'Asymmetric Volatility Transmission in International Stock Markets', *Journal of International Money and Finance*, 14: 747–62.

Lagoarde-Segot, T. and Lucey, B. M. (2007), 'Capital Market Integration in the Middle East and North Africa', *Emerging Markets Finance and Trade*, 43: 34–57.

Lewis, K. K. (1999) 'Trying to Explain Home Bias in Equities and Consumption', *Journal of Economic Literature*, 37: 571–608.

Li, X-M. (2006) 'A Revisit of International Stock Market Linkages: New Evidence from Rank Tests for Nonlinear Cointegration', *Scottish Journal of Political Economy*, 53: 174–97.

Linne, T. (1988) 'The Integration of Central and East European Equity Markets into the International Capital Markets', IWH Fortschungsreihe 1, 3–23.

Manning, N. (2002) 'Common Trends and Convergence? South East Asian Equity Markets, 1988–1999', *Journal of International Money and Finance*, 21: 183–202.

Mateus, T. (2004) 'The Risk and Predictability of Equity Returns of the EU Accession Countries', *Emerging Markets Review*, 5: 241–66.

Miller, M., Muthuswamy, J. and Whaley, R. (1994) 'Mean Reversion of Standard and Poor's 500 Index Basis Changes: Arbitrage-Indexed or Statistical Illusion?' *Journal of Finance*, 49: 479–513.

Moore, T. and Wang, P. (2007) 'Volatility in Stock Returns for New EU Member States: Markov Regime Switching Model', *International Review of Financial Analysis*, 16: 282–92.

Nasseh, A. and Strauss, J. (2000) 'Stock Prices and Domestic and International Macroeconomic Activity: A Cointegration Approach', *Quarterly Review of Economics and Finance*, 40: 229–45.

Ng, T. H. (2002) 'Stock Market Linkages in South-East Asia', *Asian Economic Journal*, 16: 353–77.

Phengpis, C. and Apilado, V. P. (2004) 'Economic Interdependence and Common Stochastic Trends: A Comparative Analysis between EMU and Non-EMU Stock Markets', *International Review of Financial Analysis*, 13: 245–63.

Phengpis, C., Apilado, V. P. and Swanson, P. E. (2004) 'Effects of Economic Convergence on Stock Market Returns in Major EMU Member Countries', *Review of Quantitative Finance and Accounting*, 23: 207–27.

Phylaktis, K. and Ravazzolo, (2002) 'Measuring Financial and Economic Integration with Equity Prices in Emerging Markets', *Journal of International Money and Finance*, 21, 879–904.

Rockinger, M. and G. Urga (2001) 'A Time Varying Parameter Model to Test for Predictability and Integration in the Stock Markets of Transition Economies', *Journal of Business and Economic Statistics*, 19: 73–84.

Sarantis, N. (2001) 'Nonlinearities, Cyclical Behaviour and Predictability in Stock Markets: International Evidence', *International Journal of Forecasting*, 17: 459–82.

Schotman, P. C. and Zalewska, A. (2006) 'Non-Synchronous Trading and Testing for Market Integration in Central European Emerging Markets', *Journal of Empirical Finance*, 13: 462–94.

Stephon, P. S. and Larsen, K. S. (1991) 'Tests of Exchange Market Efficiency: Fragile Evidence from Cointegration Tests', *Journal of International Money and Finance*, 10: 561–70.

Syriopoulos, T. (2007) 'Dynamic Linkages between Emerging European and Developed Stock Markets: Has the EMU Any Impact?' *International Review of Financial Analysis*, 16, 41–60.
Voronkova, S. (2003) 'Instability in the Long-Run Relationships: Evidence from the Central European Emerging Stock Markets', Discussion Paper, Symposium on International Equity Market Integration, Institute for International Integration Studies, Dublin.
Voronkova, S. (2004) 'Equity Market Integration in Central European Emerging Markets: A Cointegration Analysis with Shifting Regimes', *International Review of Financial Analysis*, 13: 633–47.
Yang, J. and Bessler, D. A. (2004) 'The International Price Transmission in Stock Index Futures', *Economic Inquiry*, 42: 370–86.

7
Cross-Country Versus Cross-Regional Convergence in the European Union: An Empirical Exploration

Menbere Workie Tiruneh

7.1 Introduction

The successful completion of European integration may by any measure be considered as one of the best achievements in modern European history. In spite of some outstanding pitfalls (i.e., monetary union despite fiscal decentralisation, and not no unanimity when it comes to foreign policy issues.), overall the integration process should be considered a turning point and milestone as a response to the process of globalisation and regional integration elsewhere in the world. This allows and will continue to allow the entire group much better bargaining power on the global stage, politically, economically and in other strategic areas. The implications for European transition economies are several in nature.

First, the transformation of a planned economy to market systems would have taken much longer without the incentives to join the EU. Second, the political pressure stemming from the Maastricht Criteria required these countries to standardise their economies. This, too, would probably have taken much longer time to achieve without political consensus and the support of the population. Third, the significant amount of funds (structural, regional and cohesion) channelled from advanced European Union members to help transition economies finance the transformation process played a pivotal role as these economies were strongly identified as being severely undercapitalised, especially at the outset of the transition process. Assuming these resources have been effectively allocated, one would expect transition economies to achieve higher growth rates in order to narrow gaps in their living standards against advanced EU members.

It should be emphasised, however, that there are outstanding issues linked to the sustainability of growth dynamics thus far, given the changing nature of the global economic landscape due to the ongoing global financial crisis. In this regard, as was argued by the OECD (2000), while one of the policy goals for transition economies is to achieve sustained and high rates of economic growth to enable them to close the gap, there is ample evidence of persisting cross-country variation within the transition economies themselves. While some transition economies managed quickly to achieve relatively sustainable economic growth and narrow their income per capita gap compared to other advanced EU economies, others are still caught in a poverty trap. Some countries' poor performance to a large extent is a reflection of their terrible initial conditions, whereas others simply failed to undertake firm and quick economic, institutional and political reforms.

The objective of this chapter is to analyse empirically the extent to which transition economies have managed to scale down their living-standard gaps against those of advanced EU member states. The chapter also explores empirically whether cross-country convergence may or may not have a 'trickle-down effect' on regional convergence within countries. Since data are not available for EU regional funds channelled to transition economies, this chapter cannot test the impact of these funds on the growth dynamics of these economies. When it comes to theoretical models and empirical strategies, I follow the neoclassical growth framework based on the seminal work of Solow (1956), extended by among others, Barro (1991), Sala-i-Martin (1994) and Barro and Sala-i-Martin (1995) and Mankiw, Romer and Weil (1992).

The chapter is structured as follows. Section 7.2 briefly discusses the basic Solow growth framework, and elaborates on the concepts of convergence and measurement issues. Section 7.3 briefly discusses selected previous empirical studies and is followed by section 7.4 which deals with data computation and observations. Section 7.5 discusses the results from various perspectives, and section 7.6 comprises conclusions and some policy implications.

7.2 The basic issues in growth and convergence debates

One of the most frequently asked questions in economics has been linked to why some countries are growing faster than others; why some countries are poorer than others; what should be done to reduce cross-country and cross-regional income disparities, and so on. The second most important question is one associated with measurement issues. In this regard, one way of measuring the speed at which countries are moving not only towards their own steady states but also towards the income per capita level of other countries goes back to Solow's (1956) growth framework. In this framework, countries with a high savings rate and a low population growth are predicted to experience higher per capita income than those in the opposite camp (Solow, 1956), *ceteris paribus*. This seminal work was quickly adopted by other economists and has therefore been the subject of constant extension.

Following Sala-i-Martin (1994, 1996a and 1996b), convergence in the context of economic growth is said to occur in a cross-section of economies, if there is a negative relationship between the growth rate of income and the initial level of income. In other words, in a cross-section of economies, convergence takes place if those economies with lower income per capita at the beginning of the observation period manage to outperform the growth rates of those with higher income per capita during the period under consideration. This, then, would suggest that the poorer the economy, the more quickly it would be expected to grow over a longer time horizon, and vice versa. Similarly, Baumol (1994) defines convergence as tantamount diminishing to the degree of economic inequality among countries. Nonetheless, as is often the case, it turns out that there are significant disputes among growth scientists regarding the theory of economic growth and convergence (Workie, 2007).[1]

The convergence debate is also considered vital as it is concerned with the gaps in living standards between countries, that is, whether these gaps are narrowing or widening across countries and over time (Pritchett, 1996). Sala-i-Martin (1996) and Barro and Sal-i-Martin (1995), using β-convergence and σ-convergence concepts, elaborate in the convergence debate more broadly.[2] Sala-i-Martin (1996, p. 1025) points out that the lack of convergence means that the degree of cross-country income inequality not only fails to disappear, but rather tends to increase over time (σ-divergence); and that economies (nations) which are predicted to be richer a few decades from now are the same countries (nations) that are rich today (β-divergence).[3] Moreover, despite the persisting disputes among economists on the determinants of long-run growth, the convergence debate has also substantial implications for policymakers both in developed and in transition economies. One of the key questions in this regard is to measure the extent to which EU funds that have been channelled to the new EU members and external aid to other developing countries have helped them to achieve accelerated growth.

7.3 The Solow-Swan model and the convergence debate: A brief theoretical review

Almost all recent empirical research on cross-country and/or cross-regional convergence and growth issues starts with the Solow growth framework. In this work, I will also first briefly summarise the basic model before presenting its empirical counterpart.

As is well known, the Solow model is a closed economy framework, where output (Y) is a function of input variables, such as labour (L) and capital (K). This can formally be written as

$$Y = F(K, L) \tag{1}$$

Three basic assumptions are linked to this model:

1. The production function in equation. (1) assumes positive and marginal products with respect to each input variable:

$$\frac{\partial F}{\partial K} > 0, \frac{\partial F}{\partial L} > 0; \frac{\partial^2 F}{K^2} < 0, \frac{\partial^2 F}{\partial L^2} < 0 \tag{1.1}$$

   Equation (1.1) indicates that whereas each input variable contributes positively towards boosting the output that is produced, its marginal productivity falls over time as more and more of it is added, *ceteris paribus*.
2. The production function exhibits constant returns to scale, indicating a proportionate increase in output as a result of changes in all input variables. This can formally be written as:

$$F(\lambda K, \lambda L) = \lambda.F(K, L), \text{ for all } \lambda > 0 \tag{1.2}$$

3. The third assumption is referred to as the so-called 'Inada conditions':

$$\begin{aligned} \lim_{K \to 0}(F_K) &= \lim_{L \to 0}(F_L) = \infty \\ \lim_{K \to \infty}(F_K) &= \lim_{L \to \infty}(F_L) = 0 \end{aligned} \tag{1.3}$$

The Inada conditions expressed in equation (1.3) state that whereas production in the absence of input variables is impossible, their excessive abundance also their marginal product diminishes over time, *ceteris paribus*. The assumption of constant returns to scale in equation (1.2) is also consistent with the balanced growth path along which capital and effective labour grow at the same rate. It is also helpful to rewrite the production function in equation (1) in its intensive form:

$$Y = F(K, L) = L\left(\frac{K}{L}, 1\right) = Lf(k) \tag{1.4}$$

where

$k = \frac{K}{L}$ = capital-labour ratio; and

$y = \frac{Y}{L}$ per capita income.
Now, the production function in equation (1) can be written in its intensive form:

$$y = f(k) \tag{1.5}$$

The change in the capital stock with a constant savings rate:

$$\dot{K} = I - \delta K = s.F(K, L, t) - \delta K \tag{1.6}$$

$$\frac{\dot{K}}{L} = s.f(k) - \delta k \tag{1.7}$$

$$\dot{k} \cong \frac{\partial\left(\frac{K}{L}\right)}{\partial t} = \frac{\dot{K}}{L} - nk$$

$$\dot{k} = s.f(k) - (n + \delta)k \tag{1.8}$$

Finally, the growth rate of k can be approximated as:

$$\gamma_k = \frac{\dot{k}}{k} = s.f(k)/k - (n + \delta) \tag{1.9}$$

Following Barro and Sala-i-Martin (1995, p. 22), the long-run growth rates in the Solow-Swan model are determined entirely by exogenous factors. The fundamental conclusion about long-run growth, therefore, is negative, simply because the long-term growth rates are independent of the savings rates and the level of the production function. Nevertheless, the model is very important in providing us with sound information about the transitional dynamics of growth, which indicates the per capita convergence of an economy towards its own steady-state value or towards the per capita incomes of a cross-section of economies (Barro and Sala-i-Martin, 1995, in Workie 2007).

7.3.1 The absolute and relative convergence hypotheses

The absolute (unconditional) convergence

Following Barro and Sala-i-Martin (1995), equation (1.9) implies that the derivative of y_k with respect to k is negative:

$$\frac{\partial y_k}{\partial k} = s.\left[f'(k) - f\left(\frac{k}{k}\right)\right] / k < 0 \tag{1.10}$$

This implies that, *ceteris paribus*, smaller values of k are linked to larger values of its corresponding growth (y_k). This suggests (provided that countries have similar rates of savings (s), growth of population (n), rate of depreciation (δ) and production function and they have the same steady state values of k and y; then, if the only difference across countries is the initial capital per capita (k), the model predicts that countries with less capital per capita tend to grow faster than those with a relatively higher level of capital per capita. Therefore, the hypothesis that nations with lower capital per capita tend to grow faster than those with higher capital per capita without imposing any restriction is referred to as 'absolute (unconditional) convergence' (Barro and Sala-i-Martin, 1995).

The convergence debate may also be further elaborated using equations. In equation (1.8) there are basically two components: Whereas the $(\delta + n)$ part represents the rate of depreciation and the growth rate of the population, the $s,f(k)/k$ component represents the savings curve. From equation (1.8), it also implies that the growth rate is rewarded by the savings rate whereas it is penalised by the elements that constitute the depreciation curve. Assumption (1.1) discussed earlier also indicates that the savings curve is downward sloping, whereas the Inada conditions (equation (1.3)) ensure that the saving curve is vertical at $k = 0$ and it approaches the horizontal axis as k tends to infinity.

The assumption behind the absolute (unconditional) β-convergence hypothesis is that countries or economies under consideration are moving to the same steady states (k^*). Then, if the only difference between them is the initial capital stock (real GDP per capita), poor regions are predicted to grow faster than rich counterparts over a longer time period. In other words, the growth rate of the poor economies towards the steady state is predicted to be faster than the growth rate of the richer counterparts that are, in fact, closer to the steady state (the terminal value).

Some reasons in favour of the absolute convergence hypothesis include (Sala-i-Martin, 2000; in Workie, 2007):

- the first is linked to the 'common-force' mechanism introduced by Baumol (1986), where at some stage due to circumstances inherent in the growth process, a set of variables influences a number of economies and drives them all in the same general direction. 'It is as though a common terminal point (the steady state) is equipped with something analogous to a magnet that draws toward itself all economies whose histories it affects'. Following Baumol (1994)', 'the unusual thing about this magnet is that it exerts the greatest force not on the economies closest to the terminal point but on those that are farthest from it'. Hence, convergence occurs- the economies initially farthest from the terminal are driven to move towards it most rapidly, which is a defining characteristic of a convergence hypothesis (in Baumol's terminology, a 'common-force convergence');
- since poor economies have a lower level of initial capital (capital-labour ratio), any additional investment would quickly push these economies towards the steady state, and
- although the above two factors are based on the assumption that all economies have similar economic parameters but different initial capital stock, there is a third reason without the underlying assumption: the contagion model of convergence predicts that because of contagion (say, imitation of production), the laggards tend to grow faster than those in an advanced stage of economic development.[4]

There has however, been a growing opposition to the absolute β-convergence hypothesis, for a number of reasons. The core assumption of the absolute convergence hypothesis is that the sole difference between nations is their initial levels of capital. However, in reality, this is just not the case always. In fact, nations are different from each other in so many other respects, including the level of technology, the propensity to save natural endowments, institutional constraints, among other things. This leads to what has come to be known as the 'absolute convergence fallacy'. Therefore, the relative or conditional convergence took this stage of the discussion.

The relative (conditional) convergence hypothesis

The absence of broader empirical evidence in favour of absolute convergence across economies makes the traditional absolute convergence hypothesis fruitless as a measure of the speed of transition towards the steady state. Therefore, the idea of conditional convergence has been introduced.[5] As was discussed, if a rich economy has a higher savings rate relative to a poor counterpart (an assumption more realistic than the previous one), then the rich economy might be proportionately further from its steady state position. Under such circumstances, it should be the rich rather than the poor economy that is predicted to grow faster towards its own steady state.

There are some additional arguments against the absolute convergence hypothesis (or in favour of the conditional convergence hypothesis) (Workie, 2007):

- Poor economies have lower savings rates (due to lower income) compared to rich ones and therefore they have lower rates of investment, and poor subsequent economic growth.
- Rich countries, as opposed to their poor counterparts, have high growth rates, despite their high initial capital-to-labour ratio, thanks to persistent innovation.
- Capital is not moving from economies where it is abundant to those where it is scarce, as was predicted by the contagion model of convergence, due mainly to risk and uncertainty in most poor nations.
- Finally, scarce qualified human capital in poor countries caused by a lack of education makes the possible transfer of technology and know-how from rich to poor countries slow and difficult.

7.3.2 Empirical specifications

The β-Convergence hypothesis

The Solow-Swan growth model that makes possible measuring the coefficient of β, whose value determines whether or not convergence has occurred in a cross-section of economies, could be summarised as follows (see Sala-i-Martin, 1996, p. 1334):

$$\frac{1}{T}\left[\frac{\ln\left(y_{i,t}\right)}{\ln\left(y_{i,t-1}\right)}\right]=\alpha+\left[\frac{-\left(1-e^{-\beta T}\right)}{T}\right]*\ln\left(Y_{i,t-1}\right)+\mu_{i,t}, \tag{1.11}$$

Where

α and β – are constants,

$0<\beta<1$, and $\mu_{i,\,t}$ is the error term with, same variance (σ_{μ}^{2}) for all economies and is assumed to have mean zero, and is independent over time and across economies. Then convergence occurs if β>0 and is statistically significant, as this implies an inverse relationship between the annual growth rate ln $(Y_{i,t}/Y_{i,\ t-1})$ and the initial level of real per capita income ln $(Y_{i,\ t-1})$. Following Sala-i-Martin (1996), the coefficient on the initial per capita level $(1\text{-}e^{\beta T})/T$, which is the slope of the initial GDP per capita level, is an expression that declines with the length of the time interval T for a given β. In other words, if the linear relation between the growth rate of real GDP per capita and the initial GDP per capita level are estimated, then the coefficient is predicted to be smaller the longer the time period over which the growth rate is averaged. The reason for this is that the growth rate declines as income increases. To calculate the β-coefficient from the regression, one may linearise the model as follows:

$$b = -\left[\frac{1-e^{-\beta T}}{T}\right] \tag{1.11a}$$

The implied β that measures the speed of convergence may then be computed using the following approximation (equation 1.11b):

$$\beta = -\frac{\ln(1 = bT)}{T} \tag{1.11b}$$

The σ-convergence hypothesis

The second model has been developed to measure the cross-sectional dispersion of income using a sample variance of the log of income (σ-convergence):

$$\sigma^2 = \frac{1}{n}\sum_{i=1}^{n}\left[\ln\left(Y_{i,t}\right) - \mu_t\right]^2 \tag{1.12}$$

Where,

μ_t the sample mean of the log of $(Y_{i,\ t})$, and $Y_{i,t}$ is the log of the GDP per capita level of country *i* at time period *t*. The main argument here is that if countries are converging in terms of income per capita, the cross-sectional dispersion of their income should fall over time.

At the outset of the empirical test for the convergence hypothesis, there was a heated debate regarding the relationship between β-convergence and σ-convergence (apparently first introduced by Sal-i-Martin). The central point of controversy was the presumption that β-convergence be a necessary prerequisite for σ-convergence. The thinking behind this is that if there is convergence, the growth rate should fall over time (because when an economy is getting richer, the predicted growth rate will be much smaller, and vice versa). However, later it was acknowledged that β-convergence is a necessary, but not a sufficient, condition for σ-convergence to take place; either because of overtaking or of divergence.

7.4 A brief review of previous empirical research

Baumol (1986) has been one of the first (if not the first) growth economist to examine convergence across 16 industrialised countries (covering the period 1870–1979) using Madison's 1982 data. The results of the regression suggest that there was perfect convergence across these groups of economies, especially after World War II. De Long (1988) and Romer (1986) (in Sala-i-Martin, 1996b) demonstrate, however, that Baumol's attempt at measuring convergence was might not have been accurate due mainly to the following: the first dispute is related to sample selection, where historical data are constructed retrospectively. The economies that have long data series are naturally those that are more industrialised; secondly, because of the first reason, Baumol has been accused of being biased. For example, Quah (1996) criticises the traditional empirical analysis growth and convergence for overemphasising physical capital and de-emphasising endogenous technological progress and externalities that are main determinants of growth and convergence.

Similarly, Sala-i-Martin (1994, 1996a) shows that β-convergence across the US, Japan and five European nations is strikingly similar (about 2% per year).[6] Based on the above results, the author reaches two conclusions: First, the speeds of convergence are surprisingly similar across data sets. Second, as a result of the first conclusion, the degree to which national governments use regional cohesion policies is very different, and the fact that the speeds of convergence are very similar across countries suggests that public policy plays a very small role in the overall process of regional convergence. This has been the subject of criticism by development economists and others.[7]

Nevertheless, as is usual in economics, there is ongoing dispute in the whole debate about the absolute and conditional convergences hypotheses. One of the most serious criticisms comes from Quah (1996a), who interprets the neoclassical definition of convergence as a 'basic empirical issue, one that reflects – among other things – polarization, income distribution, and inequality' (p. 1354). In an oversimplified way, Quah links the convergence debate to the question of *whether poor economies are incipiently catching up with those already richer or whether they are caught in a poverty trap.*

Quah (1996a) argues that β-convergence is uninformative as it is interested only in a comparison of mean growth across countries and not in income distribution. He further argues that cross-section regressions can represent only average behaviour, not the behaviour of the entire distribution (p. 1365). Moreover, Quah is concerned about the overall intention of the convergence debate because it fails to inform, for instance, 'whether the poorest 10% of the world are catching up with the richest 10% of the world'. He adds that studying an average economy or a representative one gives little insight into the empirical behaviour of the entire cross-section. In his view, for such cross-section dynamics to be interpretable, one needs a theoretical model that makes predictions on them (p. 1368). His model then makes predictions on cross-section dynamics by taking three observations (p. 1368): countries endogenously select themselves into groups and thus do not act in isolation; specialisation in production allows the exploiting of economies of scale; and ideas are an important engine of growth.

From this hypothesis, two key results emerged. First, coalitions (convergence clubs) – form endogenously – the model delivers prediction on coalition membership across the entire cross-section of economies and, secondly, different convergence dynamics are generated depending on the initial distribution of characteristics across countries. In these potential dynamics, explicit convergence clubs can be characterised as:

- polarisation – the rich are getting richer while the poor are getting poorer and the middle class is vanishing;
- stratification – when more than two coalitions form (multiple modes in the income distribution across countries); and
- overtaking and divergence – two economies initially on roughly equal footing separated over time, so that one eventually becomes wealthier than the other, a conclusion that is in line with the argument why β-convergence may not necessarily be a prerequisite for σ-convergence.

(Quah 1996, p. 1368)

Galor (1996), for his part, argues along the same line as Quah. He classifies convergence into three groups: the absolute convergence hypothesis, which is convergence of per capita income across countries regardless of their initial conditions; the conditional convergence hypothesis, which assumes convergence in per capita income across countries with identical structural parameters and regardless of their initial situation; and, finally, the 'club convergence hypothesis' (predicts polarisation, persistent poverty, and clustering), in which case there is per capita income convergence across countries with identical structural parameters provided that the countries also have similar initial conditions (p. 1056). Similarly, Bernard and Jones (1996) also dispute the current convergence debate on the ground that it neglects to take into account the role of technology in the process of convergence.[8] Although plenty of essential points are addressed by those who dispute the convergence debate, particularly regarding the claim of the 'magic 2%' convergence, there is a bulk of empirical literature that proves the existence of conditional convergence in a cross-section of economies, controlling for other factors that determine long-run economic growth.

7.5 Data description, samples and results

The data source for real GDP per capita (in purchasing power standard) is Eurostat and is based on NUTS_3. The period for which data (especially regional data) have become available is 1995–2006. While data for real GDP per capita is available for the EU-26 (except Luxembourg) countries, regional data is either missing or not fully available for some EU member states. For some countries (i.e. Denmark), GDP data are available only for selected regions whereas others (Romania, Poland) have full data only for certain periods. Therefore, concerning regional convergence analysis (regions within individual countries), 21 EU member states for which data were available have been taken into account for this study (see Table 7.1). The computations for standard deviation and growth rates are in log scales.

7.5.1 Cross-country convergence across EU members

Regarding cross-country income per capita convergence across EU member states, the results from our analyses seem to suggest there has been modest but consistent convergence over the past decade. This is indicated by the negative relationship between average growth of real GDP per capita during the period 1995–2005 and its initial level (GDP per capita in 1995) (Figure 7.1). This seems to suggest that poorer EU member states outperformed their wealthier EU counterparts as regards growth rates of GDP per capita (GDPG) during the period under consideration (evidence of β-convergence). This modest convergence has also been confirmed by the declining trend in the dispersion of real per capita income across countries and over time (a confirmation of

Table 7.1 Income dispersion across EU (standard deviation of GDP per capita_log scale)

	1995	1996	1997	1998	1999	2000	2001	2002	2003	2004	2005	2006
EU-26	0.530	0.522	0.517	0.515	0.523	0.518	0.494	0.472	0.443	0.424	0.406	0.383
EU-12	0.411	0.400	0.404	0.405	0.417	0.412	0.389	0.368	0.345	0.328	0.318	0.292
EU-10	0.395	0.366	0.333	0.321	0.327	0.320	0.299	0.278	0.251	0.240	0.224	0.201
EU-Regions (N = 1511)	0.422	0.437	0.436	0.431	0.434	0.433	0.420	0.410	0.402	0.398	0.397	0.393

Source: own computation based on Eurostat data, 2009.

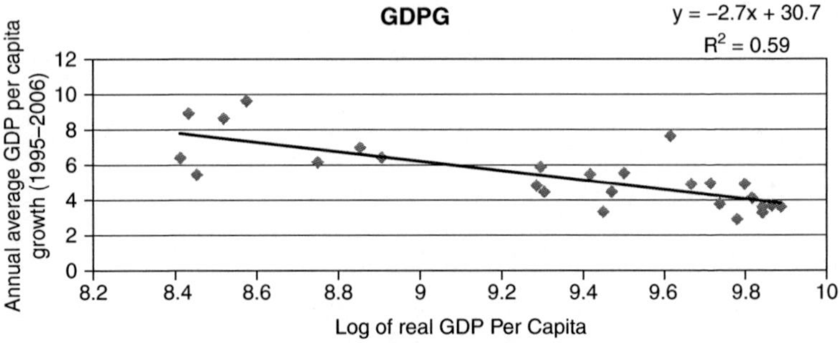

Figure 7.1 Beta convergence for EU-26 (1995–2006)
Source: Own computations based on data from Eurostat 2009.

Σ-convergence). This is indicated by the diminishing standard deviation of real GDP per capita levels during the period under investigation (Figure 7.2). Similarly, the ratio of maximum to minimum real GDP per capita level has been declining consistently during the period under consideration, again signalling some progress in the catch-up process. A declining income gap between the country with the highest (max.) real GDP per capita and the one with the lowest (min.) real GDP per capita (hence, the max./min. ratio) in EU-26 supports this conclusion (Figure 7.2).

Nonetheless, whereas cross-country convergence in the EU seems to be a positive development, it appears there is substantial cross-country variation in terms of both the magnitude of the income gap and the speed with which transition economies are getting closer to the income per capita levels of advanced EU member states. The convergence process seems to be most visible across the EU-10 member states, where not only is average income disparity within this group is lower compared to the EU-26 or EU-12, but it has also been declining significantly faster (Figures 7.3 and 7.4 and Table 7.1).

In spite of the overall trend in the process of convergence across EU countries, there is a significant cross-country variation in the transition economies themselves. Whereas some countries in this group have achieved outstanding results (Cyprus, Malta, Slovenia and the Czech Republic), others are still struggling to minimise their income gap against EU-15. In this regard, Romania, Bulgaria, Lithuania, and Estonia seem to have a long way to go towards reducing their income gaps against advanced EU member states.

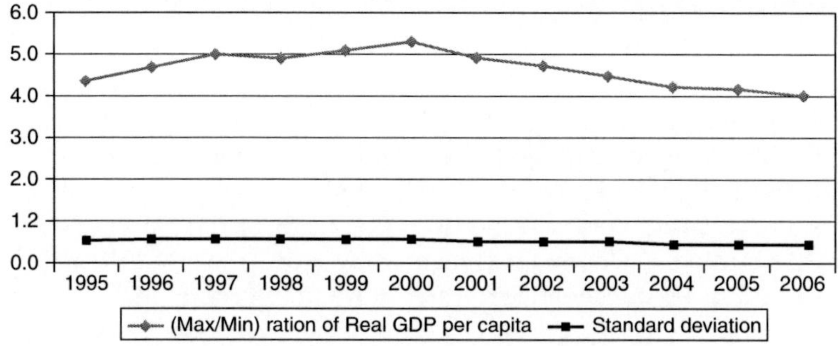

Figure 7.2 Sigma convergence for EU-26 countries (1995–2006)
Source: Own computations based on data from Eurostat 2009.

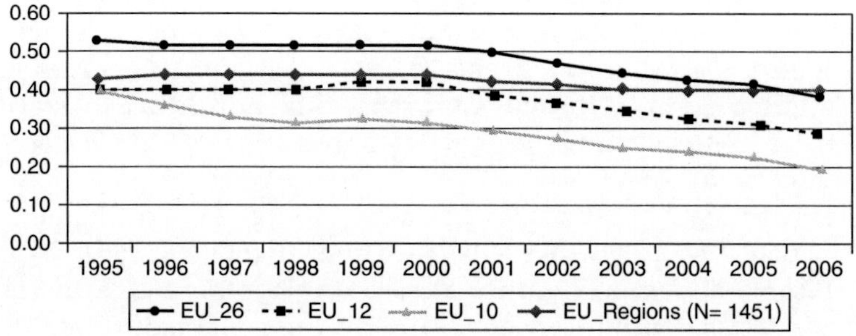

Figure 7.3 Standard deviation of income per capita in EU (1995–2006 and log scale)
Source: Own computation based on Eurostat data, 2009.

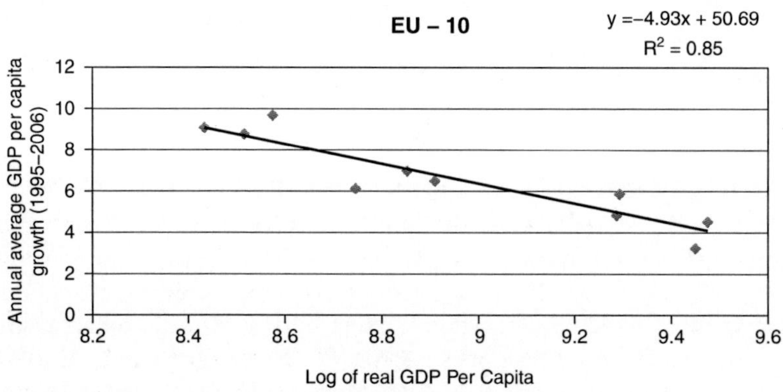

Figure 7.4 Beta Convergence in EU-10 (1995–2006)
Source: Own computations based on Eurostat data.

From a different perspective, convergence across EU regions seems to be relatively stronger compared to cross-country convergence in the EU. As is shown in Figure 7.3, whereas there was a significant trend in cross-regional divergence (standard deviation of real GDP per capita rising or remaining smooth in 1996–2001), the dynamics took a reverse direction roughly after the year 2002. This may suggest that transition economies have benefited from both the yields of the market-friendly policies put in place during the negotiating process to join EU and from the EU funds used to finance the transformation process.

7.5.2 Cross-regional convergence in the European Union

One of the most interesting issues to look at is whether the cross-country convergence discussed earlier may have been replicated at the regional level. In this regard, the results from both β-convergence (an inverse relationship between growth and its initial level) and σ-convergence (a declining trend in income per capita dispersion) seem to suggest there has been substantial regional convergence within the wider EU (Figures 7.5 and 7.6).

From our analyses based on the data of 1510 regions in the EU during the period 1995–2006 substantial declining trends emerged regarding income dispersion (Figure 7.5). Likewise, the same data indicate a negative relationship between real GDP per capita growth and the level of initial GDP per capita. This implies that, despite still-persisting cross-regional variation, poorer regions within the wider EU have achieved relatively higher growth dynamics compared with their wealthier counterparts (Figure 7.6). Although there are uncertainties about the sustainability of this trend given the turbulence in the world economy, this performance is indeed in line with the objectives of individual countries within the EU as well as the long-term goals of the EU as a growing club of influence.

7.5.3 The absence of a 'trickle-down effect' in regional convergence: country-by-country case

From our results, it is apparent that regional convergence within countries does not seem to be in line with cross-country convergence in the EU. As mentioned earlier, while modest but consistent cross-country convergence seems to be a reality across EU-26 member states, regional convergence within individual member states seems to have experienced a serious setback over the past decade or so. In this respect, the most seriously affected countries in terms of regional divergence are the

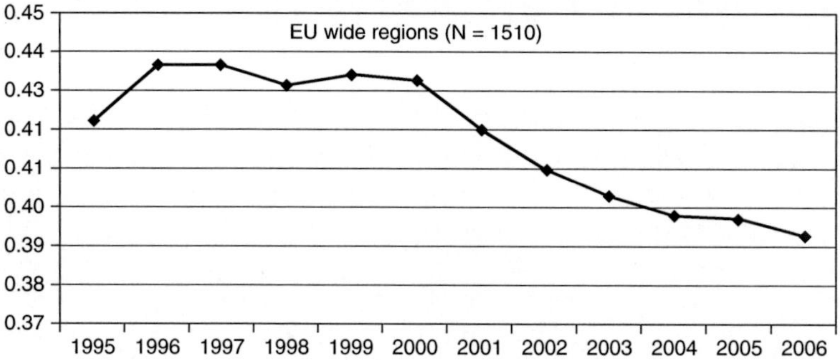

Figure 7.5 Cross-regional convergence in selected EU regions (1995–2006)
Source: Own computation based on Eurostat data, 2009.

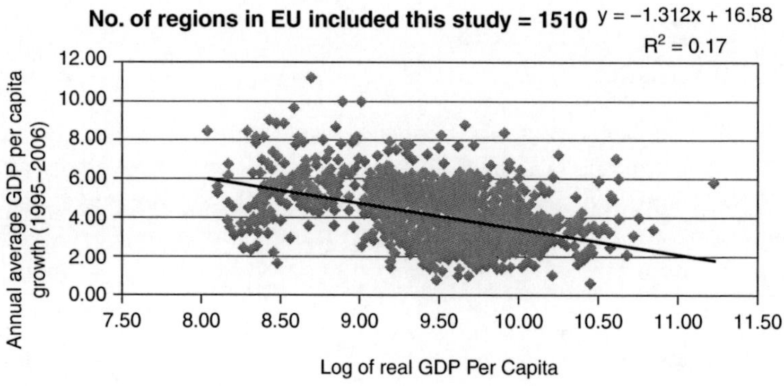

Figure 7.6 Beta convergence in the EU regions (real GDP per capita, PPS and NUTS_3)
Note: There are 1510 regions taken into account in this analysis. Regions of countries included in this analysis: Austria, Belgium, The Czech Republic, Germany, Spain, Finland, France, Greece, Hungary, Ireland, Italy, Lithuania, Latvia, Poland, Portugal, Sweden, Slovenia, Slovakia, and United Kingdom
Source: Own computation based on EUROSTAT data.

new EU member states. Of those countries for which regional data were available, Romania, Bulgaria, Lithuania, Slovakia, Poland, Hungary and Slovenia seem to have failed to downsize the scale of income dispersion between their respective regions.

In contrast to the new EU member states, some advanced EU members seem to have done better in narrowing regional income disparity. In this respect, Portugal, Greece and partially Spain and Germany have shown substantial progress in this area, whereas the UK and France seem to have lower levels of regional disparity without significant change. One of the surprising outcomes in this analysis is Ireland, which has managed to surpass the average income level of the EU-15 in less than 10 years' time, but failed to reduce its regional income disparity. In all the countries under investigation, regional disparities turn out to be less dramatic once capital cities or conglomerates are excluded (Tables 7.2 and 7.3).

One of the arguments behind stronger regional convergence in Portugal, Spain and Greece (despite its current financial troubles) is often linked to the regional funds they were receiving from advanced European countries in the 1980s. In this regard, the analogy for new EU members is clear: if they effectively allocate EU funds in areas and sectors of the economy where they have the highest level of productivity, they should achieve higher and more sustainable growth dynamics, which should accelerate the catch up process.

7.6 Conclusion

Although the beginning of European integration dates back to the 1950s, its most crucial stage of development came into effect after the fall of communism in the early 1990s. The main objective of the integration process is to create a stronger and homogeneous club that can serve to mitigate the challenges of globalisation and regional integration elsewhere in the world. The results of this and other studies show this has been a mutually rewarding process both for advanced EU Members in terms of expanding their business operations and for transition economies which benefited from financial and other technical supports from advanced EU members. In this regard, the results seem to indicate persistent though modest convergence across EU member states implying that poorer EU members had recorded higher growth rates compared to their wealthier counterparts. Similarly, data for 1511 regions across the EU during the period 1995–2006, suggest there was a significant reduction in income dispersion across regions, indicated by a continuous fall in the standard deviation of income per capita. Nonetheless, given the magnitude of the income gap, this will take most transition economies and regions in the EU more time to match their richer co-members' income levels.

The results of this study reveal that in spite of modest but consistent convergence across countries in the European Union, this does not seem to replicate itself in inter regional convergence within individual member states. While some countries (such as, Spain, Greece, and

Table 7.2 Standard deviation of real GDP per capita for new EU members (log scale)

		1995	1996	1997	1998	1999	2000	2001	2002	2003	2004	2005	2006
Romania	1.	0.166	0.184	0.195	0.210	0.233	0.264	0.247	0.269	0.263	0.259	0.300	0.314
Slovakia	1.	0.367	0.358	0.367	0.367	0.367	0.374	0.377	0.385	0.388	0.392	0.433	0.432
	2.	0.310	0.304	0.310	0.311	0.312	0.317	0.319	0.323	0.327	0.332	0.366	0.375
Slovenia	1.	0.174	0.175	0.170	0.168	0.178	0.177	0.185	0.189	0.203	0.202	0.203	0.212
Hungary	1.	0.243	0.261	0.281	0.289	0.307	—	0.303	0.315	0.315	0.313	0.332	0.345
	2.	0.205	0.223	0.244	0.254	0.271	—	0.260	0.268	0.272	0.268	0.283	0.292
Czech Rep.	1.	0.144	0.145	0.156	0.174	0.185	0.193	0.204	0.208	0.208	0.203	0.207	0.212
	2.	0.042	0.045	0.043	0.051	0.059	0.067	0.071	0.073	0.070	0.070	0.067	0.077
Poland	1.	0.197	0.198	0.211	0.225	0.259	0.267	0.251	0.265	0.259	0.268	0.273	0.276
Bulgaria	1.	0.149	0.475	0.502	0.461	0.501	0.488	0.485	0.495	0.550	0.559	0.244	0.276
Latvia	1.	—	0.288	0.321	0.368	0.398	0.420	0.488	0.429	0.411	0.452	0.424	0.398
Lithuania	1.	0.151	0.149	0.184	0.192	0.202	0.220	0.237	0.257	0.265	0.270	0.289	0.305

Note: 1. Including the capital city (or cities).
2. Without capital cities.
Source: Own computation based on Eurostat data, 2009.

Table 7.3 Standard deviation of real GDP per capita for advanced EU members (log scale)

		1995	1996	1997	1998	1999	2000	2001	2002	2003	2004	2005	2006
Ireland	1.	0.220	0.216	0.245	0.257	0.255	0.266	0.272	0.296	0.289	0.266	0.274	0.276
	2.	0.173	0.158	0.195	0.209	0.210	0.222	0.229	0.260	0.243	0.207	0.209	0.212
Portugal	1.	0.261	0.253	0.266	0.261	0.260	0.267	0.258	0.266	0.262	0.260	0.262	0.257
	2.	0.240	0.232	0.245	0.237	0.237	0.243	0.233	0.243	0.238	0.235	0.238	0.235
Italy	1.	0.278	0.278	0.271	0.269	0.264	.	0.276	0.268	0.266	0.266	0.260	0.257
	2.	0.278	0.278	0.271	0.269	0.264	.	0.275	0.267	0.265	0.265	0.259	0.256
Sweden	1.	0.095	0.104	0.120	0.125	0.135	0.132	0.127	0.124	0.122	0.125	0.130	0.125
	2.	0.074	0.079	0.093	0.094	0.103	0.102	0.099	0.094	0.093	0.094	0.099	0.096
Austria	1.	0.250	0.249	0.247	0.245	0.247	0.251	0.246	0.245	0.242	0.241	0.247	0.246
	2.	0.239	0.238	0.237	0.234	0.237	0.241	0.236	0.234	0.232	0.232	0.240	0.239
Greece	1.	0.220	0.231	0.220	0.218	0.212	0.232	0.227	0.226	0.215	0.224	0.224	0.236
	2.	0.221	0.232	0.222	0.220	0.213	0.228	0.222	0.218	0.208	0.215	0.216	0.227
Spain	1.	0.202	0.206	0.214	0.216	0.219	0.217	0.214	0.212	0.203	0.198	0.195	0.193
	2.	0.199	0.203	0.211	0.212	0.215	0.213	0.211	0.209	0.199	0.195	0.191	0.190
France	1.	0.192	0.194	0.194	0.192	0.197	0.204	0.202	0.200	0.202	0.197	0.200	0.200
	2.	0.164	0.165	0.164	0.162	0.167	0.175	0.173	0.171	0.173	0.169	0.172	0.172
Netherlands	1.	0.172	0.179	0.175	0.174	0.170	0.175	0.178	0.182	0.183	0.189	0.194	0.202
	2.	0.162	0.168	0.164	0.161	0.156	0.163	0.166	0.168	0.169	0.174	0.180	0.190
UK	1.	0.237	0.246	0.257	0.266	0.270	0.280	0.274	0.279	0.278	0.274	0.274	0.276
	2.	0.226	0.235	0.245	0.254	0.258	0.268	0.262	0.267	0.265	0.261	0.261	0.263
Germany	1.	0.339	0.335	0.334	0.340	0.335	0.336	0.334	0.327	0.327	0.324	0.327	0.329
	2.	0.335	0.331	0.330	0.336	0.331	0.333	0.331	0.324	0.323	0.320	0.324	0.325
Belgium	1.	0.259	0.261	0.266	0.265	0.269	0.272	0.274	0.278	0.282	0.288	0.285	0.288
	2.	0.226	0.228	0.235	0.234	0.238	0.241	0.244	0.248	0.253	0.260	0.258	0.261

Note: 1. Including the capital city (or cities).
2. Without capital cities.

Source: Own computation based on Eurostat data, 2009.

Portugal) have managed to reduce regional disparities substantially, others seem to lag behind in narrowing regional disparities in their respective countries. In this respect, there is a long way to go to scale down both cross-country and cross-regional disparities in the EU. This implies that whereas the benefits ensuing from European integration clearly contributed to fostering regional convergence, transition economies should proceed with reform programs, including investments in information and communication technologies, education, and other infrastructure, thus generating not only higher but also more sustainable economic growth in order to narrow their income gaps against those of their wealthier co-members.

Notes

This chapter is a part of the research project, 'Analysis of Regional Disparity in SR and Prognosis of Future Development'. It is financed by the Slovak Agency for Science and Research_APVV, No. APVV-0649-07.

1. Advocates of the endogenous growth model and other development economists in fact reject the hypothesis of convergence.
2. β-convergence occurs if economies that are poorer are predicted to grow faster that richer ones. On the other hand, σ-convergence occurs if the dispersion of income per capita across countries declines overtime. The two concepts are broadly discussed later in the chapter.
3. See Sala-i-Martin (1994, 1996), and Barro and Sala-i-Martin (1995) for the detailed distinguishing between sigma and beta convergence.
4. William Baumol et al. (1994) 'Convergence of Productivity: Cross-National Evidence' Oxford Press Inc.
5. Conditional β-convergence exists if the partial correlation between growth and initial income is negative. In contrast, a set of economies displays absolute β-convergence if the coefficient on initial income is negative in univariate regression (Sala-i-Martin, 1996, p. 1330).
6. The results for 48 US states from 1880–1920 indicate that dispersion of per capita personal income net of transfers declined from 0.54 in 1880 to 0.33 in 1920, then rose to 0.40 in 1930 due to the adverse shock to agriculture in 1920s. The dispersion continued declining to 0.35 in 1940 and to 0.24 in 1960, to 0.17 in 1970 and 0.14 in 1976. The same observation for 47 Japanese prefectures for the period (1955–87) of per capita income, shows that the dispersion of personal income increased from 0.47 in 1930s to 0.63 in the 1940s which was caused by explosion in military expenditure during that period. The cross-prefectural dispersion has decreased substantially since 1940. It fell to 0.29 by 1950, to 0.25 in 1960, 0.23 in 1970 and it hit a minimum of 0.12 in 1978. However, income dispersion was observed to constant since then (Sala-i-Martin 1996, p. 1338).
7. For a broader discussion of the determinants of convergence in OECD countries, see, OECD 2009 and the study by the European parliament (2007).

8. There cross-country analysis on dispersion of labour productivity and dispersion in technology for 14 OECD countries indicates that first, countries are heterogeneous in their level of technology, and secondly, the change in the dispersion of labour productivity overtime matches with closely with the dispersion of technology (p. 1041).

References

Barro, R. J. (1991). 'Economic Growth in a Cross-Section of Economies', *The Quarterly Journal of Economics*, 106(2), 407–43.

Barro, R. J. and Sala-I-Martin, X. (1991). 'Convergence across States and Regions', *Brookings Paper on Economic Activity*, 1, 107–58.

Barro, R. J. and Sala-I-Martin, X. (1992). 'Convergence', *Journal of Political Economy*, 100(2), 223–51.

Barro, R. J. and Sala-I-Martin, X. (1995). *Economic Growth*, Boston, MA: McGraw Hill.

Baumol, W. J., Nelson, R. R. and Wolff, E. N. (eds) (1994). *Convergence of Productivity: Cross-National Studies and Historical Evidence*, New York: Oxford University Press.

Caselli, F., Esquivel, G. and Lefort, F. (1996). 'Reopening the Convergence Debate: A New Look at Cross-Country Growth Empirics', *Journal of Economic Growth*, 1(3), 363–89.

European Parliament (2007). 'Regional Disparities and Cohesion: What Strategies for the Futire?'. IP/B/REGI/IC/2006_201.

Galor, O. (1996). 'Convergence? Inferences from Theoretical Models', *The Economic Journal*, 106(437), 1056–69.

Mankiw, N. G., Weil, D. N. and Romer, D. (1992). 'A Contribution to the Empirics of Economic Growth', *The Quarterly Journal of Economics*, 107(2), 407–37.

Pritchett, L. (1996). 'Forget Convergence: Divergence Past, Present and Future', *Finance and Development*, 33(4), 40–3.

Quah, D. T. (1996a). 'Empirics for Economic Growth and Convergence', *European Economic Review*, 40(6), 1353–75.

Quah, D. T. (1996b). 'Twin Peaks: Growth and Convergence in Models of Distribution Dynamics', *The Economic Journal*, 106(437), 1045–55.

Sala-I-Martin, X. (1994). 'Cross-Sectional Regressions and the Empirics of Economic Growth', *European Economic Review*, 38(3–4), 739–47.

Sala-I-Martin, X. (1996a). 'Regional Cohesion: Evidence and Theories of Regional Growth and Convergence', *European Economic Review*, 40(6), 1325–52.

Sala-I-Martin, X. (1996b). 'The Classical Approach to Convergence Analysis', *The Economic Journal*, 106(437), 1019–36.

Solow, R. M. (1956). 'A Contribution to Theory of Economic Growth', *The Quarterly Journal of Economics*, 70, 65–94.

Tsangarides, C. G. (2000). 'Revisiting Growth and Convergence: Is Africa Catching Up?' Africa Region Working Paper Series No. 10, The World Bank Group.

OECD (2000). *Catching Up and Falling Behind: Economic Convergence in Europe*, Economic Survey of Europe, No. 1.

OECD (2009). OECD Regions at a Glance, www.oecd.org/publishing/corrigenda

Workie, M. (2007). *From Debt Crisis to Growth Crisis: Is External Debt the Cause of the Effect of Africa's Marginalization*, Saarbrücken, Germany: VDM Verlag Dr. Muller.

8

Price- and News-Based Measures of Financial Integration among New EU Member States and the Euro Area

J. Babecký, J. Frait, L. Komárek and Z. Komárková

8.1 Introduction

In a monetary union, the integration of financial markets (e.g., money, foreign exchange, bond, and equity markets) plays a key role in assuring the effective transmission of common monetary policy. The importance of conducting an assessment of the degree of financial integration across the euro area member countries is stressed by both central banks and academic institutions – see, among others, Trichet (2008, 2007, 2006, 2005), Papademos (2008a, 2008b), and Yam (2006). The more integrated financial markets are, the more effectively monetary policy is transmitted through the financial system, particularly within the European monetary union. As financial markets expand, their fluctuations have stronger effects on real economic variables such as private consumption. Thus, along with a number of benefits, financial integration brings certain costs. It is widely believed that the benefits outweigh the costs, provided that mechanisms for controlling for financial stability are implemented.[1]

Joining the euro area without a sufficient degree of financial market integration can cause problems with the transmission of the common monetary policy and common shocks. A high degree of financial market integration implies that euro area-wide shocks dominate; hence, the common monetary policy can be effectively applied to react to common shocks. On the other hand, in the case of weak financial market integration local (i.e., country-specific) shocks prevail, which diminishes the effectiveness of the common monetary policy. In the case of new EU member states which are committed to adopting the euro at some point, it is especially important to analyse the alignment of their markets, including the financial ones, with those of the euro area countries.

This chapter is unique, within the financial integration literature, in its simultaneous focus on a number of markets, several integration measures and periods with different institutional and economic settings. We focus on the financial integration of money, foreign exchange, government bond, and stock markets in five new EU member states (the Czech Republic, Hungary, Poland, Slovakia, and Slovenia) and selected old EU members (Germany, Austria, Portugal, and Sweden) with the euro area.[2] Notice that whereas stock markets are relatively minor compared to the other three markets, as stock markets grow in size, they represent an increasingly important but not yet well-examined segment of the financial system. We test for the existence and determine the degree of financial integration of the selected new member states in relation to the euro area. The empirical analysis is conducted at the country level using national indices.

How can the degree of financial market integration be measured in practice? Financial integration, which is a broad concept, can be quantified using three main dimensions, namely price-based, news-based, and quantity-based measures. In this paper we focus on the first two classes of measure. Price-based measures could be viewed as a direct check of the law of one price on the condition that the compared assets have similar characteristics. They can be quantified through the use of time series techniques. Our evaluation consists of (1) the application of the concept of β-convergence to identify the speed of integration; and (2) the application of σ-convergence to measure the level of integration. We perform our analysis on weekly returns, collected for the period from January 1995 to January 2009 for the foreign exchange and stock markets, January 2001 to January 2009 for the money market, and January 2002 to January 2009 for the government bond market (bond market henceforth).

Price-based measures provide evidence of financial integration between the Czech Republic, Hungary, Poland, Slovakia, and Slovenia vis-à-vis the euro area. The results unambiguously point to the existence of β-convergence comparable to that observed in Portugal, Austria, and Germany. Moreover, the speed at which shocks dissipate is quite high, specifically less than half a week. We do not observe a major impact of EU enlargement or the announcement thereof on β-convergence. In fact, the high speed of β-convergence was achieved much earlier, namely, during the 1990s. Regarding the effect of the recent financial turmoil, the results are less clear-cut. Next, the dynamics of the σ-convergence suggest overall convergence, yet there is a clear indication of an increase in volatility since the second half of 2007. Furthermore, transmission of shocks is substantial, with the highest impact being observed on the stock markets. Overall, taking the results together, we find evidence of increasing integration of the new EU members' markets towards the levels of the mature euro area economies.

The news-based approach aims at determining whether the returns on assets across countries and segments of financial markets are influenced by local or worldwide news. This enables us to identify existing market imperfections such as frictions and barriers, because in the integrated area new information of a local character should have a smaller impact on particular assets than global news. To the extent that the markets are not integrated, local news may continue to influence asset prices significantly. To operationalise the news-based approach, the price movements of benchmark assets are used as a proxy for global news. This approach was applied to foreign exchange, government bond, and stock markets in the Czech Republic, Slovakia, Hungary, Poland, and Sweden compared to the euro area. The results indicate considerable propagation of shocks across the financial markets under review. At the same time, this propagation was changing relatively slowly during the period analysed, with only limited evidence of increasing transmission in recent years.

The chapter is organised as follows. Section 8.2 briefly discusses the various approaches to measuring financial integration and provides examples of empirical evidence for the four financial segments covered by our study. Sections 8.3 and 8.4 give methodological details on the chosen indicators of price- and news-based convergence. The data used in this study are discussed in section 8.5. Section 8.6 presents the results and section 8.7 concludes.

8.2 Financial integration: Concept and evidence

8.2.1 Indicators of financial integration[3]

Baele et al. (2004) propose to quantify financial integration using three main dimensions, namely: (i) price-based, (ii) news-based, and (iii) quantity-based measures.[4] The first class of measures could be viewed as a direct check of the law of one price on the condition that the compared assets have similar characteristics. Price-based measures can then be quantified by means of, for example, β- and σ-convergence. The second class of measures makes it possible to identify existing market imperfections such as frictions and barriers, because in the integrated area new information of a local character should have a smaller impact on particular assets than global news. The third class of measures quantifies the effects of mainly legal and other non-price frictions and barriers from both the supply and demand sides of the investment decision-taking process.

(i) Price-based measures

The price-based approach constitutes a direct check of the law of one price, which in turn must hold if financial integration is complete. If assets have sufficiently similar characteristics, we can base these measures on direct price or yield comparisons.[5] Otherwise we need to take into account differences in systematic (or non-diversifiable) risk factors and other important characteristics. Given these considerations, we can construct a number of specific integration measures. The cross-sectional dispersion (σ-convergence) of interest rate spreads or asset return differentials can be used as an indicator of how far away the various market segments are from being fully integrated. Similarly, β-convergence, a measure borrowed from the growth literature, is an indicator of the speed at which markets are integrating. In addition, measuring the degree of cross-border price or yield variation relative to the variability within individual countries may be informative with respect to the degree of integration in different markets.

(ii) News-based measures

These measures are designed to distinguish information effects from other frictions or barriers. In a financially integrated area, portfolios should be well diversified, and the degree of systematic risk should be identical across assets in different countries. Hence, common or global news (i.e., the arrival of new economic information of a common or global nature) should dominate in affecting prices. To the extent that the markets are not integrated, local news may continue to influence asset prices significantly.

In our study we explore indicators of financial integration belonging to the class of price-based and news-based measures. If the law of one price did not apply, there would be scope for arbitrage. If we assume a fully integrated market with no barriers (economic, legal, cultural, etc.), then any investor will be able to use this arbitration opportunity, causing the law of one price to apply again. Nevertheless, we also acknowledge the limitations associated with such an approach.

8.2.2 Evidence from the key segments of the financial system

(i) FX market

Aguilar and Hördal (1998) try to evaluate eligibility for the introduction of the euro by means of correlation analysis of national currencies against US dollar and alternative benchmarks. The application of a similar methodology can be found in the study by Castrén and Mazzotta (2005). Babetskaia-Kukharchuk, Babetskii, and Podpiera (2008) use dynamic correlations to analyse convergence in exchange rate volatilities between the NMS and the euro area. Komárková and Komárek (2007) evaluated the FX market integration of the selected new EU Member States (the Czech Republic, Hungary, Poland, and Slovakia) by means of an analysis of harmonisation (standard and rolling correlation analysis), the concept of β-convergence (state-space model and panel regression analysis), and the concept of σ-convergence.

(ii) Money market

Money market integration has been studied – with application to the euro area countries – by, for example, Baele et al. (2004) and Adam et al. (2002). Adam et al. (2002) investigate the speed and degree of financial integration using the concept of β- and σ-convergence on 3M interbank rates. The authors show that this segment of the money market became strongly integrated before the introduction of the euro. Similarly, Baele et al. (2004) investigate financial integration on the unsecured, secured, and interest rate swap segments of the market. A high degree of financial market integration is found among the euro area countries; the introduction of the euro played an important role in this process.

(iii) Bond market

The integration of the bond market has been analysed by Adam et al. (2002), Adjaouté and Danthine (2003), Codogno et al. (2003), Kim et al. (2004), Baele et al. (2004), and Barr and Priestley (2004). Barr and Priestley (2004) investigate the question of how strongly bond yields are determined by world versus local factors. The authors argue that the world bond market is not integrated, as world factors have only a 70 per cent influence on the development of domestic returns. Codogno et al. (2003) find that movements in yields on the government bond market are explained by changes in international risk factors.

(iv) Stock market

A European perspective of financial market integration, oriented primarily towards the capital market, is included in European Commission (1999) and Hartmann, Maddaloni, and Manganelli (2003). Ayuso and Blanco (1999) find that financial market integration between stock markets in the euro area increased during the 1990s. An analysis of sectoral and national effects on the European capital market is presented by Baca, Garbe, and Weiss (2000) and Heston and Rouwenhorst (1995).

Bekaert, Harvey, and Lumsdaine (2000) search for the steps of world equity market integration by identifying structural breaks in the size of international capital flows. Portes and Rey (2000) and Martin and Rey (2001) analyse the timing and geographical pattern of cross-border equity flows and the size of the asset market. Bekaert and Harvey (1995) attempt to remedy this problem by constructing a time-varying measure of financial market integration. Using data on equity returns, they find that a number of markets exhibit time-varying integration, thus allowing them to identify the reasons for rejecting the international CAPM, which instead assumes perfectly integrated markets.

Adam et al. (2002) show that the most appropriate indicators of stock market integration, based on stock returns, require the specification and estimation of sophisticated asset pricing models, which make them inadequate for prompt policy analysis and evaluation. Alternatively, this study proposes a simpler indicator based on the dynamics of the correlation of stock market returns in EU countries. While the correlations are easy to compute and update, they have no necessary relation to the degree of financial integration, since they may also reflect changes in the correlation structure of real and policy shocks in the individual countries. This implies that correlations measure the degree of financial integration only if the stochastic process of common shocks is constant over time. This is an issue of serious concern, given that Europe is undergoing a process of real economic integration.

8.3 Price-based measures of financial integration

8.3.1 β-convergence

Following Adam et al. (2002), we apply the concepts of β-convergence and σ-convergence to assess the state of financial market integration in the selected EU countries.[6] The concept of β-convergence enables identification of the speed at which shocks are eliminated on the individual financial markets. A negative β-coefficient signals the existence of convergence, and the magnitude of the β-coefficient expresses the speed of convergence, that is, the speed of elimination of shocks to the yield differential vis-à-vis the euro area. The higher the absolute value of the β-coefficient, the higher the speed of convergence.

For quantification of β-convergence, it is useful to apply common regression analysis or the panel estimate method, in the form of the equation:

$$\Delta R_{i,t} = \alpha_i + \beta R_{i,t-1} + \sum_{l=1}^{L} \gamma_l \Delta R_{i,t-l} + \varepsilon_{i,t} \qquad (1)$$

where $R_{i,t} = Y_{i,t} - Y_{i,t}^{B}$ is the difference between the asset yields of country i and a selected reference territory (a benchmark, the euro area stock index) at time t, Δ is the difference operator, α_i is a dummy variable for the respective country, L is the maximum lag length, and $\varepsilon_{i,t}$ is a white noise disturbance. The size of coefficient β may be interpreted as a direct measure of the convergence speed. A negative β-coefficient indicates the occurrence of convergence, and the absolute value of the β-coefficient indicates the convergence speed. The β coefficient can take values ranging from 0 to –2. The closer the absolute value of the β coefficient to 1, the higher the speed of convergence, and if $\beta = 0$ or $\beta = -2$, no convergence is observed. β values from 0 to –1 indicate monotonous convergence, whereas fluctuating convergence occurs for values from –1 and –2.

8.3.2 σ-convergence

The concept of σ-convergence captures the differences between the yields on identical assets in different countries at a given time, identifying the degree of integration vis-à-vis the euro area achieved in the individual financial market segments in the countries under review at that time. Sigma-convergence arises if and when the σ- coefficient falls to zero. Beta-convergence may be accompanied by σ-divergence, so both concepts must be tracked concurrently in order to observe financial integration. To quantify σ-convergence, a calculation is used of the (cross-section) standard deviation (σ), according to the formula:

$$\sigma_t = \sqrt{\left(\frac{1}{N-1}\right)\sum_{i=1}^{N}\left[\log(Y_{i,t}) - \mu_t\right]^2} \tag{2}$$

where $Y_{i,t}$ is the asset yield for country i at time t, μ_t is the sample (cross-section) mean of $\log(Y_{i,t})$ at time t, and i stands for separate countries ($i = 1, 2, \ldots, N$). For the purposes of this analysis, we introduce $N = 2$, that is, we examine the evolution of σ-convergence over time between the euro area and one of the countries under review. σ takes only positive values in theory. The lower the value of σ, the higher the level of convergence. In theory, full integration is reached when the standard deviation is zero, whereas high (several digit) values of σ reflect a very low degree of integration.

8.4 News-based measures of financial integration

An important sign of financial market integration is that asset prices respond to common (global) news to such assets rather than to local news, that is, news typical of a specific country. If markets are financially integrated, yields on financial assets of different countries but having the same risk characteristics should depend on global rather than local news. The news-based approach thus aims at determining whether the returns on assets across countries and segments of financial markets are influenced by local or worldwide news. In practice, however, it is difficult to measure news. To operationalise the news-based approach, Baele et al. (2004) argue that the price movements of benchmark assets are a good reflection of all relevant common news. The news-based approach is relevant to studies on foreign exchange, government bond, and stock markets. Following Baele et al. (2004), the degree of integration of shocks can be estimated using the following regression:

$$\Delta Y_{i,t} = \alpha_{i,t} + \gamma_{i,t}\,\Delta Y_{b,t} + \varepsilon_{i,t} \tag{3}$$

where $Y_{i,t}$ represents the return on specific assets (currencies, bonds, interbank rates, and stock exchange indexes) in country *i* at time *t*, and *b* denotes the benchmark country (Germany for the government bond market, otherwise the euro area). α_i is the country-specific constant (converging to zero), Δ is the time difference operator, and ε is the white-noise disturbance (country-specific shock). The parameter γ is a measure of convergence. We do not use any lags, since news spreads much more quickly (i.e., within minutes) compared to the frequency of our data (daily or weekly). The time-varying parameter γ can be estimated by the Kalman filter in a similar way to parameter β in equation (1).

The magnitude of parameters γ expresses the degree of identical response of an asset of a selected country and a comparable benchmark asset to assumed news. Simply stated, parameter γ shows to what extent a certain asset of a selected region responds to news in the same way as the benchmark asset, assuming that the benchmark asset responds to global news only. The higher the value of the parameter, the higher the integration of the assets under comparison. As in reality credit, liquidity, and foreign exchange risks are not identical across individual countries and assets, the change in the yield on a local asset is not expected to be explained fully and solely by the impact of global (common) news.

Notice that the above-described measures of market integration are based on the idea that markets are efficient, which is not true in reality – see Shleifer (2000). Inefficiencies could be present even in clearly integrated markets. Although a comprehensive analysis of market inefficiencies is beyond the scope of this paper, we intend to address the issue of inefficiencies by looking at the country- and sector-specific risk premiums. This can be done in two ways. First, we can compare country risk assessments performed by different agencies with our results (β- and σ-coefficients). The objective of such a comparison is to check whether countries with higher risk have different betas and sigmas compared to lower-risk countries. Second, we can examine whether the risk premiums are due to primarily country- or sector-specific factors. In other words, we can check whether the risk premiums are related to a particular sector across all the countries considered, or whether the risk premiums are country-specific instead. This can be done by analysing cross-sectoral dispersion in both sector and country index returns. Finally, in order to understand and interpret the empirical results better, we discuss the institutional developments in the countries of our sample.[7]

8.5 Data

The calculations were made using weekly data (averages of daily data) from Thomson Datastream, covering January 1995 to January 2009 for the foreign exchange and stock markets, January 2001 to January 2009 for the money market, and January 2002 to January 2009 for the bond market (see Table 8.1). Three-month interbank rates were used for the money market, national currencies quoted against the US dollar for the foreign exchange market, five-year government bonds for the bond market, and national stock indices for the stock market. Table 8.1 summarises the data coverage.

8.6 Results

8.6.1 Price-based measures of financial integration

January 1995–July 2007

The results of the β-convergence analysis, as applied to the individual segments of the financial market, are given in Table 8.2. The results show that yields on the Czech and Hungarian stock and bond markets converged towards those on corresponding euro area financial instruments relatively quickly in this period, at a faster pace than in Portugal and Austria. Hungary, Slovakia, and Slovenia have a comparable degree of stock market convergence as the selected euro area countries such as Austria and Portugal. On the foreign exchange market, the speed of convergence of all five new EU member states is broadly comparable. On the money market the speed of convergence is somewhat lower in the Czech Republic and Slovakia.[8] Yield convergence towards the euro area (towards Germany in the case of bond markets) occurred in all the countries under review. In this period, the absolute values of the β-coefficient

Table 8.1 Data coverage

	Money market	**Foreign exchange market**	**Bond market**	**Stock market**
	1999–2009	**1995–2009**	**2002–9**	**1995–2009**
CZ	PRIBK3M	PRUSDSP	BMCZ05Y-(RY)	CZPXIDX
AT	n.a.	n.a.	BMOE05Y-(RY)	ATXINDX
DE	n.a.	n.a.	BMBD05Y-(RY)[B]	DAXINDX
PT	n.a.	n.a.	BMPT05Y-(RY)	POPSI20
HU	HNIBK3M	HNUSDNB	BMHN05Y-(RY)	BUXINDX
PL	POIBK3M	POUSDSP	BMPO05Y-(RY)	POLWIGI
SI	SJIBK3M	SJUSDSP	n.a.	SLOESBI
SK	SXIBK3M	SXUSDSP	SXGOVT1-(RY)[b]	SXSAS16
SE	SIBOR3M	SDUSDSP	BMSD10Y	SWEDOMX
EU13	BBEUR3M[B]	USECBSP[B]	n.a.	DJES50I[B, a]

Note: B: benchmark; n.a.: data not available; a: DJES501 is made up of the following weights of the national stock indices of the selected euro area countries: 34.9% France, 23.3% Germany, 13.5% Spain, 12% the Netherlands, 11.8% Italy, 3.5% Finland, and 0.9% Ireland); b: data from 2002 onwards.
Source: Thomson Datastream.

were close to 1 for all the countries and markets except the money market, which means that the levelling of newly arising differences in yield differentials between the relevant national economy and the euro area can be labelled as 'fast'. A comparison of the periods 1995–2002 and 2003–7 reveals that the pace of β-convergence of the stock markets of the new EU member states under review (except Slovakia) increased over time. The speed of convergence of the money market increased in the Czech Republic and Hungary; the pace of convergence of the foreign exchange market was faster, particularly in the countries heading towards the euro area – Slovakia and Slovenia. Nonetheless, the new EU member states are generally achieving high levels of β-convergence of their financial markets towards the euro area.

The results of the σ-convergence analysis for the individual segments of the financial market and the countries under review vis-à-vis the euro area (Germany[9] for the bond markets) are shown in Figure 8.1. The results of σ-convergence across the individual markets of the new EU member states show that the highest degree of integration was achieved in the money and foreign exchange markets. The Czech financial market seemed to be the most integrated (especially in the case of the foreign exchange and stock markets) compared to the markets in the other new Member States. Only the Slovenian money and foreign exchange markets achieved a higher degree of integration; this is linked to Slovenia's completed euro adoption process.[10] However, significant

Table 8.2 Beta coefficients

	Money market			Foreign exchange market			Bond market		Stock market		
	1999–2002	2003–7/2007	8/2007–1/2009	1995–2002	2003–7/2007	8/2007–1/2009	2001–7/2007	8/2007–1/2009	1995–2002	2003–7/2007	8/2007–1/2009
CZ	–0.57	–0.65	–0.36	–0.94	–1.11	–0.85	–0.73	–1.15	–0.76	–0.94	–0.87
AT	n.a.	n.a.	n.a.	n.a.	n.a.	n.a.	–1.12	–0.74	–0.90	–0.88	–0.47
DE	n.a.	n.a.	n.a.	n.a.	n.a.	n.a.	B	B	–0.79	–0.79	–1.30
PT	n.a.	n.a.	n.a.	n.a.	n.a.	n.a.	–0.81	–0.56	–0.89	–1.04	–1.12
HU	–0.42	–0.84	–0.99	–0.89	–0.95	–0.82	–0.87	–0.67	–0.80	–0.85	–1.23
PL	–0.77	–0.52	–0.62	–0.91	–0.78	–0.34	–0.82	–0.79	–0.80	–0.91	–0.75
SI	n.a.	n.a.	n.a.	n.a.	n.a.	n.a.	n.a.	n.a.	–0.77	–0.83	–0.88
SK	–0.77	–0.55	–0.56	–1.09	–0.98	–0.61	–0.77	–0.90	–0.74	–0.69	–1.14
EU13	B	B	B	B	B	B	n.a.	n.a.	B	B	B

Note: B: benchmark; n.a.: data not available. All estimations were significant at the 1% level.
Source: Authors' calculations based on Thomson Datastream data.

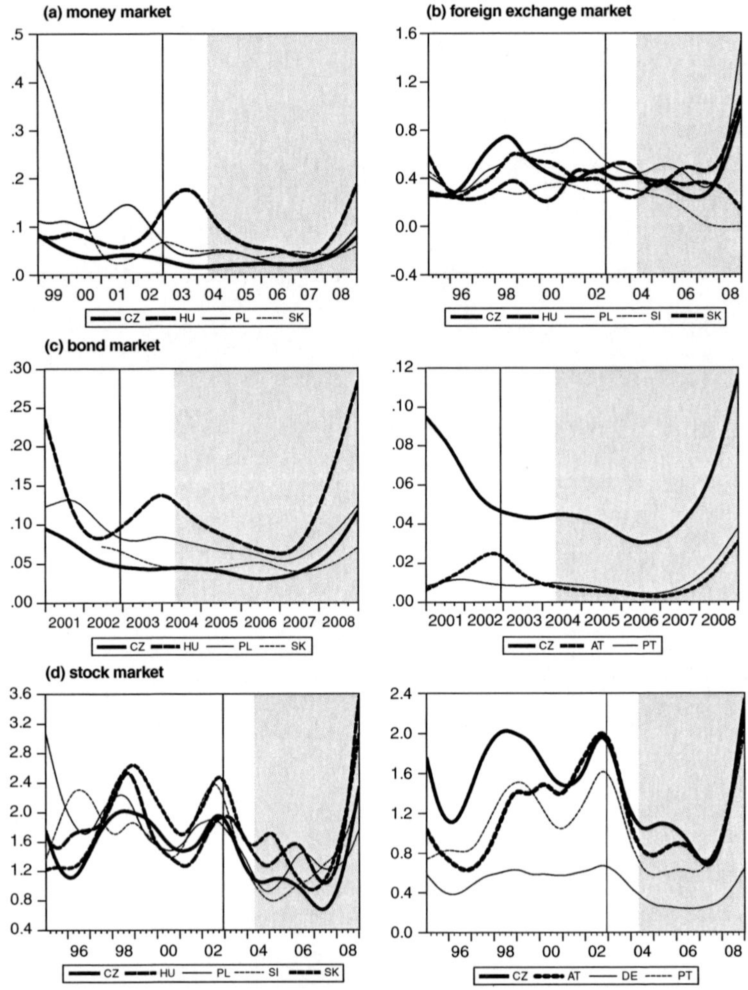

Figure 8.1 Sigma coefficients
Note: Lower standard deviation values (vertical axis) correspond to a higher convergence level. The grey area represents the period after EU enlargement on 1 May 2004 and the vertical line represents the announcement thereof on 12–13 December 2002.
Source: Authors' calculation based on Thomson Datastream data.

differences in the yields on the Slovenian stock market persisted. The foreign exchange markets may have seemed more volatile until August 2007, but the σ values were very low there, reflecting the already relatively strong integration of these markets. Regarding stock markets, the degree of integration achieved in the Czech Republic was comparable to that observed in Portugal, Austria, and Germany. The same could not yet be said in the case of the bond markets. Overall, it can be seen that gradual trend σ-convergence of stock, bond, and money markets had been taking place in all the observed countries since 2001–2.[11]

August 2007–January 2009

The relevant columns of Table 8.2 (August 2007–January 2009) and the relevant parts of Figure 8.1 describe the developments on the individual markets in the period affected by the financial crisis. The calculations show that most countries recorded a slowdown in convergence of yields towards those in the euro area. Since 2007, the integration of money and foreign exchange markets has accelerated only in Slovakia; this is connected to its preparations for euro adoption. From the point of view of the degree of integration of the individual markets with the euro area, it is clear that the present financial crisis has contributed with mixed intensity to divergent developments in the given period on all markets except the money market. However, with the exception of the foreign exchange market, where the indicator for the Czech Republic was affected by strong koruna appreciation in the period under review, the impact of the current crisis on the Czech economy was rather lower compared to the other economies of the Central European region, Hungary in particular. This can be put into context with the solid economic performance of the Czech economy and the confidence in the Czech currency.

8.6.2 News-based measures of financial integration

In the application of news-based measures, we focus on four Central European economies (Czech Republic, Hungary, Poland, Slovakia) plus Sweden, compared to the euro area, or Germany in the case of the government bond market. The results for the Central European countries indicate that (i) parameter γ turns out to be slowly changing over time, thus documenting a relative constancy of shock propagation across individual markets and countries; (ii) the transmission of shocks across markets and countries is characterised by a dominantly symmetric (positive) response (except for the Hungarian government bond market); (iii) on average, the strongest transmission of shocks occurs on the stock markets, whereas the lowest propagation is on the government bond markets (γ being close to zero); (iv) sensitivity to the transmission of news or shocks across individual countries varies, which is due to country-specific risk premiums or monetary policy regimes, thus questioning the statement of similar behaviour of financial markets in the countries of Central Europe; (v) on average, the lowest sensitivity to shocks is observed for Slovakia (however, notice that Slovakia is characterised by the shallowest markets), followed by the Czech Republic and then Poland and Hungary closing the ranking. Overall, the results show that the 'integration coefficients' for individual markets are significant, with the stock market being characterised by the highest sensitivity to the transmission of news (i.e., being most integrated, in our terms). The differences in credit, liquidity, and monetary risks, as well as the chosen monetary policy, of the sample countries, which in addition increase from the beginning of the financial crisis, thus play an important role in the process of financial integration. In particular, the degree of integration on the money market may reflect the alignment of the selected states' monetary policies with that of the euro area. Thus, idiosyncratic local news (a change in the monetary policy rate of the relevant state) may prevail far more on the money market than on the stock market.

By comparing the results of financial integration for Central European countries and Sweden it follows that the Swedish economy is much

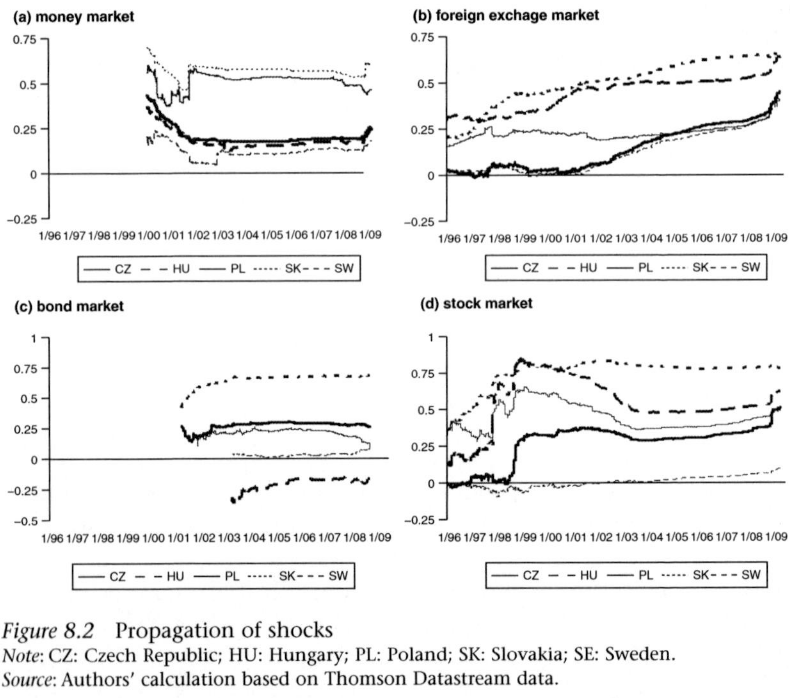

Figure 8.2 Propagation of shocks
Note: CZ: Czech Republic; HU: Hungary; PL: Poland; SK: Slovakia; SE: Sweden.
Source: Authors' calculation based on Thomson Datastream data.

strongly integrated with the euro area, which is in accordance with economic intuition. In the case of Sweden, European news still prevails (high gamma coefficient).

8.7 Conclusion

In this chapter we empirically examined the price- and news-based measures of financial integration. For the price-based measures, we analysed the speed (by means of β-convergence) and level (by means of σ-convergence) of the financial integration in five new EU member states (Czech Republic, Hungary, Poland, Slovakia, and Slovenia) and three old EU members (Germany, Austria, and Portugal) in comparison with the euro area as a whole. The results showed both strong β-convergence and σ-convergence in all markets up to the beginning of the financial crisis in August 2007. All markets exhibited a substantial degree of integration. The situation changed during the current financial turmoil. The calculations showed that most of the markets in all countries recorded a lower convergence level towards the euro area. One exception was the convergence of the foreign exchange market in Slovakia and Slovenia with the euro area, arising from the euro adoption process in these two countries.

Regarding the news-based approach, the results demonstrated considerable propagation of shocks across the four financial markets considered. Financial integration, measured by the strength of shock/news transmission, was highest for the stock market, followed by the foreign exchange, money, and government bond markets. Nevertheless, the propagation of shocks was changing rather slowly, with only limited evidence of increasing transmission in recent years.

Taking all measures altogether, we found evidence of relatively strong and gradually increasing financial market integration of the new EU member states' markets towards the levels of the euro area economies. However, the results clearly indicated differences between individual Central European countries – evidenced, for example, by the insensitivity of the shallow Slovak stock markets, the asymmetric reaction of the Hungarian government bond market, and differences in the magnitude of β-, σ-, and shock convergence. The group of Central European new EU Member States was thus far from being homogeneous.

Notes

The research is supported by Czech National Bank Research Project No. C2/09 and partly by the Grant Agency of the Czech Republic under Project

No. 402/08/0067. We thank participants at the CICM conference at London Metropolitan Business School for valuable comments. This research was also supported by the Czech National Bank project no. C8/2007, Grant Agency of the Czech Republic no. 402/08/0067 and Internal Grant Agency of The University of Finance and Administration in Prague no. 7720/2010.

This chapter represents the authors' own views, which do not necessarily reflect those of the Czech National Bank. All errors and omissions remain entirely the fault of the authors.

1. A detailed discussion of the costs and benefits of financial integration is provided by Agénor (2003).
2. Slovenia joined the euro area on 1 January 2007 followed by Slovakia on 1 January 2009. However, since our sample covers largely January 1995 to January 2009, we consider Slovenia and Slovakia together with the non-euro area EU member states.
3. Chen and Knez (1995) and Baele et al. (2004) provide more details, including in particular the weaknesses of each of the proposed measures.
4. The aim of these measures is to quantify the effects of frictions faced by the demand for and supply of investment opportunities. Where they are available, we will use statistics giving information on the ease of market access, such as cross-border activities or listings. This paper will not cover such analysis.
5. Since asset pricing models are difficult to estimate and require long time series to provide reliable estimates, Adam et al. (2002) and Baele et al. (2004) consider the correlation of stock market returns as an alternative indicator.
6. The terms beta-convergence and sigma-convergence originate from the literature on economic growth and its dynamics; see, for example, Barro and Sala-i-Martin (1992).
7. There are alternative measures of stock market integration based on GARCH (linear and non-linear) type analysis – see Hardouvelis, Malliaropulos, and Priestley (2006), Capiello et al. (2006) and Bekaert et al. (1997). The degree of stock market integration could also be assessed upon the co-dependence between two random variables (called the co-movement box) – see Capiello, Gérard, and Manganelli (2005) or by using the Dynamic Conditional Correlation (DCC) method originally proposed by Engle (2002) and subsequently extended by Capiello, Engle, and Sheppard (2003). Another alternative methodology for testing financial market integration based on the intertemporal asset-price model with time-varying discount factors is proposed by Flood and Rose (2005).
8. Yields on money market assets are affected to some extent by the monetary policy decisions of the state in question, so the validity of the law of one price is somewhat limited. Therefore, the speed of beta-convergence is lower on the money market than on the other markets.
9. Interpretation of the values for Germany should also take into account the fact that the data for Germany have a significant weight in the calculation of the data for the euro area.
10. The developments in Slovakia also reflect the adoption of the single currency in January 2009.
11. This may have been due to the announcement that these countries would join the European Union (12–13 December 2002). This period is illustrated by a vertical line in Figure 8.1.

References

Adam, K., Japelli, T., Menichini, A., Padula, M., and Pagano, M. (2002) *Analyse, Compare, and Apply Alternative Indicators and Monitoring Methodologies to Measure the Evolution of Capital Market Integration in the European Union*. European Commission, pp. 1–95.

Agénor, P. R. (2003) 'Benefits and Costs of International Financial Integration: Theory and Facts', *World Economy*, vol. 26, no. 8, pp. 1089–118.

Aguilar, J., and Hördahl, P. (1998) 'Exchange Rates and Currency Options as EMU Indicators', *Sveriges Riksbank Quarterly Review*, 2, pp. 58–81.

Ayuso, J., and Blanco, R. (2000) 'Has Financial Market Integration Increased during the Nineties?' *Journal of International Financial Markets, Institutions and Money*, vol. 11, no. 3, pp. 265–87.

Baca, S. P., Garbe, B., and Weiss, R. A. (2000) 'The Rise of Sector Effects in Major Equity Markets', *Financial Analysts Journal*, September/October, pp. 35–40.

Babetskaia-Kukharchuk, O., Babetskii, I., and Podpiera, J. (2008) 'Convergence in Exchange Rates: Market's View on CE-4 Joining EMU', *Applied Economic Letters*, 15(5), pp. 385–390.

Baele, L., Ferrando, A., Hördahl, P., Krylova, E., and Monnet, C. (2004) 'Measuring Financial Integration in the Euro Area', *Occasional Paper Series*, no. 14, European Central Bank, pp. 1–93.

Barr, D. G., and Priestley, R. (2004) 'Expected Return, Risk and the Integration of International Bond Markets', *Journal of International Money and Finance*, 23(1), pp. 71–97.

Barro, R. J., and Sala-I-Martin, X. (1992) 'Convergence', *Journal of Political Economy*, vol. 100, pp. 223–51.

Bekaert, G., Campbell, R. H., and Lumsdaine, R. L. (2000) 'Dating the Integration of World Equity Markets', *Journal of Financial Economics*, vol. 65, no. 2, pp. 203–47.

Bekaert, G., and Harvey, C. R. (1995) 'Time-Varying World Market Integration', *Journal of Finance*, vol. 50, pp. 403–44.

Castrén, O., and Mazzotta, S. (2005) 'Foreign Exchange Rate Option and Returns Based Correlation Forecasts Evaluation and Two Applications', *ECB Working Paper*, No. 447.

Chen, Z., and Knez, P. J. (1995) 'Measurement of Market Integration and Arbitrage', *The Review of Financial Studies*, vol. 8, no. 2, pp. 287–325.

Codogno, L., Favero, C., and Missale, A. (2003) 'Government Bond Spreads', *Economic Policy*, October, pp. 503–32.

European Commission (1997) 'The Impact of the Introduction of the Euro on Capital Markets', *Euro Papers*, no. 3 (July). European Commission, Brussels.

European Commission (1999) *Financial Services: Implementing the Framework for Financial Services: Action Plan*. COM (1999) 232, Brussels, May 11.

Hardouvelis, G., Malliaropulos, D., and Priestley, R. (2006) 'EMU and European Stock Market Integration', *Journal of Business*, vol. 79, no. 1, pp. 365–92.

Hartmann, P., Maddaloni, A., and Manganelli, S. (2003) 'The Euro Area Financial System: Structure, Integration and Policy Initiatives', *Oxford Review of Economic Policy*, Spring 2003, vol. 19, no. 1, pp. 180–213.

Heston, S. L., and Rouwenhorst, K. G. (1995) 'Industry and Country Effects in International Stock Returns', *The Journal of Portfolio Management*, Spring, pp. 53–58.

Kim, S. J., Lucey, B. M., and Wu, E. (2004) 'Dynamics of Bond Market Integration Between Existing and Accession EU Countries', *Institute for International Integration Studies Discussion Paper*, No. 25/June.

Komárková, Z., and Komárek, L. (2007) 'Integration of the Foreign Exchange Markets of the Selected EU New Member States', *Politická ekonomie*, no. 3, 2007.

Martin, P., and Rey, H. (2004) 'Financial Super-Markets: Size Matters for Asset Trade', *Journal of International Economics*, vol. 64, no. 2, pp. 335–61.

Papademos, L. (2008a) 'Financial Integration, Financial Innovation and Development', speech at the Second Symposium of the ECB-CFS Research Network on 'Capital Markets and Financial Integration in Europe', Frankfurt am Main, 13 February 2008.

Papademos, L. (2008b) 'Financial Integration in Europe', presentation by Mr. Lucas Papademos at the press briefing on the occasion of the publication of the second edition of the ECB Report on financial integration in Europe, Frankfurt am Main, April 29, 2008.

Portes, R., and Rey, H. (2005) 'The Determinants of Cross-Border Equity Flows', *Journal of International Economics*, vol. 65, no. 2, pp. 269–96.

Trichet, J.-C. (2005) 'European Financial Integration and the Management of Inflation Expectations by the European Central Bank', Remarks at the conference 'The euro: one currency, one financial market' organised by the European Commission, New York, April 19, 2005.

Trichet, J.-C. (2006) 'Two Successes of the Euro – the Single Monetary Policy and European Financial Integration', speech at the Conference on experience with and preparations for the euro, Linz, May 11, 2006.

Trichet, J.-C. (2007) 'Major Issues Related to the Process of European Financial Integration – the Regional and Global Perspective', keynote luncheon remarks at the conference 'Transatlantic Roundtable on Finance and Monetary Affairs', at the invitation of the European Institute, Washington, DC, April 13, 2007.

Trichet, J.-C. (2008) 'Financial Integration in Europe and Important Financial Sector Issues', keynote speech at the Second Symposium of the ECB-CFS research network on 'Capital Markets and Financial Integration in Europe', Frankfurt am Main, February 13, 2008.

Yam, J. (2006) 'Financial Integration and Regulation', remarks at the conference 'The Euro: Lessons for European and Asian Financial Markets', Hong Kong, February 24, 2006.

9

Exports and Economic Growth of East European Economies, 1996–2007

Shahdad Naghshpour and Bruno S. Sergi

9.1 Introduction

The argument whether export causes growth dates back to Ricardo and the comparative advantage. According to this theory, free trade increases the production of traded goods due to lower costs for each country. The assumption that the goods are 'normal goods' ensures that lower prices induced by increased production increase the utility of the citizens of each trading partner. Of course, in order to increase production in the export sector, the production of other sector(s) must be reduced. The 'logical' choice is therefore the production of imported goods. Needless to say, in order for trade to occur, the trading countries must engage in both the import and export of goods. The net effect of increased exports and imports is positive, resulting in increased production, which is defined as growth.

In reality, however, growth is a relative concept. If a country grows by 2 per cent while all the other countries grow by 3 per cent or more, has the country actually grown? Another factor to consider is the income generated from trade. As a result of differences in elasticity of demand, an increase in production may or may not necessarily increase a country's income and, hence, its ability to import and increase the utility of its citizens. Some goods, such as unprocessed coffee beans, are price elastic. An increase in the output of price-elastic goods reduces total revenue. Another influencing factor is the income elasticity of a good. If a good is income inelastic, its demand does not increase as much with an increase in income. For income-inelastic goods an increase in output reduces the revenue. Contrary to the common belief that the demand for food, necessary for survival, should increase as income increases, the reality is that food, in general, is income inelastic. An increase in income increases expenditure on food by a proportionally smaller amount; therefore, a country exporting food might have a problem when its trading partners grow. Consequently, the empirical results are inconclusive.

During the eighteenth and the nineteenth centuries primary goods were in relatively high demand due to the Industrial Revolution. Many of the agricultural goods also benefited from increased demand due to population growth in the newly industrialised countries. One example of such items is coffee. It could be produced only in certain regions, of which only limited parts were capable of producing for export due to capacity, transportation, and other necessary arrangements, both financial and logistical. Before long, many of the countries that specialised in the export of the primary goods faced competition from other countries with similar capabilities, as well as countries in other parts of the world, where they managed to produce comparable goods. A good example is the rubber produced in Southeast Asia. To aggravate the problem, the advent of new technology, such as synthetic fibre, eliminated the relative scarcity and inelastic demand enjoyed by the original exporters of the primary goods (Adekola and Sergi, 2007).

The deterioration in terms of trade for developing countries, especially in Latin America, Africa, and parts of Asia, proved detrimental to the development ambitions of the exporters of primary goods. The possibility of growth via primary goods has been discounted since the 1960s. After the Second World War almost all countries that exported primary goods experienced a decline in economic growth. In many years, in many countries, the economic growth was, in fact, negative in part due to the abovementioned problem and in part due to a substantial increase in the population growth rate and hence the ensuing population increase. The outcome put a damper on the value of exports as the growth engine. In response to the writings of scholars such as Prebisch (1959), many underdeveloped countries decided against trade with the former colonial powers of the West, and curtailed their exports as much as possible. Instead, the domestic production of industrial products was encouraged and government support, aid, and policy shifted towards import substitution. During this period, however, there were yet others who advocated export-led growth (Maizels 1968). The issue raised by Maizels (1968) might have been the main problem that Prebisch was trying to combat – Maizels wrote about the 'Sterling-based' countries, which were all former colonies of England.

9.2 Literature review

Since the last decade of the twentieth century, the idea of export-led growth has re-emerged; however, this time round the emphasis has been on the industrial production of consumer goods that are of interest to developed nations. By then there was no doubt about the consequences of specialising in primary goods and depending on revenues from them to achieve economic growth. Trade causes benefits and losses to participating countries. In the exporting country, the exporters gain. The demand for their product increases and, hence, the prices, and therefore the return to exporters increases. The consumers of the exported goods lose due to the higher prices that erode their consumer surplus. On the other hand, the price of imported goods declines, which helps consumers of such goods while hurting their producers. The importers also gain as a result of increased revenue. However, it can be shown that the gain to the winners outweighs the loss to the losers (Krugman and Obstfeld, 2009). The theory takes into account the amount of the gain based on the elasticity of demand and supply in each country. Factor mobility equalises factor prices among trading partners, short of transportation costs and some friction. It is argued that free trade is also capable of equalising the prices of goods and services, which in turn can translate into factor price equilibrium among the trading partners (Krugman and Obstfeld, 2009). These gains are very important to a country and its citizens, and can improve the overall economic wellbeing of the country. However, there is no way to assess whether the overall utility of the citizens of the country has increased or to assess the increase in the rate of economic growth. The reasons for these two outcomes are different. The inability to assess the utility outcome for a country lies in the fact that there is no way to compare the level of utility gain and loss between two people. A utility reduction caused by a one-dollar loss to one person may be less than, equal to, or greater in magnitude than the utility gain caused by a one-dollar gain for another person. The reason for the inability to increase the rate of growth stems from the fact that the gains from trade are one-off gains. These gains are static and affect only the level of the measure of growth, such as gross domestic product (GDP), and not the rate of growth of such measures. In order for a country to increase its economic growth via trade, it must increase its trade every year. Even this might not be sufficient, especially if the counter-argument that growth increases exports is considered. The evidence is that countries with a higher GDP experience greater trade. Although there is ample evidence of a relationship between GDP and trade, as expected, the direction of causality is not always unidirectional.

There is a lively discussion about the effect of trade on economic growth and development. In accordance with neoclassical tradition, Maizels (1968: p. 54) acknowledges the contributions of factors of production and indicates that in developing countries there are at least three main bottlenecks. These bottlenecks are the low skills of labour, the shortage of domestic savings that hampers domestic investment, and the limitation on imports and net borrowing. Maizels acknowledges that 'limitation on supply of skills adversely affects growth' (Chenery and Strout, 1966). However, he stipulates that 'it seems probable that for the majority of overseas Sterling countries. ... [t]he effective limitation [on] growth, which is a form of a trade or a savings constraint, comes into operation before the skill limit imposes [a] ceiling on the possible rate of growth' (Maizels 1968: p. 67). Maizels argues that one way, if not the best way, to promote development is through exports, which would also expand domestic savings (Sergi, 2003a; Sergi and Vit, 2004). The possibility of a link between growth and trade has been evidenced by Balassa (1991) and Kreuger (1993) for East Asia, and Sergi (2003b) for Eastern Europe. On the other hand, Amsden (1989) argues that the interventionist policies of East Asian governments were more effective in promoting growth than trade openness. Rodrik (1995) attributes the success of those countries to their industrial policies.

The above argument is about the dynamic effects of trade on growth. The claim is that trade not only causes a one-off gain in GDP, but also changes the competitiveness of the exporting sectors, which continues to increase growth. The argument is that an increase in trade increases competition, at least in the exporting sector under normal conditions. It is possible that increased exports come from an existing monopoly or a new monopoly to form as a result of increased opportunity to grow. The latter would be the case when a substantial economy of scale exists. An example of the former is the Microsoft Corporation: An increase in the export of computer operating systems and software helped Microsoft to consolidate its domestic monopoly and extend it to the international market instead of increasing competition in the domestic or international market. The impact on the import sector could also be an increase or a decrease in competition. The first intuition is that an increase in import increases competition, but the Microsoft case provides a clear counter-example to the claim. Among the remaining domestic producers of imported goods, if any remain after the establishment of trade, it is more likely that the outcome is reduced competition.

In order to compete with imported goods, a firm that survives has to be the best or among the better ones to compete globally, the remaining domestic producers must be efficient, which usually means they have to produce on a large scale. An increase in imports leaves smaller portions for domestic producer(s), which when combined with the need to produce at larger scale means there is little chance for many domestic producers, especially in the Third World countries that have relatively smaller markets due to the size of the country and the low purchasing power of its consumers.

At least since 1776, when Smith published *The Wealth of Nations* the idea of economic competition being good has been revered and considered good without question. However, according to Scharfstein (1988), increased competition is detrimental to innovation, whereas Hicks posits that it is conducive to innovation. Scharfstein (1988: p. 151) claims that the price elasticity of demand does not play any role in the outcome. Grossman and Helpman (1991) point out that trade increases prices in the export sector and reduces them in the import sector: therefore it both increases and decreases respective profits in the corresponding sectors. The change in profits is the incentive for innovation. The point made by Scharfstein is not about other aspects of competition or whether it is good for the economy and the welfare of its citizens. The point is that it is not good for innovation. The counter-arguments of the other references are also limited to the issue of innovation. An astute student of development would know that a discussion of innovation is important because of the central role it plays in economic growth. Solow (1956) chose to make improvements to technology, the ramification of innovation, exogenous. However, he did not exclude technology from the neoclassical growth model. In fact, advances in technology accounted for the disproportionate degree of economic growth in Solow's model. The contribution of later research has been in making technology an endogenous component of the growth theory. This is the foundation of endogenous growth theory (Romer, 1990). If trade increases competition, and if increased competition cradles innovation, and increased innovation increases output, then an increase in trade would result in economic growth. This dynamic role of trade is the engine of growth. As Lipsey (2009) states, technological advance is a necessary condition for sustained economic growth, where technologies and institutions co-evolve in a system of mutual causation. Sustained growth began with the Industrial Revolution, which was the culmination of three trajectories of technological advances in steam power, electric power, and the mechanisation of textile manufacturing. These advances stretched over several centuries. Growth then became sustained when the West 'invented how to invent'. A necessary condition for the Industrial Revolution was western science, the roots of which lie as far back as the scholastic philosophers and the medieval universities. Its absence elsewhere is sufficient reason why no other place developed its own indigenous industrial revolution.

Maizels (1968: p. 29) points out that 'insofar as the relative importance of the subsistence (or non-monetary) sector varies from one country to another, the multiplier effect of a given export expansion on the rest of the economy is likely to differ, since the subsistence producers may not react to any substantial extent, in either output or demand, to changes in the (monetary) export sector'. Nevertheless, he states that the expansion of trade, at least in the sterling currency countries, will affect economic growth. Maizels also speculates that due to differences in the 'balance between government and private sector' in these countries the impact of export expansion should be different. At least in countries with a shortage of foreign exchange an increase in exports would increase the possibility of importing intermediate goods needed for production (MacKinnon, 1964; Chenery and Strout, 1966). The intermediate goods or capital goods are goods used in the production of other goods. In other words, these are machines used in factories and are not demanded for consumption to derive direct utility. An important distinction exists between developed and underdeveloped countries with regard to the intermediate goods. In most of the underdeveloped countries and for most productions, the country depends on foreign intermediate goods. According to Jones (2002: p. 125), the invention of new capital goods or the importation of such goods from more developed countries could be an engine of growth for a country.

Another argument in favour of an export-based policy is that competition with foreign firms, contact with other producers, and learning by doing would improve the efficiency of the export sector, if not the entire economy (Bhagwati, 1978; Krueger, 1978). In addition, Jung and Marshall (1985) state that 'export growth may represent an increase in demand for country's output and thus serve to increase real GNP'. They cite Schenzler (1982) for evidence. One argument in favour of an export-oriented policy is that exports not only add to the GDP, that is, a static aspect of its contribution to GDP, but also result in improved production capacity, economies of scale, innovation, and efficiency (Balassa 1978; Feder 1982; Esfahani 1991). According to Feder (1982: p. 59), 'there are substantial differences between marginal factor productivities in export-oriented and non-export-oriented industries, such that the former have higher factor productivity'. Balassa (1978) examines 11 developing countries that had already, by 1970, established an industrial base. According to Balassa (1978: p. 181), 'export-oriented policies lead to better growth performance than policies favoring import substitution'. The main factor is the market size that, in the case of the latter, is limited. Balassa studies the effect of export growth on the growth of a GNP net of exports to measure the direct effect. For the total effect, that is direct plus indirect effects, the relationship between GNP growth and export growth is examined. The method of analysis is Spearman rank correlation. The method does not account for other factors that affect a change in the growth rate. The countries used differ from one another in many respects. Korea, Singapore, and Taiwan adopted export-oriented policies in the early 1960s and continued with them throughout the period (1960–73) under study. They had provided free trade for exports, but also provided some incentives for import substitution. Argentina, Brazil, Colombia, and Mexico continued import substitution incentives throughout the study period, but began export-oriented incentives in the mid-1960s. Israel and Yugoslavia began export incentives early on in the period, but did not continue later. Israel depends heavily on aid from the US, whereas Yugoslavia was a socialist country during the study period. It is not clear to what extent the exports would influence other parts of the economy in a planned economy. Chile and India maintained import substitution policy throughout the study period. Finally, if these countries were at different levels of development in the 1960s, the less-developed countries would have grown faster than the more developed countries, based on the neoclassical theory of growth (Solow, 1956), which would affect the rate of growth regardless of positive, zero, or negative effects of trade on GNP. This is the subject of the vast amount of research termed 'income convergence' (Naghshpour, 2009).

One shortcoming of Balassa (1978) is that trade policy is not the only factor that affects economic growth, and not accounting for other factors is misleading. For example, Balassa (1978: p. 185) states that 'in most of the countries domestic investment was rising rapidly during the period under consideration and its effects were not yet fully absorbed in the national economy.' Balassa points out that the outcome is not far from the 0.06 of 1 per cent reported by Krueger (1978: ch. XI). Balassa (1978) acknowledges the possibility of the importance of other factors and cites Michalopoulos and Jay (1973), who add domestic and foreign investment, and labour to export data. They use data from 39 countries over the seven years from 1960 to 1966. Both studies report that 'a one percent increase in the rate of growth of exports is associated with a 0.04 of 1 percent increase in the rate of growth of GNP. Although the result is statistically significant, it does not provide much evidence in support of effectiveness of the contribution of export on growth'.

There are at least two major distinct methods. One approach is the use of regression analysis, which usually incorporates the production function (Michaely, 1977; Balassa, 1978, 1985; Ram, 1985, 1987; Salvatore and Hatcher, 1991). It is not clear, however, whether the increase in exports causes the increase in GNP, or vice versa. These studies have not been able to settle the argument. Another problem with these studies is that they do not necessarily agree on the determinants of GNP growth, and are thus susceptible to the possibility of spurious results. Time series studies using the unit root and co-integration analysis can establish the causality between exports and GNP as established by Jung and Marshall (1985), Chow (1987), Bahmani-Oskooee and Alse (1993), and Chandra (2002). The preferred causality test is that of Granger (1969) and Sims (1972). However, Granger (1969) warns about excluding relevant variables, which can result in spurious causality. In a special case, the exclusion of relevant variables results in invalid inference (Caporale and Pittis, 1997). However, Love and Chandra (2004) and Sharma and Panagiotidis (2004), using the same methods in the case of India, cast doubt that trade openness increases the growth rate.

In most underdeveloped countries the problem is not a lack of trade but the instability of exports, especially the exports of commodities. Many underdeveloped countries rely on one or two primary goods. At least since the second half of the twentieth century, the demand for these goods has been volatile. This volatility is detrimental to planning economic development programmes because the necessary foreign exchange fluctuates a lot. This problem is addressed by Coppock (1962), MacBean (1966), Glezakos (1973), Knudsen and Parnes (1975), and Lim (1976), but they do not address the issue of causality. They demonstrate that export instability adversely affects economic growth. Olzer and Harrigan (1988) demonstrate that there is a negative relationship between instability and growth, whereas Love (1992) and Sinha (1999) establish the direction of causality from export instability to economic growth. However, as early as 1967, Emery suggests that the relationship between trade and economic growth is bidirectional. Nevertheless, he acknowledges the important role that exports play in growth.

Emery (1967: p. 475) argues that per capita data should be used on the grounds that population increase, especially in agrarian countries, is a main contributor to the growth of income. Instead of using per capita gross national product (GNP), Emery chooses to calculate the rate of growth in GNP and subtract from it the rate of growth in the population. In agriculture-based countries, a population increase can also reduce the exports as the land is converted from producing export goods to producing food for domestic use. In such cases it would seem that there is an inverse relationship between exports and economic growth.

There is vast literature on the subject of 'determinants of growth' that differs from the above literature. The research in this area focuses on the neoclassical theory of growth dating back to Ramsey (1928), Solow (1956), Swan (1956), Cass (1965), and Koopmans (1965). This literature focuses on the issue of convergence more closely and more directly than the literature cited earlier. One implication of this convergence perspective is that the further a country is from its steady state the faster it grows. Arrow (1962) and Sheshinski (1967) added the idea of 'learning by doing' into the model. Later, Romer (1986) and Lucas (1988) expanded the idea by formally incorporating the notion of human capital in the model, which is commonly known as the endogenous growth theory. Barro and Sala-i-Maritn (1997) point out that the endogenous growth theory does not predict conditional convergence, for which view there is strong empirical support. Therefore, they extended the theory to accommodate the possibility. These models typically include many socioeconomic factors such as the rate of literacy, life expectancy, democracy index, government consumption, level of GDP, geographical location, inflation rate, rule of law, and fertility, to name but a few. However, the present study focuses on the previously cited literature to examine the impact of trade in a fashion that is comparable to the existing literature.

9.3 Model

Based on the literature review, there are several acceptable approaches to determining the impact of trade on growth. As explained in the literature review, the first approach here is that of Balassa (1978, 1985) and similar works. In this model the per capita rate

$$GDP = \beta_0 + \beta_1 \frac{X_m}{X} + \beta_2 \frac{l}{L} + \beta_3 \frac{S_T}{Y} + \beta_4 \frac{S_D}{Y} + \beta_5 \frac{x}{X} + \beta_6 \frac{Y}{P} + \beta_7 IXP + \varepsilon \quad (1)$$

where

$\frac{X_m}{X}$ is the base year share of manufactured goods in total exports

$\frac{l}{L}$ is the growth rate of labour

$\frac{S_T}{Y}$ is the sum of current account balances over the period as a percentage of base year GNP

$\frac{S_D}{Y}$ is the sum of gross domestic investments less current account balance over the period as a percentage of base year GNP.

$\frac{x}{X}$ Indicates a change in merchandise exports over the period as a percentage of the base year value.

$\frac{Y}{P}$ represents per capita GNP

IXP is the absolute change in exports to absolute change in GNP over the study period.

Balassa (1985) starts with a basic model based on Michalopoulos and Jay (1973). He regresses the growth rate in per capita GNP on several combinations of the above listed variables. The first model uses the two capital-formation variables and the growth rate of labour over the period 1973–8 for 43 developing countries. Then he adds the growth rate of exports, the GNP of the base year, and the share of manufacturing exports in the base year. The sum of gross current account balances for the period proves statistically insignificant in explaining the growth rate of per capita GNP. The same is true for the growth rate of labour for most of the models. The other capital formation variable, namely the sum of gross domestic investment less current account balances for the period as a percentage of the base year GNP, is the only variable that is significant in all the models. The remaining variables are added one at a time and prove to be statistically significant. An earlier work (Balassa, 1978) also includes a variable named *IXP*, which is the absolute change in exports to an absolute change in GNP over the study period. The variable is marginally significant with a t-value of 1.86. The study is replicated here for the countries of the former Communist Bloc in Eastern Europe.

9.4 Data and analysis

For Balassa's (1978, 1985) models the data are obtained from the World Development Index. There are data for all 22 countries that were either part of the Soviet Union or the Eastern Bloc and became independent countries after the collapse of communism and are located in Eastern Europe. Russia is excluded because of its major economic collapse after the regime change. However, the length of the series varies vastly. Some countries, such as Poland and Hungary, have data for all variables as far back as the 1970s. Others, such as Serbia, have data from somewhere between 1997 or 1999 and 2007. In some cases there are no data for some variables. For the sake of uniformity only those 19 countries with data from 1996 to 2007 for all variables have been included: Albania, Armenia, Azerbaijan, Belarus, Bulgaria, Croatia, Czech Republic, Estonia, Georgia, Hungary, Latvia, Lithuania, Macedonia, Moldova, Poland, Romania, Slovak Republic, Slovenia, and Ukraine. All the variables in Balassa (1978, 1985), except the per capita GNP, are calculated according to the article; the data consist of levels and rates.

The main claim is that export plays a major role in growth. However, it is not the level of export that matters because a one-off change in exports has a one-time static impact on growth. Therefore, instead of the level of exports, the change in exports is used. Furthermore, to account for differences in the starting level of exports for different countries the change is represented as a percentage of the base year. In order to be consistent with the cited literature, this variable is shown as x/X in Table 9.1. To isolate the role of manufacturing in growth, a separate variable is incorporated, shown as X_m/X in Table 9.1. The actual variable is the share of manufactured goods in total exports at the base year. Countries with a relatively higher percentage of manufactured goods in their exports bundle are more developed than those with lower percentages. According to the neoclassical growth theory, such countries grow more slowly than less-developed countries, other things being equal. This *ceteris paribus* requirement is especially important in the case of technological advancements. Technological advancement, be it original or borrowed, is the undisputed source of sustained growth in all growth models. The model should also account for the efforts of the country to improve its capacity to produce. Two variables account for two different aspects of this factor: one is the sum of current balances over the period; the other is the sum of gross domestic investments less the current account balance over the period. Both of these variables are expressed as a percentage of GNP to account for differences in the levels of investment before the study period. The first model is the setup of Balassa (1985). The growth rate of labour is the last component necessary in terms of the neoclassical growth theory. The expected sign of the growth rate of labour is negative. Other things being equal, when there are more workers, more capital is needed to maintain the level

Table 9.1 Regression of growth on savings, labour, and exports, 1996–2007

Variable	Coefficient	t -value	P-value
Intercept	–53.70	(–0.39)	0.71
$\frac{X_m}{X}$	1.59	(0.93)	0.37
$\frac{l}{L}$	–0.83	(–0.34)	0.74
$\frac{x}{X}$	0.03	(0.2)	0.84
$\frac{S_T}{Y}$	0.79	(1.48)	0.16
$\frac{S_D}{Y}$	0.70	(2.31)	0.04
$\frac{Y}{P}$	–0.03	(–2.27)	0.04

Note: R^2 = .83, adjusted R^2 = 0.74, $F_{6,\,12}$ = 9.61, model *P*-value = 0.0005.

of productivity as before. On the other hand, the expected signs of the capital variables are positive –as more and more capital is accumulated, the economy grows faster. The expected sign of the level of economic output is negative, because at a higher level of production the rate of growth declines. The most general model, with all six variables, is included. The results are displayed in Table 9.1.

The model is good, indicating that the variables explain a variation in growth rates among Eastern European countries well. The overall model is highly statistically significant and R^2, and even the adjusted R^2, are high. Balassa (1985) does not indicate whether the reported R^2 are adjusted. Regardless, the above values are much higher than the highest R^2 of 0.465 reported on by Balassa (1985), which corresponds to the same formulation as the above model. All the variables have the correct signs.

Contrary to the neoclassical growth theory, the more industrialised countries have a higher growth rate. This reflects the fact that these countries have a higher production capacity and fewer production bottlenecks. This also reflects their better infrastructure, which enables them to increase production. The increase in labour reduces the growth rate, whereas increase in capital accumulation, that is, investment, increases the growth rate. The more advanced a country is, the lower its growth rate, as is to be expected. Finally, the larger the increase in the export compared to the base year, the faster the country grows.

For the period 1996 to 2007, the only two significant variables are the per capita GNP and the sum of gross domestic investments less current account balances. However, Balassa reports on four statistically significant results for coefficients versus the two here. The models with fewer variables reported in Balassa (1985) are examined but no major change is noticed, so they are not reported on here owing to space constraints. Part of the reason for this outcome is the fact that the variables excluded from Balassa's model are those that are not significant in the present model. Therefore, their exclusion does not affect the outcome of the model. Also not reported, for the same reasons, is the result of adding the *IXP* variable to the model that Balassa (1978) uses. Balassa adds another variable, introduced by Feder (1982), which consists of the product of the averages of exports and GNP for the study period. Although Balassa finds statistically significant values in all the models except one, the present study finds that most of the variables fail on statistical significance. In fact, inclusion of the variable makes all the variables in the model statistically insignificant. Nevertheless, the adjusted R^2 is greater than 0.72. This is a textbook example of multi-colinearity. Therefore, for the sake of space, the results are omitted. The methods used by Balassa (1978;1985) and Feder (1982) use different measures by averaging some of the variables over the study period. The former also includes the initial value of some of the variables as explanatory variables. The present study uses 12 years of observation instead of the 6 used by Balassa and the 10 used by Feder. The Feder study uses countries that are homogenous with regard to their level of industrialisation; the scope of its conclusions is also restricted accordingly and limited to the countries at levels of industrialisation comparable to those in the study. Balassa uses both the least developed and the newly industrialised countries; therefore, the data are less homogenous than either Feder's data or the data used in the present study, whose homogeneity lies in its historical political system, but not necessarily in the level of growth or industrialisation. Therefore, as such, it lies somewhere in the middle of the above two studies. The above analysis reveals several shortcomings in the ability to explain the growth rate of the Eastern European countries since their independence.

9.5 Panel data analysis

9.5.1 Fixed-effect model

Although the variables have explanatory power, the model is less than desirable. One possibility is that both the model and the theory are incorrect. Another possibility is that the tool itself needs improvement. At least the nature of the data warrants further examination. The data, which cover several countries over many years, lend themselves to panel data analysis. In this section both the random-effects and the fixed-effects analysis are discussed. The model is:

$$S_{it} = \alpha_0 + \alpha_1(GDP_t - EXP_t) + \alpha_2 EXP_t + U_i + \varepsilon_{it} \;\; \forall i = 1\ldots18 \text{ and } t = 1\ldots13$$

where
S is the gross domestic savings
GDP is the gross domestic product
EXP is exports
ε_{it} is the random error.

The subscript '*t*' represents the year. The results are displayed in Table 9.2 below. The values in parentheses are the *t*-values and those in square brackets are the corresponding *p*-values.

The fixed-effects model allows different intercepts for each country, while keeping the slope the same for all countries. According to Table 9.3, both the *GDP* minus exports and the exports are both highly significant. The *F*-test for the model is $F_{(2,214)} = 1648.34$. According to the variance fraction of *U*, the error term, 46 per cent of the variances in the data is due to variances between the countries. The test statistic for the individual effect (country level) is $F_{(17,\ 214)} = 7.34$, which indicates that the use of pooled time series cross-section analysis would have been incorrect due to the differences between countries. The within and between R^2 are 0.94 and 0.99, respectively. The overall $R^2 = 0.98$.

9.5.2 Between estimators

When the countries are different, as is shown above for this study, it means that the averages for the countries are also different. One way of analysing such cases is to use their means in the regression. This is also known as the 'between estimators' method. In this model the

Table 9.2 Results for the fixed-effects model

GDP- Export	Export	Sigma *U*	Sigma ε	Variance fraction of *U*
0.11 (8.64) [0.000]	0.31 (33.49) [0.000]	1.49E10	1.61E10	0.46

Table 9.3 Results for the random-effects model

GDP – Export	Export
0.11 (8.33) [0.000]	0.35 (16.11) [0.000]

random errors are assumed to be independent of the endogenous variables. The results are shown in Table 9.3 below. The values in parentheses are the *t*-values and those in square brackets are the corresponding *p*-values.

There is a slight change in coefficients, but both are still statistically significant. The Wald test with two degrees of freedom is 4624 and significant. The fraction of the variance due to the country effect is smaller in this case.

9.5.3 Error component model

The modified Wald test for group-wise heteroskedasticity using the fixed-effect model is rejected, which indicates that variances among countries are not identical. Therefore, the error component model is tried next. The results for this error component model are listed in Table 9.4. The values in parentheses are the *t*-values and those in square brackets are the corresponding *p*-values.

The model is also tested using the maximum likelihood estimator. The results are almost identical, except for a slight increase in the variance of the random error *U*, which decreases from 1.49E10 to 1.07E10. The Breusch and Pagan (1980) test for random effects results in a chi-squared value of 103.8, which is statistically significant. This indicates that the variances between the countries are also dissimilar, and the data should not be pooled. Note that the estimate for variance of *U* is much smaller than that of the variance for ε. The Hausman test results in a chi-square statistic of 9.15, which is significant at the 0.01 level, indicating that the differences in coefficients are not systematic.

Table 9.4 Results for error component model

GDP Exports	Exports	Sigma *U*	Sigma ε	Variance fraction of *U*
0.12 (14.26) [0.000]	0.31 (37.83) [0.000]	1.07E10	1.61E10	0.31

9.6 Conclusions

The present study examines the contribution of which shows that growth in the East European countries. This study uses Maizels' model that exports could be an engine of growth and considers four alternative models; the data are combined to take advantage of panel data analysis. All subsequent models confirm Maizels' claim via statistically significant results for exports among other variables. Although the idea of export as a growth engine is theoretically feasible; exports are nevertheless a function of the importing country's demand and purchasing power. Furthermore, it is not clear how the expansion of exports would translate into the overall growth of a country. Maizels, an advocate of trade-based growth, expands the theoretical foundation of the idea and provides some examples from members of the Overseas Sterling Area in the 1960s. Theoretical analysis indicates that the outcome of the impact is an empirical question. We consider empirically four alternative models, starting with the Balassa (1985) model. In this model the export variables fail statistical significance. Hence, the data are combined to take advantage of panel data analysis. All subsequent models confirm Maizels' claim via statistically significant results for exports among other variables.

References

Adekola, Abel and Bruno S. Sergi (2007). *Global Business Management: A Cross-Cultural Perspective*. Aldershot: Ashgate.

Amsden, Alice H. (1989). *Asia's Next Giant: South Korea and late Industrialization*, New York: Oxford University Press.

Arrow, Kenneth, J. (1962). 'The Economic Implications of Learning by Doing', *Review of Economic Studies* 29 155–73.

Bahmani-Oskooee, Mohsen and J. Alse. (1993). 'Export Growth and Economic Growth: an Application of Co-integration and Error-Correction Modeling', *Journal of Developing Areas* 27 535–42.

Balassa, B. (1991). *The Structure of Protection in Developing Countries*. Baltimore: Johns Hopkins University Press.

Balassa, Bela. (1985). 'Export Policy Choices and Economi Growth in Developing Countries after the 1973 Oil Shock', *Journal of Development Economics* 83 23–5.

Balassa, Bela. (1978). 'Exports and Economic Growth, Further Evidence', *Journal of Development Economics* 5 181–9.

Barro, Robert, J. and Xavier, Sala-i-Martin (1997) 'Technological Diffusion, Convergence, and Growth', *Journal of Economic Growth* 2 (1) 1–27.

Bhagwati, J. (1978). *Foreign Trade Regimes and Economic Development: Anatomy and Consequences of Exchange Control Regimes*, New York: National Bureau of Economic Research.

Caporale, G. M. and N. Pittis. (1997). 'Causality and Forecasting in Incomplete Systems', *Journal of Forecasting* 16 425–37.

Cass, D. (1965). 'Optimum Growth in an Aggregative Model of Capital Accumulation', *Review of Economic Studies*, 32, 233–40.
Chenery, Hollis, B. and Alan, M. Strout. (1966). 'Foreign Assistance and Economic Development', *American Economic Review* 56 (4) part 1 679–733.
Chow, P. C. Y. (1987). 'Causality between Export Growth and Industrial Development', *Journal of Development Economics*, 26 55–63.
Chandra, R. 2002. 'Export Growth and Economic Growth: An Investigation of Causality in India', *Indian Economic Journal*, 49 64–73.
Coppock, J. D. (1962). *International Trade Instability*, New York: McGraw Hill.
Emery, R. (1967). 'The Relation of Exports and Economic Growth', *Kyklos; Internationale Zeitschift fur Sozialwissenschaften* 20 (4) 470–84.
Esfahani, Hadi Salehi. (1991). 'Exports, Imports, and Economic Growth in Semi-Industrialized Countries', *Journal of Development Economics* 35 93–116.
Feder, Gershon, (1982). 'On Exports and Economic Growth', *Journal of Development Economics* 12 59–73.
Glezakos, C. (1973). 'Export Instability and economic Growth: A Statistical Verification', *Economic Development and Cultural Change* 3 815–28.
Granger, C. (1969). 'Investigating Causal Relations by Econometric Models and Cross-spectral Methods', *Econometrica* 37 424–38.
Grossman, G. and E. Helpman. (1991). *Innovation and Growth in the Global Economy*. Cambridge, MA: The MIT Press.
Jung, W. S. and P. J. Marshall. (1985). 'Exports, Growth and Causality in Developing Countries', *Journal of Development Economics* 18 1–12.
Knudsen, O. K. and A. Parnes. (1975). *Trade Instability and Economic Development – An Empirical Study*, Lexington, MA: Lexington Books.
Koopmans, Tjalling, C. (1965). 'On the Concept of Optional Economic Growth', *The Economic Approach to Development Planning*. Amsterdam: North-Holland.
Kreuger, Anne, O. (1993). *Economic Policies at Cross-Purposes: The United States and Developing Countries*, Washington: The Brookings Institution.
Krueger, Anne, O. (1977). *Foreign Trade Regimes and Economic Development: Liberalization Attempts and Consequences*. Cambridge, MA: Ballinger Press for the National Bureau of Economic Research.
Krugman, Paul and Maurice Obstfeld. (2009). *International Economics Theory & Policy*, Boston: Pearson.
Lim, D. (1976). 'Export Instability and Economic Growth: A Return to Fundamentals', *Oxford Bulletin of Economics and Statistics* 38 735–42.
Lipsey, Richard G. (2009). 'Economic Growth Related to Mutually Interdependent Institutions and Technology', *Journal of Institutional Economics* 5(3), 259–88.
Love, J. (1992). 'Export Instability and the Domestic Economy: Questions of Causality', *Journal of Development Studies* 28 37–54.
Love, J. and R. Chandra. (2004). 'An Index of Openness and its Relationship with Growth in India', *Journal of Developing Areas* 38 735–42.
MacBean, A. I. (1966). *Export Instability and Economic Development*. Cambridge, MA: Harvard University Press.
MacKinnon, R. (1964). 'Foreign Exchange Constraint in Economic Development and Efficient Aid Allocation', *Economic Journal* 74 (294) 388–409.
Maizels, A. (1968). *Exports and Economic Growth of Developing Countries*, Cambridge: Cambridge University Press.
Michaely, M. (1977). 'Exports and Growth: An Empirical Investigation', *Journal of Development Economics* 4 45–53.

Michalopoulos, Constantine and Keith, Jay. (1973). 'Growth of Exports and Income in the Developing World: A Neoclassical View', AID Discussion Paper No. 28 (Agency for International Development, Washington, DC).
Naghshpour, Shahdad. (2009). 'Sigma Convergence in the Former Communist Europe', *The International Journal of Business and Economic Perspective* 4: (2). (2009) 24–33.
Olzer, S. and J. Harrigan. (1988). 'Export Instability and Economic Growth', Department of Economics Working Paper No. 486, University of California, Los Angeles.
Prebisch, R. (1959). 'Commercial Policy in Underdeveloped Countries', *American* Economic Review, 251–73.
Ram, R. (1985). 'Export and Economic Growth: Some Additional Evidence', *Economic Development and Cultural Change* 33 59–74.
Ram, R. (1987). 'Export and Economic Growth in Developing Countries: Evidence from Time Series and Cross-Section Data', *Economic Development and Cultural Change* 24, 51–70.
Ramsey, Fran. (1928). 'A Mathematical Theory of Saving', *Economic Journal* 38 543–59.
Romer, Paul, M. (1986). 'Increasing Returns and Long-Run Growth', *Journal of Political Economy* 94, 1002–37.
Romer, Paul M. (1990). 'Endogenous Technological Change', *Journal of Political Economy* 98, S71–S102.
Rodrik, D. (1995). 'Getting Interventions Right: How South Korea and Taiwan Grew Rich', *Economic Policy* 55–107.
Salvatore, D. and T. Hatcher. (1991). 'Inward Oriented and Outward Oriented Trade Strategies', *Journal of Development Studies* 27 7–25.
Schenzler, C. (1982). 'An Empirical Investigation of the Relationship between Growth of Gross National Product and Exports in Chile, India, and South Korea', unpublished Master's thesis (Vanderbilt University, Nashville, TN).
Sergi, Bruno S. and Vit, Karel (2004). 'How to Rationalize the Export-Saving Paradigm (the Czech Experience)', *Prague Economic Papers* XIII (2), 115–20.
Sergi, Bruno S. (2003a). 'Testing the Saving Functions of Keynes and Maizels: A Case Study on Slovakia', *Eastern European Economics* 41(3), 60–9.
Sergi, Bruno S. (2003b). *Economic Dynamics in Transitional Economies: The Four-P Governments, the EU Enlargement, and the Bruxelles Consensus*. New York: Routledge.
Sharma, S. C. and T. Panagiotidis. (2004). *An Analysis of Exports and Growth in India: Co-integration and Causality Evidence 1971–2001*, ESRC Seminar Series, Oxford: Oxford University Press.
Sheshinski, Eytan. (1967). 'Optimal Accumulation with Learning by Doing', in Karl Shell (ed.) *Essays on the Theory of Optimal Economic Growth* 31–52. Cambridge, MA: MIT Press.
Sinha, D. (1999). 'Export Instability, Investment and Economic Growth In Asian Countries: A Time Series Analysis', Discussion Paper No. 799, Economic Growth Center, Yale University.
Solow, R. M. (1956). 'A Contribution to the Theory of Economic Growth', *Quarterly Journal of Economics* 70 (1) 65–94.
Swan, Trevor W. (1965). 'Economic Growth and Capital Accumulation', *Economic Record*, 32 334–61.

10

Inflation Convergence in the New EU Member States from Central and Eastern Europe

Alina M. Spiru

10.1 Introduction

After becoming members of the European Union (EU), the main goal for Central and Eastern European (CEE) countries is to join the European Monetary Union (EMU) as soon as possible, given their status as members without an 'opt out' clause. Their EMU membership is, however, conditional on the fulfilment of the Maastricht Criteria for nominal convergence, which impose a number of benchmark values for inflation, interest rates, government deficit and public debt, and also entail exchange rate stability. These tight criteria were designed to ensure that the participation of new Member States in the EMU contributes to the stability and viability of the system.

This chapter focuses on an empirical enquiry into an important issue pertaining to the monetary integration of the CEE economies by investigating one of the facets of nominal convergence, specifically the convergence of inflation rates. Compliance with this convergence criterion is intrinsically related to the effectiveness of monetary policy in achieving disinflation. A positive result in the attempt to bring the high levels of inflation recorded at the beginning of the transition process down to close to the average of the euro countries is suggestive of monetary policy efficacy and also encourages inflation convergence.

Eleven countries form the sample considered here. In terms of macroeconomic policy design, they have been characterised by a variety of experiences: ten of them joined the EU in May 2004, eight after successfully completing the transformation of their economies (Czech Republic, Estonia, Hungary, Latvia, Lithuania, Poland, Slovakia and Slovenia), two others (Cyprus and Malta) after years of experience as market economies. The eleventh country of the sample is Romania, which joined the EU in January 2007. The composition of the sample portends a challenging assessment that will combine elements of comparative analysis and country-specific coverage.

The prospects for these economies as candidates for monetary integration will depend strongly on their ability to align themselves with the institutions and macroeconomic policies of the existing EMU members. Although structural change and institutional adaptation to EMU norms are still in progress, convergence to EMU standards has gained momentum. Therefore, the analysis conducted in this chapter represents an empirical stock-taking exercise whose main purpose is to examine the extent to which the CEE countries have been able to achieve a certain degree of convergence to EMU standards.

The Maastricht Treaty states an explicit target in terms of convergence of inflation rates: the inflation rate of a country that aims to join the monetary union should not exceed by more than 1.5 percent the average of the three lowest inflation rates in the Eurozone. Since the beginning of the 1980s and until the introduction of the euro in 2002, inflation rates have declined within the Euro area. After the inception of the single currency, however, a proliferating inflation divergence has been observable. The pertinent literature is yet to discern whether this divergence is only short-term or represents the manifestation of a more structural phenomenon. A new wave of EMU enlargement, mostly involving CEE countries, is likely to add new dimensions to this fact. Two questions become relevant in this context. First, what is the degree of inflation convergence towards EMU benchmarks that characterises the future members of the EMU? Second, what is the anticipated effect of the EMU enlargement on the inflation rates of the older members? The empirical analysis reported on in this chapter aims to provide an answer to the first question, while highlighting some issues that may be relevant to tackling the second. To this end, the methodological framework employed here builds on the literature on growth convergence and brings together several econometric techniques to address the stationarity properties of inflation differentials. The main contribution of the analysis performed in this chapter consists in employing an augmented framework, which features two classes of econometric technique – time series and panel – while encompassing two modelling paradigms: linear and non-linear. The use of the non-linear approach in this context is novel and provides results that generate new insights into the inflation convergence process. In terms of country coverage, this study includes more economies and focuses on more panels of countries in order to gain a better understanding of the impact of institutional and regional characteristics on convergence, while also paying attention to country-specific factors and cross-country differences.

The organisation of this chapter is as follows. After this introduction, a selective review of inflation convergence studies is presented in section 10.2. Section 10.3 focuses on methodology. Section 10.4 presents the data and reports the empirical findings of the analysis. Section 10.5 discusses the results from a policy perspective, whereas section 10.6 concludes.

10.2 Empirical studies on inflation convergence: A selective review

The primary interest in this section lies in reviewing the techniques employed to examine inflation convergence. From a methodological point of view, one can classify existing attempts into two broad categories: time series approaches and panel studies. Whereas the first approach has dominated most of the early contributions, the second started to gain popularity when the enhanced power of panel methods over their univariate time series counterparts was widely documented.

The time series-based strand of the literature examines inflation convergence among European economies by employing several techniques. In one of the first attempts to study the degree of convergence in inflation rates of the European Monetary System (EMS) members, Koedijk and Kool (1992) utilise a variant of the principal components method and test convergence by investigating the stationarity of the first largest principal component of inflation deviations from the German inflation, taken as benchmark. Hall et al. (1992) and Holmes (1998) examine inflation convergence by estimating models with time-varying coefficients, using a Kalman filter technique. Other studies (Caporale and Pittis, 1993; Thom, 1995; Siklos and Wohar, 1997; Holmes, 1998; Westbrook, 1998; Amián and Zumaquero, 2002; Mentz and Sebastian, 2003) employ cointegration analysis to identify common stochastic trends in the data on inflation rates; the existence of a common stochastic trend is regarded as evidence of convergence. To examine the convergence of inflation rates among the old EMU members, Busetti et al. (2006) use a sequence of univariate and multivariate unit root and stationarity tests that account for correlations across countries.

A second strand of the literature advocates the use of panel unit root and cointegration tests to gauge the degree of inflation convergence. Kočenda and Papell (1997) employ quarterly consumer price index

(CPI)-based inflation rates for the period 1952–94 to perform panel unit root tests on inflation convergence within the countries of the EU. They report evidence in favour of inflation convergence, mainly among countries participating from the start in the Exchange Rate Mechanism (ERM) and argue that the convergence process was not substantially affected by the 1992 and 1993 ERM crises. On the other hand, Holmes (2002), using monthly CPI-based inflation data over the interval 1972–99, finds that inflation convergence was strongest during the period 1983–90, whereas the turbulence experienced within the ERM in the early 1990s conferred some degree of macroeconomic independence to certain member countries.

Beck and Weber (2005) examine the mean-reverting behaviour of regional inflation rates for a number of EU countries over the interval 1981 to 2001. They examine both σ- and β-convergence and find that inflation dispersion among EU regions is higher than in the US or Japan. To test for mean-reverting behaviour (equivalent to β-convergence), Beck and Weber (2005) complement a univariate approach, based on the Augmented Dickey-Fuller (ADF) test, with the panel unit root test developed by Levin and Lin (1992, 1993).

The main conclusion that can be drawn by examining the evidence on inflation convergence among the EU (or EMU) economies is that the results are sensitive to the time interval under scrutiny and certain institutional arrangements. It is widely agreed that participation in the ERM has fostered inflation convergence, whereas the introduction of a single currency and a common monetary policy have generated a certain degree of divergence.

The prospect of an eastward enlargement of the EU has generated a growing interest in the issue of macroeconomic convergence of CEE economies, especially since 1995, when these countries started formally to apply for membership. The degree of nominal convergence of the CEE countries has been assessed from two angles: first, within their own groups, formed on the basis of geographical and/or institutional criteria (Kočenda, 2001; Kutan and Yigit, 2002) and second, with respect to some EU benchmarks (Brada and Kutan, 2002; Brada et al., 2002; Kutan and Yigit, 2002, 2004; Kočenda et al., 2006). From a methodological standpoint, some of the above-mentioned studies employ time series testing techniques, whereas others attempt to mediate the short time series dimension of the sample by applying panel methods. Moreover, nominal convergence is examined together with real convergence. Brada et al. (2002) argue that convergence is an evolving rather than a stable concept. To emphasise the time-varying character of convergence, they employ the rolling cointegration techniques developed by Hansen and Johansen (1999) and Rangvid and Sorensen (2002).

The findings of the studies that examine real and nominal convergence of CEE countries to EU or EMU benchmarks reveal that these countries surpassed the difficulties of the macrostabilisation process and started moving in the same direction as the EU economies. However, the results are sensitive to the methodology employed.

10.3 Methodology

The concept of convergence is inherently related to that of economic growth. Therefore, definitions and methodological approaches to convergence are rooted in the empirical growth literature, pioneered by Baumol (1986), Barro (1991) and Barro and Sala-i-Martin (1991, 1992). This literature defines two types of convergence: absolute and conditional. Absolute convergence implies that, independent of their characteristics, different economies will eventually converge to the same long-term level. With conditional convergence, all countries grow to their own steady state, which depends on underlying, country-specific factors.

In two seminal contributions, Bernard and Durlauf (1995, 1996), drawing on Carlino and Mills (1993), develop the concept of 'stochastic convergence'. This posits that, in terms of economic variables, differences between countries will always have a transitory nature. Hence long-run forecasts of the differential between any pair of countries converge to zero as the forecast interval increases (Oxley and Greasley, 1997).

Stochastic convergence can be present only if shocks to the disparity between two countries are temporary, hence their effects dissipate over time. Therefore, the stochastic approach to convergence is characterised by a testable inference: the differential series is stationary. Non-stationarity of the differential implies that any shocks to it will have a long-lasting effect, accentuating the gap between countries. Evans and Karras (1996) show that to investigate the presence of stochastic convergence one can conduct a standard unit root test for the differential series. If the null of a unit root cannot be rejected, then there is no convergence between the two countries involved in the calculation of the differential. Alternatively, if stationarity is supported by the results, then convergence is present.

Testing inflation convergence involves studying the dynamic properties of the inflation differential between two economies. If we let $\pi_{i,t}$ denote the inflation rate of country i at time t, then the inflation differential ($d_t^{i,b}$) between country *i* and a benchmark country *b* can be calculated as:

$$d_t^{i,b} = \pi_{i,t} - \pi_{b,t} \tag{1}$$

The stochastic convergence of country *i*'s inflation rate towards the benchmark value implies that:

$$\lim_{\tau \to \infty} E\,(d_{t+\tau}^{i,b} \mid \Omega_t) = \alpha,\ \forall t \tag{2}$$

where Ω_t denotes the information set available at time *t*, comprising current and past observations on the differential series. For $\alpha = 0$, expression (2) mirrors the definition of absolute inflation convergence in a stochastic environment, in the spirit of Bernard and Durlauf (1996). This definition states that absolute convergence entails equality of long-term forecasts of the two inflation series at any fixed point in time. Putting it in different words, inflation rates of two countries converge in absolute terms if the expected value of the difference between them tends to zero as time tends to infinity. If, in (2) above, α is different from zero, then convergence is conditional or relative (Durlauf and Quah, 1999), which implies that the two inflation series converge towards a time-invariant equilibrium differential.

As discussed above, an empirical test for stochastic inflation convergence can be implemented in a time series framework by examining the univariate properties of the inflation differential using a unit root test. Both absolute and conditional convergence require a stationary inflation differential. Whereas absolute convergence implies that the auxiliary regression of the test does not include an intercept term, conditional convergence does not impose this restriction. As argued by Busetti et al. (2006), a simple time-series representation of conditional convergence is provided by a first-order autoregressive process:

$$d_t^{i,b} - \alpha = \rho\left(d_{t-1}^{i,b} - \alpha\right) + \varepsilon_{i,t} \tag{3}$$

which, parameterised in first differences, has the following expression:

$$\Delta d_t^{i,b} = \gamma + (\rho - 1)\, d_{t-1}^{i,b} + \varepsilon_{it} \tag{4}$$

where ε_t's are a sequence of martingale difference innovations, ρ represents the speed of convergence and $\gamma = \alpha(2-\rho)$ (where α is defined in (2) above). Representation (4) illustrates that the value of the growth rate of the inflation differential in the current period is a negative fraction of the inflation gap between two countries in the previous period, after allowing for a permanent difference (γ).

Expression (4) above corresponds to the maintained regression of the standard Dickey-Fuller (DF) test. However, in empirical studies on inflation convergence, the ADF test, a generalisation of the DF test that accounts for serial correlation in the residuals, provides a more suitable representation. Commonly applied in univariate analyses of inflation convergence, the auxiliary regression of the ADF test requires additional lagged values of the inflation differential ($\Delta d^{i,b}$) in specification (4) above, having the following expression:

$$\Delta d_t^{i,b} = \gamma + (\rho - 1)\ d_{t-1}^{i,b} + \sum_{j=1}^{p_i} \varphi_{ij} \Delta d_{t-j}^{i,b} + \varepsilon_t \tag{5}$$

Within the confines of representation (5), inflation convergence can be examined by conducting a unit root test, which evaluates the null hypothesis $H_0\!:\rho = 1$, against the alternative $H_A\!:\rho < 1$. Müller and Elliott (2003) argue that the power properties of this unit root test depend on an initial condition, that is, how far $d_0^{i,b}$ is from α. If the hypothesis under scrutiny is that of absolute convergence and consequently α is assumed to be equal to zero, a test based on an ADF regression with no intercept term performs relatively well, with a high initial value of the differential leading to enhanced power properties of the test (see Harvey and Bates, 2003 and Müller and Elliott, 2003, for a formal demonstration, and Busetti et al., 2006, for an empirical illustration). As a result, a specification that does not include a constant term is appropriate for testing the null of no convergence against the alternative hypothesis that two inflation series are converging in absolute terms, since it provides an improvement in power. However, testing absolute convergence is of interest when inflation differentials pertain to countries that are already members of a monetary union. In this study, the conditional form of convergence is employed, this being appropriate in view of CEE countries' inflation history since the beginning of the transition.

As highlighted in section 10.2, from a methodological standpoint, the focus of empirical studies on inflation convergence has gradually moved on from time series to panel data techniques. The latter provide more sophisticated devices to address the issue of convergence. In a panel setting, the time series dimension is augmented with the information contained in the cross-sectional one. This implies that non-stationarity from the time series can be dealt with and combined with the increased data and power that the cross-sectional dimension brings to the analysis. As a result, the inference about existence of unit roots, relevant to assessing convergence, becomes more accurate. Such outcome is particularly important in the case of CEE economies, where time series data are available over a short span, but similar data may be obtained across a cross-section of countries.

Panel unit root tests not only mediate the time dimension problem that arises in small samples, but are also characterised by enhanced power properties in comparison with their univariate counterparts. It is now a widely documented fact that commonly applied standard unit root tests, such as ADF, have low power in distinguishing the unit root null from a stationarity alternative, tending to over-reject the alternative of stationarity. In a convergence-testing framework, this is equivalent to offering more empirical support to divergence between countries.

In this study, two panel unit root tests are conducted to assess the extent of convergence of CEE inflation rates. The first is the test proposed by Im, Pesaran and Shin (IPS, 1997, 2003), which it addresses the convergence properties of a panel as a whole. The second test employed here, developed by Breuer, McNown and Wallace (SURADF, 2002), sheds light on the convergence performance of each panel member. These two testing frameworks complement each other, enabling one to derive convergence results not only for the panel as a whole, but also for individual countries. Their features facilitate a comprehensive analysis, which can focus on country-specific aspects. Moreover, both tests allow for heterogeneity in convergence rates.

To conduct the IPS test, an ADF-type regression is specified and estimated for each inflation differential, as follows:

$$\Delta d_t^{i,b} = X_{it}^{'}\gamma_i + \phi_i d_{t-1}^{i,b} + \sum_{j=1}^{p_i} c_{i,j}\Delta d_{t-j}^{i,b} + u_{i,t} \tag{6}$$

where $i = 1,\ldots,N$ and $t = 1,\ldots,T$. N is the cross-sectional dimension of the panel, whereas T is the time dimension. X_{it} is a vector of deterministic components. In the framework of equation (6), the null hypothesis of a unit root, $H_0: \phi_i = 0, \forall i$, is tested against the alternative $H_A: \phi_i < 0$, for $i = 1,\ldots,N_1$ and $\phi_i = 0$, for $i = N_1 + 1,\ldots,N$. Here, $\phi_i = \rho_i - 1$, where ρ_i is used as a measure of the speed of inflation convergence. The specification of the vector of deterministic components (X_{it}) is important in empirical applications. If no deterministic components are allowed in (6) above, then the IPS procedure tests absolute convergence between inflation rates, which is equivalent to assuming that the two inflation rates used in the calculation of the differential are characterised by identical steady states. When a constant term is included in (6), then one can distinguish two cases. In the first case, the constant is restricted to be equal across panel members ($X_{it} = 1$ and $\gamma_1 = \gamma_2 = ... = \gamma_N = \gamma$), which suggests that inflation rates are characterised by the same growth rate. The second case allows for different constant terms, which is equivalent to a model with fixed effects, suitable for representing conditional convergence. If the vector of deterministic components includes a constant and a term trend, where the constant is not the same across panel members, then there is a time-changing disparity between inflation rates.

In the empirical analysis carried out in this chapter, I consider a constant term as the only deterministic component in the specification of (6) and, therefore, adopt a representation that corresponds to a model with fixed effects. From a conceptual viewpoint, this representation allows for idiosyncrasies and examines the evidence of conditional convergence in a framework characterised by heterogeneity across countries.

The *t*-bar test statistic proposed by Im, Pesaran and Shin (1997, 2003) can be computed as an average of the *t*-statistics on the coefficients ϕ_i that resulted from the estimation of ADF-type maintained regressions, illustrated in equation (6), for all countries in the panel.

An important drawback of the IPS testing technique is that it builds on the assumption that the error terms u_{it} in (6) are individually and identically distributed, IID $(0, \sigma_\varepsilon^2)$. If the residual terms are contemporaneously correlated, this assumption is no longer valid, and the IPS test is characterised by significant size distortions, as demonstrated by Maddala and Wu (1999) and Strauss and Yigit (2003). To account for cross-dependencies across panel members, Im, Pesaran and Shin (1997, 2003) suggest the following solution: introduce a common time effect by decomposing the error term in (6) into a common time effect and an idiosyncratic random effect that is independently distributed across groups. To remove the common time effect, one needs to subtract the cross-sectional mean from each panel member. However, simple demeaning to account for the presence of contemporaneous cross-correlations does not remedy the size distortions in a satisfactory way (Strauss and Yigit, 2003).

Taylor and Sarno (1998) argue that panel unit root tests that focus on the stationarity properties of the panel as a whole, such as the IPS test, have an important drawback: the null of (joint) non-stationarity might be rejected due to the strong stationarity of one panel member, which induces rejection of the unit root null. This critique pertains to the results delivered by the IPS test, in cases where the panel under scrutiny comprises a mixture of convergent and non-convergent inflation rates.

When the results of the IPS test are interpreted, if the sample test statistic exceeds its critical value, it may not be the case that all members of the panel are stationary. The IPS testing framework does not allow one to distinguish how many and which members of the panel contain a unit root, which may constitute a serious drawback.

One of the objectives of the analysis conducted here is to shed light on the individual experiences, in terms of inflation convergence performance, of the selected countries, while exploiting the advantages of panel approaches over univariate ones. To this end, I complement the IPS testing framework with the series-specific panel unit root test proposed by Breuer, McNown and Wallaces (SURADF, 2002). By employing a Seemingly Unrelated Regressions (SUR) framework, the testing procedure developed by Breuer, McNown and Wallace (2002) leads to an improvement in the power of univariate time series tests, without sacrificing much series-specific information.

To conduct the SURADF test, ADF-type regressions, illustrated in (6) above, are specified for each panel member (similar to IPS). In a subsequent step, these regressions are estimated using a SUR approach, and individual unit root tests are conducted for each member of the panel. The SUR framework allows taking into consideration contemporaneous cross correlations among panel members, circumventing one of the drawbacks of the IPS test. The trade relations and institutional arrangements that exist among the CEE countries considered in this chapter suggest that a panel unit root test which accounts for cross-correlations is required to ensure an accurate assessment. Since it accounts for cross-correlations among panel members, which are specific to each panel, the SURADF test statistic is characterised by a non-standard distribution, and so the critical values of this test need to be generated by Monte Carlo simulations tailored to the panel under scrutiny.

10.4 Data and empirical results

This chapter uses a dataset that comprises monthly observations on prices (represented by CPIs) for the following countries: Cyprus, the Czech Republic, Estonia, Germany, Greece, Hungary, Latvia. Lithuania, Malta, Poland, Romania, the Slovakia and Slovenia. The data are obtained from the *International Financial Statistics* compiled by the International Monetary Fund. The data cover the interval January 1993 to December 2004. The pre-1993 period is excluded from analysis for two reasons: first, in order to avoid the early years of transition and the instability that characterised them and, second, for countries which have gained separate identities only recently (such as the Czech Republic and Slovakia), data are available only from January 1993. Therefore, to construct balanced panels, in line with the requirements of the panel unit root tests conducted in this study, the beginning of the sample is fixed at January 1993.

Based on the monthly CPI observations, annualised[1] inflation rates are calculated as log differences:

$$\pi_t = \ln CPI_t - \ln CPI_{t-12} \tag{7}$$

Several reasons motivate the choice of countries. The first is related to the common features that characterise their economies. The beginning of the 1990s marked a turning point in the evolution of these economies, representing the moment when the transition process from a communist system to a fully fledged market economy started. This radical transformation required the implementation of various fiscal and monetary policy steps within distinctive macroeconomic stabilisation strategies. However, besides the inherent peculiarities of their stabilisation attempts, the transition process these countries underwent shared several common features, related mainly to institutional reforms, price liberalisation, the choice of an appropriate exchange rate regime, and the attempt to contain corrective inflation. At the same time, these economies tried to establish a framework for international trade and cooperation to foster the transition process. They developed trade relations with each other and this fact provides a second reason to expect a certain degree of convergence within their groups. Bilateral trade relations, involving flows of capital and goods, play a coordinating role in the economic development of the countries involved. Ben-David (1996) provides insights into this issue, bringing evidence that income convergence prevails as a feature of countries that engage in extensive trade relations with one another.

For the purposes of this empirical analysis, six panels are constructed as follows: *CEFTA*[2] (the Czech Republic, Hungary, Poland, the Slovakia and Slovenia), the extended CEFTA (*ECEFTA*: the Czech Republic, Hungary, Poland, Romania, the Slovakia and Slovenia), the Baltic States (*BALTICS*: Estonia, Latvia and Lithuania), the first wave group,[3] comprising only former transition economies (*FIRST8*: the Czech Republic, Estonia, Hungary, Latvia, Lithuania, Poland, the Slovakia and Slovenia), the complete first wave group (*FIRST10*: Cyprus, the Czech Republic, Estonia, Hungary, Latvia, Lithuania, Malta, Poland, the Slovakia and Slovenia), and a panel that includes all former transition economies (*ALL9*: the Czech Republic, Estonia, Hungary, Latvia, Lithuania, Poland, Romania, the Slovakia and Slovenia). Therefore, panels are formed on the basis of both institutional and geographical criteria.

To examine inflation convergence, inflation differentials of the selected countries are identified with respect to the following four benchmarks: Germany, Greece, the Euro area and their group average, where the groups are those described above. Germany is chosen as a benchmark to represent the core EU standards, since it has a remarkable experience in terms of low inflation. In this regard, this work is related to that on the Bundesbank's domination of the EMS (see, e.g., von Hagen and Fratianni, 1990; Karfakis and Moschos, 1990; MacDonald and Taylor, 1991; Kutan, 1991; Kirchgässner and Wolters, 1993; Hafer et al., 1997). Greece, a more recent member of the EMU, is chosen to represent the peripheral countries of the EU and facilitate comparisons between results. Since Germany and Greece have been used as benchmarks by other convergence studies (Brada and Kutan, 2001; Brada et al., 2002; Kutan and Yigit, 2004), I introduce a third benchmark, representative of an average inflation rate for the euro area, calculated based on a weighted average CPI for the euro area, reported by Eurostat.

Table 10.1 provides some descriptive statistics, such as averages and standard deviations, for the inflation rates considered in this study. Looking at the average values, we can see that the lowest average inflation rate prevailed in Germany, followed by the Eurozone. Not surprisingly, inflation tended over this period to be higher in the transition economies than elsewhere.

Univariate unit root test results

To test for mean-reverting behaviour (β-convergence) in inflation differentials, I start by conducting the standard ADF unit root test. This test will also serve as a benchmark for comparison of the results of subsequent panel unit root tests and assist in the selection of the lag order for the specification of panel-based unit root tests.

If we can reject the null hypothesis of a unit root and therefore detect stationarity (and convergence), any shock that causes deviations from equilibrium[4] has a temporary nature and its impact will eventually die out. The speed at which this process takes place can be directly derived using the estimated value of the speed of convergence ($\hat{\rho}$). Given $\hat{\rho}$, half-lives (HL) can be calculated using the following formula:

$$HL = \frac{\ln(0.5)}{\ln(\hat{\rho})} \tag{8}$$

Table 10.1 Descriptive statistics for inflation rates

Country	Average	Standard deviation
CY	2.96	1.24
CZ	5.49	3.6
ES	11.26	11.72
HU	12.5	6.63
LA	9.12	9.46
LI	11.9	19.2
MA	2.6	1.2
PO	11.4	9.01
RO	40.55	29.11
SVK	7.94	3.07
SVL	8.68	4.17
GE	1.52	0.62
GR	5.07	2.6
EZ	1.98	0.53

Note The table reports summary statistics (average and standard deviation) of inflation rates as percentage values. CY = Cyprus, CZ = Czech Republic, ES = Estonia, HU = Hungary, LA = Latvia, LI = Lithuania, MA = Malta, PO = Poland, RO = Romania, SVK = Slovakia, SVL = Slovenia, GE = Germany, GR = Greece, EZ = Eurozone.

The results of the univariate ADF test (reported in Table 10.2) suggest that, with only a few exceptions, the inflation differentials examined in this study are unit root processes. The only country which appears consistently not to have a unit root in its inflation differentials is Romania; this result may be due to the features of its inflation series, characterised by outliers and possible structural breaks. However, this limited support for convergence has to be regarded with caution, given the low power that characterises the ADF test. In what follows, I present results derived from a panel framework.

Panel unit root test results

Table 10.3 below reports the results of the IPS t-bar test for each benchmark inflation rate and panel of countries. After calculating the standardised version of this test statistic, its level of significance is determined using critical values drawn from a standard normal distribution.

The null hypothesis of a unit root is rejected for all benchmarks and lag values for four panels: BALTICS, FIRST8, ALL9, FIRST10. However, for the CEFTA and ECEFTA panels, the results are conditional on the selected lag length and benchmark inflation rate. It may be the strong

Table 10.2 Univariate ADF unit root test results

Panel A. Benchmark: Germany

Country	k	ρ	HL	t-stat
CY	1	0.740	2.30	–4.037***
CZ	1	0.980	34.98	–1.195
ES	1	0.981	37.09	–2.319
HU	2	0.994	118.77	–0.704
LA	1	0.980	33.90	–2.336
LI	8	0.981	36.40	–2.221
MA	1	0.810	3.29	–3.331**
PO	5	0.983	41.26	–2.246
RO	1	0.962	17.72	–3.147**
SVK	0	0.938	10.87	–2.235
SVL	1	0.978	31.03	–1.522

Panel B. Benchmark: Euro area

Country	k	ρ	HL	t-stat
CY	1	0.763	0.21	–3.764***
CZ	1	0.981	3.07	–1.239
ES	3	0.975	2.25	–3.483**
HU	2	0.995	11.59	–0.669
LA	1	0.979	2.80	–2.400
LI	8	0.979	2.76	–2.328
MA	1	0.875	0.43	–2.638
PO	6	0.985	3.73	–2.192
RO	5	0.964	1.56	–2.990**
SVK	1	0.934	0.85	–2.473
SVL	1	0.978	2.60	–1.663

Note: k denotes the lag length selected for the ADF specification (determined using the data-driven procedure suggested by Campbell and Perron (1991), with an upper bound of 8, given the short time dimension of the sample), ρ is the speed of convergence, while HL represents the half-life of shocks. The half-lives are expressed in months and indicate how many months it takes for a shock to the inflation differential to dissipate by a half. The auxiliary regression of the ADF test contains a constant as the only deterministic component. Country codes are given in Table 10.1. *** indicates significance at 1%; ** at 5%; * at 10%.

Table 10.3 IPS test results for inflation differentials

Panel A Benchmark: Germany

Lag	CEFTA	ECEFTA	BALTICS	FIRST8 CEECs	ALL 9 CEECs	FIRST10
1	−1.401	−1.692	−3.400***	−2.150***	−2.261***	−2.457***
2	−1.565	−1.894	−3.314***	−2.221***	−2.367***	−2.526***
3	−1.753	−2.050*	−3.733***	−2.496***	−2.608***	−2.671***
4	−1.696	−1.751	−3.795***	−2.483***	−2.432***	−2.671***
5	−1.934	−2.107**	−3.494***	−2.519***	−2.569***	−2.685***
6	−2.089*	−2.221***	−3.610***	−2.659***	−2.684***	−2.796***
7	−2.202**	−2.34***	−4.276***	−2.980***	−2.985***	−3.135***
8	−2.444***	−2.484***	−3.815***	−2.958***	−2.928***	−3.104***

Panel b Benchmark: Euro area average

Lag	CEFTA	ECEFTA	BALTICS	FIRST8 CEECs	ALL9 CEECs	FIRST10
1	−1.47	−1.749	−3.476***	−2.222***	−2.324***	−2.44***
2	−1.637	−1.953	−3.397***	−2.297***	−2.435***	−2.49***
3	−1.797	−2.08**	−3.797***	−2.547***	−2.652***	−2.644***
4	−1.776	−1.818	−3.946***	−2.589***	−2.527***	−2.742***
5	−2.022	−2.183**	−3.593***	−2.611***	−2.653***	−2.712***
6	−2.174*	−2.295***	−3.712***	−2.751***	−2.768***	−2.832***
7	−2.289**	−2.417***	−4.486***	−3.113***	−3.107***	−3.209***
8	−2.547***	−2.57***	−4.002***	−3.093***	−3.047***	−3.179***

Note: *** indicates significance at 1%; ** at 5%; * at 10%.

rejection of non-stationarity for the Baltic States that drives these results, if we look also at the CEFTA and ECEFTA results.

Table 10.4 presents two measures of convergence calculated using the IPS test results: the speed of convergence and the corresponding half-life (HL). The speed of convergence is measured by the convergence coefficient ρ. The closer ρ is to 1, the slower the convergence of the inflation rate to the chosen benchmark. Interpreted in terms of the half-life of shocks, convergence is faster when the value of the half-life is smaller, which implies that the impact of a shock causing a deviation from equilibrium (proxied by the benchmark value) will die out more rapidly. Table 10.4 illustrates that, regardless of the inflation benchmark considered, convergence is faster in the case of the new EU members that had a longer history as fully fledged market economies, Cyprus and Malta. They are followed by Slovakia, Slovenia and two of the Baltic

Table 10.4 The IPS test: Estimates of convergence coefficients and half-lives

Country	ρ(GE)	HL (GE)	ρ(GR)	HL (GR)	ρ (EA)	HL (EA)
CY	0.62	1.45	0.949	13.24	0.64	1.55
CZ	0.967	20.66	0.915	7.8	0.968	21.31
ES	0.962	17.89	0.954	14.72	0.963	18.38
HU	0.991	76.67	0.98	34.31	0.992	86.3
LA	0.949	13.24	0.938	10.83	0.945	12.25
LI	0.981	36.13	0.975	27.38	0.979	32.66
MA	0.755	2.47	0.929	9.41	0.829	3.7
PO	0.977	29.79	0.974	26.31	0.977	29.79
RO	0.962	17.89	0.96	16.98	0.963	18.38
SVK	0.899	6.51	0.926	9.02	0.901	6.65
SVL	0.944	12.03	0.915	7.8	0.946	12.49
Average	ρ (GE)	HL (GE)	ρ (GR)	HL (GR)	ρ (EA)	HL (EA)
CEFTA	0.956	29.13	0.942	17.05	0.957	31.31
ECEFTA	0.957	27.26	0.945	17.04	0.958	29.15
BALTICS	0.964	22.42	0.956	17.64	0.962	21.10
FIRST8	0.959	26.62	0.947	17.27	0.959	27.48
ALL9	0.959	25.65	0.949	17.24	0.959	26.47
FIRST10	0.905	21.68	0.946	16.08	0.914	22.51

Note: ρ denotes the speed of convergence, while HL represents the half-life. The reported values are calculated for a lag of 8 in the specification of the ADF-type maintained regression. The half-lives are reported in months and years (in brackets) and indicate how many months (years) it takes for a shock to the inflation differential to dissipate by a half. Country codes are given in Table 10.1.

States, Latvia and Lithuania. Convergence is definitely slower in the cases of Hungary, Poland, the Czech Republic, Romania and Lithuania.

The second panel of Table 10.4 reports average values of the speed of convergence and half-lives for the six panels examined in this study. They illustrate that when the benchmark inflation is the German one, convergence is fastest for the panel that comprises the new EU members (FIRST10), followed by CEFTA. The Baltic panel is characterised by the slowest convergence. A change in the benchmark value of inflation to the Greek inflation changes the ranking, with CEFTA and ECEFTA panels showing the fastest convergence and the Baltics the slowest. If the benchmark is an average Eurozone inflation rate, then convergence is fastest for the new EU members (FIRST10), followed by CEFTA and

Table 10.5 SURADF test results for inflation differentials with respect to Germany

Panel: ALL 9 CEECs

Country	ρ	HL	t-stat	CV		
				1%	5%	10%
CZ	0.975	27.67	−1.522	−3.772	−3.168	−2.856
ES	0.958	16.19	−4.604***	−3.758	−3.158	−2.856
HU	0.991	76.99	−1.138	−3.804	−3.213	−2.898
LA	0.906	7.00	−3.869**	−3.897	−3.194	−2.877
LI	0.978	31.46	−2.756	−3.748	−3.138	−2.832
PO	0.969	21.99	−4.603***	−4.068	−3.421	−3.095
RO	0.978	31.27	−1.720	−3.763	−3.177	−2.805
SVK	0.935	10.24	−2.304	−3.758	−3.131	−2.807
SVL	0.942	11.58	−3.737**	−3.889	−3.254	−2.925

Note: ρ denotes the speed of convergence, HL the half-life calculated in number of months, t-stat the t-statistic on the lagged value of the inflation differential in the ADF regressions, while CV stands for the critical values. Country codes are given in Table 10.1.

ECEFTA. The panel with the Baltic states is again characterised by the lowest speed of convergence.

In view of the sensitivity of some of the above results to lag length selection, and to look at the inflation convergence performance of each country, it is instructive to conduct a second test, the SURADF, which allows a more flexible approach in terms of lag specification. In the representation of this test, I use different lag structures for each panel member, where the lags are the same as those used in the specification of the univariate ADF test. They are determined, as before, by employing the data-dependent, top-down procedure devised by Campbell and Perron (1991). Table 10.5 displays the findings of the SURADF testing approach when inflation convergence is tested against a German inflation benchmark.[5]

When the benchmark is represented by Germany, convergence in inflation rates occurs consistently for Poland and Slovenia (in five out of six panels) and also for two Baltic economies, Estonia and Latvia (in four out of six panels). In the case of the new EU member states with a tradition as market economies, convergence in inflation rates to the German benchmark occurs for Cyprus, whereas Malta is close to converging. The results indicate that the Slovakia is also close to converging, whereas the Czech Republic, Hungary and Romania do

Table 10.6 SURADF test results for inflation differentials with respect to Greece

Panel: ALL 9 CEECs

Country	ρ	HL	t-stat	CV		
				1%	5%	10%
CZ	0.964	18.72	−1.609	−3.755	−3.257	−2.927
ES	0.955	15.17	−4.075***	−3.870	−3.219	−2.883
HU	0.980	33.68	−1.954	−4.031	−3.394	−3.072
LA	0.875	5.18	−4.388***	−3.947	−3.332	−3.029
LI	0.976	28.96	−2.443	−3.928	−3.343	−3.004
PO	0.964	19.09	−4.265***	−4.198	−3.559	−3.254
RO	0.972	24.49	−2.137	−3.735	−3.094	−2.772
SVK	0.948	13.05	−2.259	−3.799	−3.115	−2.820
SVL	0.933	10.04	−2.978	−4.060	−3.355	−3.007

Note: ρ denotes the speed of convergence, HL the half life calculated in number of months, t-stat the t-statistic on the lagged value of the inflation differential in the ADF regressions, while CV stands for the critical values. Country codes are given in Table 10.1.

not exhibit convergence in any of the panels. Lithuania displays convergence only in the Baltics panel, which shows the greatest degree of homogeneity among all the panels considered in this study, with all three members converging in their inflation rates to the German benchmark. These findings are, in general, in accord with those of Kutan and Yigit (2004).

Table 10.6 illustrates the inflation convergence performance of the countries included in this study when the benchmark economy is represented by Greece, the last country to join the EMU before the CEECs.[6] In comparison with Germany, Greece exhibited higher inflation rates throughout the interval under scrutiny. In various empirical assessments, Greece is generally viewed as a peripheral EMU economy. This being so, the macroeconomic performance of the CEE EMU candidates is often compared to that of Greece.

When the benchmark economy is Greece, convergence in inflation rates occurs consistently for Estonia and Latvia (in all panels that include them). Poland also exhibits convergence, whereas Slovenia is close to converging. Similarly to the case when Germany is selected as benchmark, the Baltic panel displays the highest degree of homogeneity, with all three Baltic states converging. However, when other countries are included, Lithuania ceases to exhibit convergence. The change in benchmark does not alter, in qualitative terms, the

Table 10.7 SURADF test results for inflation differentials with respect to Euro area benchmark

Panel: ALL 9 CEECs

Country	ρ	**HL**	**t-stat**		**CV**	
				1%	**5%**	**10%**
CZ	0.979	32.49	−1.394	−3.759	−3.137	−2.796
ES	0.964	19.05	−4.123***	−3.760	−3.114	−2.801
HU	0.995	129.88	−0.735	−3.715	−3.155	−2.809
LA	0.905	6.97	−3.891**	−3.896	−3.215	−2.900
LI	0.977	30.23	−2.743	−3.806	−3.167	−2.826
PO	0.971	23.76	−4.576***	−3.901	−3.272	−2.951
RO	0.979	32.73	−1.691	−3.745	−3.137	−2.812
SVK	0.941	11.41	−2.116	−3.678	−3.094	−2.753
SVL	0.949	13.19	−3.483**	−3.737	−3.143	−2.804

Note: ρ denotes the speed of convergence, HL the half life calculated in number of months, t-stat the t-statistic on the lagged value of the inflation differential in the ADF regressions, while CV stands for the critical values. Country codes are given in Table 10.1.

results obtained in the cases of the Czech Republic, Hungary and Romania. Slovakia is, in all panels, closer to converging than these three economies. The inflation rates of Cyprus and Malta do not exhibit convergence to the Greek one, which shows that, in their cases, a change in the benchmark matters for the inflation convergence performance.

When a Euro area average inflation rate is considered as the benchmark value, convergence occurs in the cases of Cyprus, Estonia, Latvia, Poland and Slovenia. The results are reported in Table 10.7.[7] The Baltic panel again exhibits the highest degree of homogeneity, in that all three inflation rates converge to the Euro area benchmark. Slovenia converges, albeit at 10 percent. Lithuania is close to convergence. Negative results in terms of convergence are uncovered for the Czech Republic, Hungary, Malta and Romania.

To summarise the results reported so far, the empirical evidence consistently shows that a number of countries, namely Estonia, Latvia and Poland, display inflation convergence regardless of the Euro area inflation benchmark considered. At the other end of the convergence spectrum, the Czech Republic, Hungary and Romania do not exhibit convergence in inflation rates to any of these benchmarks. The evolution of inflation in Romania, with values that peaked several times as a result of several unsuccessful stabilisation attempts and remained in the double-digit range until 2004, may account for its poor performance in terms of inflation convergence. In the cases of the Czech Republic and Hungary, an explanation is more difficult to find. The Czech inflation rates have constantly been below those recorded by Estonia, which displayed a consistent inflation convergence. Therefore, in the light of this argument, an explanation may be sought in the way inflation convergence is defined from the viewpoint of an applied econometrics approach, as a process of reducing differentials. This may be complemented with insights offered by a look at patterns in the evolution of inflation over the sample under scrutiny, which reveals a rather volatile evolution of Czech inflation over the period analysed, with values that have been much below the benchmark in some years and much above them in others. For Hungary, a possible explanation also lies in the inflation patterns during the interval under scrutiny, with several reversions in trend and a rather disappointing inflation performance over the last few years of the sample period. Compared with the other countries considered in this analysis, Lithuania has been an outlier in terms of inflation performance. In spite of this, the results indicate that in a panel that also includes the other two Baltic states, Estonia and Latvia, Lithuania exhibits convergence in terms of inflation to all three benchmarks considered. This may be due to the strong correlations that exist among the three Baltic economies, correlations that have been accounted for by the testing methodology applied in this study.

A fourth benchmark employed in this study is that of the average inflation of the groups considered. The results pertaining to convergence to these benchmarks are presented in Table 10.8.[8]

They illustrate that the strongest convergence occurs in the case of the Baltic states (Estonia, Latvia and Lithuania), which form the most homogeneous panel, a finding that reinforces previous results. At the other extreme are situated the CEFTA and ECEFTA panels, where, with the exception of Poland, the member countries do not converge in their inflation rates to the group average. The panel that comprises the eight CEE economies which joined the EU in May 2004 also evinces a high degree of homogeneity, in that convergence to the group's average inflation occurs for five countries (the Czech Republic, Estonia, Hungary, Poland and the Slovak Republic), whereas the other three (Latvia, Lithuania and Slovenia) are characterised by divergence. This result supports, to some extent, their admittance into the EU as a group. However, one can notice that countries that exhibit convergence to this group's inflation average are, with the exception of Slovakia, those who formed the initial first wave of accession economies. Latvia and Lithuania were originally members of the second wave. Their upgrading to the first wave of accession was decided based on their macroeconomic performance. However, their performance in terms of convergence to the average inflation of the group may suggest that their inflation experiences may have been different from those of the other first-wave CEE economies.

Adding Romania to the group that comprises the other eight former transition countries does not significantly change the results, except for one rather puzzling outcome: convergence in inflation rate to the group's average also occurs in the case of Romania, besides the Czech Republic, Estonia, Hungary and Poland. As it is evident that Romania represents more of an outlier within this group, the impact of its high inflation rates on the group's average may solve the puzzle.

The panel that comprises the ten new EU members is also characterised by homogeneity, with most of its members (the Czech Republic, Estonia, Hungary, Lithuania, Malta, Poland and Slovenia) converging to the group's average inflation. This result tends to support their accession to the EU as a group.

Table 10.8 SURADF test results for inflation differentials with respect to group averages

Panel: ALL 9 CEECs

Country	ρ	HL	t-stat		CV	
				1%	5%	10%
CZ	0.944	11.98	−4.247	−4.041	−3.375	−3.063
ES	0.946	12.48	−3.740	−4.067	−3.488	−3.212
HU	0.932	9.86	−4.828	−3.944	−3.360	−3.063
LA	0.963	18.57	−2.486	−4.014	−3.425	−3.094
LI	0.976	28.24	−2.564	−4.046	−3.474	−3.159
PO	0.934	10.12	−3.152	−3.885	−3.284	−2.991
RO	0.961	17.21	−5.345	−5.606	−5.075	−4.727
SVK	0.966	19.82	−3.229	−4.206	−3.585	−3.271
SVL	0.972	23.99	−2.928	−4.005	−3.437	−3.158

Note: ρ denotes the speed of convergence, HL the half life calculated in number of months, t-stat the t-statistic on the lagged value of the inflation differential in the ADF regressions, while CV stands for the critical values. Country codes are given in Table 10.1.

The case for non-linear inflation convergence

In what follows, to complement the results reported on so far, I will add a new dimension to the empirical analysis performed in this study by investigating the potential presence of non-linear features in the inflation convergence process. A non-linear adjustment is characterised by changes in the speed of convergence. Panel unit root techniques, which belong to the family of linear modelling frameworks, cannot account for this feature. In the applied econometrics literature, non-linear representations have mainly been used to illustrate the dynamic adjustment of the real exchange rates to equilibrium or the dynamics of macroeconomic variables over the business cycle. However, their main features make them suitable for assessing potential changes in the speed of inflation convergence.

In designing a modelling framework, which considers not only a linear adjustment but also a non-linear one, I build on a remark made by Beck and Weber (2005), who, using regional data, investigate the dynamics of inflation convergence in the Eurozone before and after the introduction of the single currency. They apply the panel unit root test developed by Levin and Lin (1992, 1993) and find evidence in support of mean reversion (β-convergence) in inflation rates for both sub-samples. The estimated convergence speed (common for all panel units) indicates a large value for the half-life of shocks. Moreover, the results show that the speed of convergence has decreased since the introduction of a common monetary policy. These findings motivate Beck and Weber (op.cit.) to discuss the possibility of a process with non-linear features that would accurately describe the documented change in the speed of convergence. However, they do not proceed any further to formally test for the presence of non-linearities in the dynamics of convergence.

Intuitively, a non-linear adjustment makes sense if one considers the EU accession, in May 2004, of the economies considered in this study. Non-linearities may have been induced by policy actions, when more effective disinflationary measures have been implemented by the CEE monetary authorities to ensure compliance with EU benchmarks. Such policy interventions are likely to increase the speed of convergence, as their main objective is to bring inflation down when it surpasses a certain threshold. Moreover, the non-linear adjustment induced by policy actions may also be characterised by asymmetry, as policymakers are more concerned about increases in inflation than declines. Furthermore, as suggested by Killian and Taylor (2001) for the case of exchange rates, the heterogeneity of economic agents' beliefs and expectations could induce non-linearity. A similar argument may apply also to inflation rates, given the crucial role played by inflation expectations, especially in the case of the former European transition economies. The potential for non-linear convergence of CEE countries' inflation rates towards EU benchmarks is examined here in an attempt to shed more light on the results delivered by linear modelling frameworks used so far in this chapter.

The investigation of non-linear features in the inflation convergence of the case study countries considered here is carried out for the inflation differentials calculated with respect to Germany. This choice is motivated by the arguments in favour of non-linearity presented above, which suggest that German inflation is more likely to be viewed as a benchmark by the monetary authorities of the countries that aspire to become EMU members.

To examine the presence of non-linearities, I apply a battery of linearity tests, developed by Luukkonen et al. (1988), Teräsvirta (1994) and Escribano and Jorda (1998, 2001). These tests are conducted to investigate a potential non-linear adjustment of a Smooth Transition Auto Regressive (STAR) type. A linear specification, similar to those used by the univariate and panel unit root tests carried out in this chapter, is assessed against the alternative of STAR-type non-linearity. To avoid a spurious finding of non-linearity that may be due to the presence of outliers (quite likely to exist, given the inflation experiences of the CEE economies), I perform both the standard and the outlier-robust versions of these tests. For a thorough investigation, heteroskedasticity-robust linearity tests are also conducted.[9]

Table 10.9 summarises the results of the battery of linearity tests by indicating the STAR specification that is most likely to characterise the convergence of CEE countries' inflation rates to the German benchmark if non-linear features are present in the adjustment process. Moreover, the table sheds light on the type of adjustment: asymmetric, if a Logistic STAR (LSTAR) specification is suggested as most likely by the linearity tests, or symmetric, if an Exponential STAR (ESTAR) may represent a more adequate representation.

The results of the battery of linearity tests conducted provide evidence in support of a non-linear convergence in inflation rates for eight out of the eleven countries included in the sample under scrutiny. Exceptions are the Czech Republic, Poland and Slovakia. In analysing the outcome of these tests, I place more emphasis on their outlier-robust versions, given the patterns in the evolution of inflation rates in CEE countries

Table 10.9 Non-linear STAR models for inflation convergence

Inflation rate	Potential non-linear specification
Cyprus	ESTAR (4)
Czech Republic	Linear model
Estonia	ESTAR (12)
Hungary	LSTAR (9)
Latvia	LSTAR (1)
Lithuania	ESTAR (6)
Malta	LSTAR (4)
Poland	Linear model
Romania	LSTAR (9)
Slovakia	Linear model
Slovenia	ESTAR (7)

Note: the numbers in brackets correspond to the delay parameter, which characterises the most likely non-linear convergence model.

over the interval 1993–2004. An asymmetric, LSTAR-type non-linear adjustment may provide an adequate description of the inflation convergence process in the cases of Hungary, Latvia, Malta and Romania. ESTAR models are suitable for Cyprus, Estonia, Lithuania, Romania and Slovenia. In the case of Hungary, the outcome of the linearity tests may explain why convergence was not unveiled by the univariate and panel unit root tests that adopted a linear specification. Furthermore, the case of Romania highlights the importance of performing outlier-robust linearity tests in order to avoid a spurious finding of non-linearity. In terms of inflation experience, among the countries considered in this analysis, Romania stands out with high and volatile inflation rates. However, the outlier-robust linearity tests performed here suggest that there is potential for non-linear convergence in the case of the Romanian inflation rate.

10.5 The inflation convergence record: A look at potential explanatory factors

The main finding of the empirical analysis performed above is that convergence in inflation rates of CEE countries to EU benchmarks occurs only in a limited number of cases. Moreover, the results are country-specific and benchmark-specific. An interpretation of the whole picture is difficult. This is not surprising, given the inflation experiences of the CEE economies during the period 1993–2004. Whereas the established market economies of Cyprus and Malta make better candidates for convergence, the former transition economies of CEE offer a rather mixed picture. To explain the results, I evaluate a number of factors that may exert an impact on the convergence process.

First, the experience of current EMU members provides a very useful arena for examining the factors that underlie inflation convergence. In particular, the experience of the peripheral countries may help in drawing lessons for the CEE countries that aspire to join the monetary union.

In recent European economic history, two landmarks stand out. The first corresponds to the establishment of the EMS in 1979, with the intention of stabilising exchange rate volatility among members. The second marks the adoption of a single currency and the introduction of a common monetary policy, in 1999, marking the last stage in the creation of the economic and monetary union.

The prospect of introducing a single currency within the EU has required monetary decisions taken by the member states to be synchronised. This has provided the impetus for a regulatory framework to be established, which ranged from the EMS of 1979, with its own exchange rate mechanism (ERM I), to the Maastricht Treaty of 1992. Among other nominal convergence criteria, the Maastricht Treaty has defined explicit convergence goals for inflation rates. However, after the commencement of the Euro, a proliferating inflation divergence has been documented and significant cross-country differences have emerged. A large body of studies has addressed this topic, trying to shed light on the nature of the observed divergence (short or long lasting) and the factors that caused it. To explain this change in trend, it has been emphasised that inflation rates experienced a firm decrease as countries tried to comply with the Maastricht inflation criterion. After that, the inception of a single monetary policy generated divergence in inflation rates, as a one-size policy could not fit all experiences. If one looks at the developments discussed above in the light of the EMU accession of the new EU Member States, then more divergence can be expected to occur, as these countries will contribute to an increase in the already existing heterogeneity among member states.

Second, within the confines of the EMU, increased goods market integration and greater price transparency, generated by the Internal Market Programme and, ultimately, by the introduction of a single currency, aimed at stimulating price convergence. However, as documented by Maier and Cavelaars (2003), Euro area countries have adopted a common currency but are still characterised by different price levels for similar products. The large body of literature that focuses on testing the validity of PPP offers an explanation for this, showing that price levels between countries tend to equalise, but the adjustment process is very slow[10] (see, e.g., Froot & Rogoff, 1995).

Within a monetary union, if prices expressed in a common currency reveal initial differences across countries, then convergence to a similar level entails higher inflation in countries with lower prices. Therefore, price level convergence, also labelled 'inflation catching-up' may hinder the inflation convergence process by generating cross-country differences in inflation rates (Rogers et al., 2001; Rogers, 2002).

The differences in price levels between the Euro area and the countries that aspire to join it are more pronounced than price differentials within the Euro area. This suggests that the phenomenon of price convergence may constitute an important source of inflation differentials between current EMU members and aspiring countries.

Third, an important aspect of the price convergence process concerns adjustments in the area of non-tradable goods prices. The well-known Balassa Samuelson (BS) effect is often put forward in attempts to explain why prices of non-tradable goods might increase faster in poorer members of a monetary union, therefore generating inflation differentials with respect to richer members. The process of economic integration witnessed by CEE countries has created pressure for a Europe-wide convergence of productivity levels in the tradable goods sector. In addition, productivity levels in the non-tradable goods sector have converged at a much slower rate. Therefore, productivity increases in the tradable goods sector have outpaced those in the non-tradables sector. As a result of wage equalisation (an important assumption of the BS effect), the rise in wages in the tradables sector has determined an increase in wages, and hence prices, in the non-tradables sector of CEECs, compared to the 'old' EU members. The rise in inflation that has occurred due to high non-tradable goods inflation explains, partly, the divergence in inflation between CEE countries and 'old' EU members.

Fourth, the features of the monetary regime pursued by a country may be relevant for the inflation convergence process. This conjecture stems from the main tenet of the monetarist paradigm, which, in the words of Milton Friedman, holds that 'inflation is always and everywhere a monetary phenomenon'.

A fifth aspect that may shed some light on the inflation convergence performance of EMU accession countries is the design of fiscal policy. Kutan and Yigit (2004) argue that when CPI is used to calculate inflation rates, the stance of fiscal policy becomes relevant to interpreting inflation convergence results, since the CPI accounts for fiscal shocks.

10.6 Concluding remarks

In this chapter I reported on a comprehensive econometric assessment of inflation convergence of CEE countries towards EU benchmarks and their group averages. After gaining the status of fully fledged market economies, these countries have been accepted as members of the EU and intend eventually to subscribe to EMU, legitimating an assessment of their inflation performance. However, their participation in the monetary union is conditional upon complying with a strict inflation criterion. To meet this criterion, the CEE countries have striven to build the appropriate institutions and implement consistent, sound and coordinated monetary and fiscal policies. Containing inflation and maintaining price stability has become increasingly important for these countries. In this context, the convergence of inflation becomes a topic of key importance.

The results reported in this chapter suggest that, while convergence can be revealed in a number of cases, there is some sensitivity associated with the testing framework, in particular whether time series or panel methods are used. Furthermore, the inflation convergence performance of the CEE countries is conditional on the chosen inflation benchmark, the composition of the panel and the correlations among members. The highest degree of homogeneity was recorded for the panel comprising the three Baltic states. Poland and Slovenia were the other CEE countries with a good performance in terms of inflation convergence.

To complement the results derived from univariate and panel unit root tests, I have conducted a set of linearity tests on the inflation differentials with respect to Germany, chosen to represent the EMU core. In this regard, the analysis performed in this chapter was characterised by an element of novelty, compared with other existing studies. While accounting for the interplay between linearity and outliers, the findings of the linearity tests highlighted a potential non-linear convergence process in all but one case, which may have been induced not only by policy interventions, but also by heterogeneity of inflation expectations among economic agents. This finding opens an interesting line of enquiry, suggesting that the process of inflation convergence in the CEE countries is characterised by non-linear features, which cannot be captured by standard linear models. The results reported here suggest that non-linear convergence, which allows for more flexibility in comparison to linear specifications, is almost ubiquitous. Therefore, an accurate representation of the convergence process of the CEE economies towards EMU norms needs to accommodate the presence of nonlinear features.

Notes

1. Since monthly observations on consumer prices are used, annualisation is congruent with deseasonalisation.
2. CEFTA represents the acronym for the Central European Free Trade Agreement, signed by former Czechoslovakia, Hungary and Poland on 21 December 1992. On 1 March 1993, CEFTA went into effect. On 1 January 1996, Slovenia joined CEFTA as a full member. On 1 July 1997, Romania also joined CEFTA.
3. I adopt this terminology in order to distinguish between the first wave of new member states, which entered the EU on 1 May 2004 (Cyprus, the Czech Republic, Estonia, Hungary, Latvia, Lithuania, Malta, Poland, the Slovakia and Slovenia), and the second wave, which comprises Bulgaria and Romania.
4. Proxied, as mentioned above, by the benchmark value of inflation.
5. For brevity, we report here only the results for the panel that comprises the nine 'new' EU members CEE (*ALL 9 CEECs*). The complete set of results can be found at http://www.lums.lancs.ac.uk/publications/viewpdf/005221/.
6. For brevity, we report here only the results for the panel that comprises the nine 'new' EU members CEE (*ALL 9 CEECs*). The complete set of results can be found at http://www.lums.lancs.ac.uk/publications/viewpdf/005221/.
7. For brevity, we report here only the results for the panel that comprises the nine 'new' EU members CEE (*ALL 9 CEECs*). The complete set of results can be found at http://www.lums.lancs.ac.uk/publications/viewpdf/005221/.
8. For brevity, we report here only the results for the panel that comprises the nine 'new' EU members CEE (*ALL 9 CEECs*). The complete set of results can be found at http://www.lums.lancs.ac.uk/publications/viewpdf/005221/.
9. For brevity, the detailed results of the sequence of linearity tests performed are not reported here. They can be found at http://www.lums.lancs.ac.uk/publications/viewpdf/005221/.
10. Price differences between countries tend to equalise where these differences reflect certain costs.

References

Amian, C. G., and A. M. Zumaquero (2002), 'Complete or partial inflation convergence in the EU?' Working Paper No.9, Centro de Estudios Andaluces, Sevilla.

Barro, R. J. (1991), 'Economic Growth in a Cross Section of Countries', *The Quarterly Journal of Economics*, 106, 407–43.

Barro, R. J., and X. Sala-i-Martin (1991), 'Convergence Across States and Regions', *Brookings Papers on Economic Activity*, 1, 107–58.

Barro, R. J., and X. Sala-i-Martin (1992), 'Convergence', *Journal of Political Economy*, 100, 223–51.

Baumol, W. (1986), 'Productivity Growth, Convergence, and Welfare: What the Long-Run Data Show', *American Economic Review*, 76, 1072–85.

Beck, G. W., and A. A. Weber (2005), 'Price Stability, Inflation Convergence and Diversity in EMU: Does One Size Fit All?' CFS Working Paper No. 30, Center for Financial Studies, Frankfurt.

Ben-David, D. (1996), 'Trade and Convergence among Countries', *Journal of International Economics*, 40, 279–98.

Bernard, A. B., and S. N. Durlauf (1995), 'Convergence in International Output', *Journal of Applied Econometrics*, 10, 97–108.

Bernard, A. B., and S. N. Durlauf (1996), 'Interpreting Tests of the Convergence Hypothesis', *Journal of Econometrics*, 71, 161–73.

Brada, J. C., Kutan, A. M., and S. Zhou (2002), 'Real and Monetary Convergence within the European Union and between the European Union and Candidate Countries: A Rolling Cointegration Approach', Working Paper No. 548, William Davidson Institute, University of Michigan Stephen M. Ross Business School.

Brada, J. C., and A. M. Kutan (2001), 'The Convergence of Monetary Policy between Candidate Countries and the European Union', Working Paper No. 7, Centre for European Integration Studies, Bonn University.

Brada, J. C., and A. M. Kutan, (2002), 'Balkan and Mediterranean Candidates for European Union membership: The Convergence of their Monetary Policy with that of the European Central Bank', Working Paper No. 456, William Davidson Institute, University of Michigan Stephen M. Ross Business School.

Breuer, J. B., McNown, R., and M. Wallace (2002), 'Series Specific Unit Root Tests with Panel Data', *Oxford Bulletin of Economics and Statistics*, 64, 527–46.

Busetti, F., Forni, L., Harvey, A., and F. Venditti (2006), 'Inflation Convergence and Divergence within the European Monetary Union', working Paper No. 574, European Central Bank, Frankfurt.

Campbell, J. Y., and P. Perron (1991), 'Pitfalls and Opportunities: What Macroeconomists should Know about Unit Roots', Technical Working Paper No. 100, National Bureau of Economic Research, Cambridge, MA.

Caporale, G. M., and N. Pittis (1993), 'Common Stochastic Trends and Inflation Convergence in the EMS', *Weltwirtschaftliches Archiv*, 129, 207–15.

Carlino, G. A., and L. Mills (1993), 'Are US Regional Incomes Converging? A Time Series Analysis', *Journal of Monetary Economics*, 32, 335–46.

Durlauf, S., and D. Quah (1999), 'The New Empirics of Economic Growth', *Econometrica*, 71, 1269–86.

Escribano, A., and O. Jordá (1998), 'Improved Testing and Specification of Smooth Transition Regression Models', in P. Rothman (ed.) *Dynamic Modeling and Econometrics in Economics and Finance, vol.1: Nonlinear Time Series Analysis of Economic and Financial Data*, Boston: Kluwer Academic Press, 289–319.

Escribano, A., and O. Jordá (2001), 'Decision Rules for Selecting between Exponential and Logistic STAR', *Spanish Economic Review*, 3, 193–210.

Evans, P., and G. Karras (1996), 'Convergence Revisited', *Journal of Monetary Economics*, 37, 249–65.

Froot, K. A. and K. S. Rogoff (1995), 'Perspective on PPP and Long-Run Real Exchange Rates', in G. Grossman, and K. Rogoff (eds), *Handbook of International Economics*, Vol. 3, 1647–88, Elsevier, Amsterdam.

Granger, C. W. J., and T. Teräsvirta (1993), *Modelling Nonlinear Economic Relationships*, Oxford: Oxford University Press.

Hafer, R. W., Kutan, A. M., and S. Zhou (1997), 'Linkage in EMS Term Structures: Evidence from Common Trend and Transitory Components', *Journal of International Money and Finance*, 16, 595–607.

Hall, S., Robertson, D., and M. Wickens (1992), 'Measuring Convergence of the EC Economies', *The Manchester School*, 60, 99–111.

Hansen, B. E. (1996), 'Inference when a Nuisance Parameter is not Identified under the Null Hypothesis', *Econometrica*, 64, 413–30.

Harvey, A. C., and D. Bates (2003), 'Multivariate Unit Root Tests and Testing for Convergence', Working Paper No.1, Department of Applied Economics, University of Cambridge.

Holmes, M. J. (1998), 'Inflation Convergence in the ERM: Evidence for Manufacturing and Services', *International Economic Journal*, 12, 1–16.

Im, K. S., Hasem Pesaran, M., and Y. Shin (1997), 'Testing for Unit Roots in Heterogeneous Panels', Working Paper, Department of Applied Economics, University of Cambridge.

Im, K. S., Pesaran, M. H., and Y. Shin (2003), 'Testing for Unit Roots in Heterogeneous Panels', *Journal of Econometrics*, 115, 53–74.

Karfakis, C. J., and D. M. Moschos (1990), 'Interest Rate Linkages within the European Monetary System: A Time Series Analysis,' *Journal of Money, Credit and Banking*, 22, 388–94.

Killian, L., and M. P. Taylor (2003), 'Why is it so Difficult to Beat the Random Walk for Exchange Rates?' *Journal of International Economics*, 60, 85–107.

Kirchgassner, G., and J. Wolters (1993), 'Does the DM Dominate the Euro Market? An Empirical Investigation', *Review of Economics and Statistics*, 75, 773–8.

Kočenda, E. (2001), 'Macroeconomic Convergence in Transition Countries', *Journal of Comparative Economics*, 29, 1–23.

Kočenda, E., and D. H. Papell (1997), 'Inflation Convergence within the European Union: A Panel Data Analysis', *International Journal of Finance and Economics*, 2, 189–98.

Kočenda, E., Kutan, A. M., and T. M. Yigit (2006), 'Pilgrims to the Eurozone: How Far, How Fast?' Economic Systems, 30, 311–27.

Koedijk, K. G., and J. M. C. Kool (1992), 'Dominant Interest and Inflation Differentials within the EMS', *European Economic Review*, 36, 925–43.

Kutan, A. M. (1991), 'German Dominance in the European Monetary System: Evidence from Money Supply Growth Rates', *Open Economies Review*, 2, 285–94.

Kutan, A. M., and T. M. Yigit (2002), 'Nominal and Real Stochastic Convergence within the Transition Economies and the European Monetary Union: Evidence from Panel Data', Working Paper No.6, Emergent Markets Group, Cass Business School, London.

Kutan, A. M., and T. M. Yigit (2004), 'Nominal and Real Stochastic Convergence of Transition Economies', *Journal of Comparative Economics*, 32, 23–36.

Levin, A., and C. Lin (1992), 'Unit Root Tests in Panel Data: Asymptotic and Finite-Sample Properties', Discussion Paper No. 23, University of California at San Diego.

Levin, A., and C. Lin (1993), 'Unit Root Tests in Panel Data: New Results', Discussion Paper No. 56, University of California at San Diego.

Luukkonen, R., Saikkonen, P., and T. Teräsvirta (1988), 'Testing Linearity against Smooth Transition Models', *Biometrika*, 75, 491–9.

MacDonald, R., and M. P. Taylor (1991), 'Exchange Rates, Policy Convergence, and the European Monetary System', *The Review of Economics and Statistics*, 73, 553–8.

Maddala, G. S., and S. Wu (1999), 'A Comparative Study of Unit Root Tests with Panel Data and a New Simple Test', *Oxford Bulletin of Economics and Statistics*, 61, 631–52.

Maier, P., and P. Cavelaars (2003), 'EMU Enlargement and Convergence of Price Levels: Lessons from the German Reunification', Working Paper No. 6, Monetary and Economic Policy Department, Netherlands Central Bank, Amsterdam.

Mentz, M. and S. P. Sebastian (2003), 'Inflation Convergence after the Introduction of the Euro', Working Paper No. 30, Center for Financial Studies, Frankfurt.

Müller, U. K., and G. Elliott (2003), 'Tests for Unit Roots and the Initial Condition', *Econometrica*, 71, 1269–86.

Oxley, L., and D. Greasley (1997), 'Time-Series Based Tests of the Convergence Hypothesis: Some Positive Results', *Economics Letters*, 56, 143–7.

J. Rangvid, and C. Sorensen (2002), 'Convergence in the ERM and Declining Numbers of Common Stochastic Trends', *Journal of Emerging Market Finance*, 1, 183–213.

Rogers, J. H. (2002), 'Monetary Union, Price Level Convergence and Inflation: How Close is Europe to the United States?', International Finance Discussion Paper No. 740, Board of Governors of the Federal Reserve System, Washington.

Rogers, J. H., Hufbauer, G. C., and E. Wada (2001), 'Price Level Convergence and Inflation in Europe', Working Paper No. 1, Institute for International Economics, Washington.

Saikkonen, P., and R. Luukkonen (1988), 'Lagrange Multiplier Tests for Testing Non-Linearities in Time Series Models', *Scandinavian Journal of Statistics*, 15, 55–68.

Siklos, P., and M. E. Wohar (1997), 'Convergence in Interest Rates and Inflation Rates Across Countries and Over Time', *Review of International Economics*, 5, 129–41.

Strauss, J., and T. M. Yigit (2003), 'Shortfalls of Panel Unit Root Testing' *Economics Letters*, 81, 309–13.

Taylor, M. P., and L. Sarno (1998), 'The Behaviour of Real Exchange Rates during the Post-BrettonWoods Period', *Journal of International Economics*, 46, 281–312.

Teräsvirta, T. (1994), 'Specification, Estimation and Evaluation of Smooth Transition Autoregressive Models', *Journal of the American Statistical Association*, 89, 208–18.

Thom, R. (1995), 'Inflation Convergence in the EMS: Some Additional Evidence. A Comment', *Review of International Economics*, 131, 577–86.

Von Hagen, J., and M. Fratianni (1990), 'German Dominance in the EMS: Evidence from Interest Rates', *Journal of International Money and Finance*, 9, 358–75.

Westbrook, J. A. (1998), 'Monetary Integration, Inflation Convergence and Output Shocks in the European Monetary System', *Economic Inquiry*, 36, 138–44.

11

Persistent Differential Inflation Rates in the New Euro Member Countries: The Phillips Curve before and after Adopting the Euro

Marjan Senjur

11.1 Introduction

The 2002 introduction of euro notes and coins (the so-called cash changeover) in 12 Euro Monetary Union (EMU) member countries did not cause inflationary pressure (Angelini and Lippi, 2007). There was also a second wave of euro-adopting countries during 2007–9. Was the introduction of the euro also non-inflationary this second time? Why does this question arise? While preparing to adopt the euro in 2005 and 2006 Slovenia had an inflation rate of 2.5 per cent. In 2007, after it had adopted the euro, the inflation rate had jumped to an average annual level of 3.6 per cent, rising further to 5.7 per cent in 2008. Both policymakers and researchers failed to foresee the rise in the inflation rate as a result of the country's adopting the euro (Weyerstrass, 2008; Weyerstrass and Neck, 2007). The data indicate that Slovenia has had significantly higher differential inflation, for example, a higher national inflation rate, in comparison to the euro area, ever since 1997. How can we explain the higher differential inflation before and after the country introduced the euro?

We may assume that the EMU consists of two groups of countries: big 'core' (developed) countries and small 'periphery' (middle developed) countries. The 'periphery' is those catching-up countries with high-trend productivity growth rates. Their growth is driven by investment and export. The productivity growth path in each individual country determines member countries' real equilibrium long-term interest rates. The long-term equilibrium real interest rate for catching-up countries is above the average in the euro zone. In the euro area the real long-term interest rate therefore differs across member countries. The nominal interest rate is, in turn, equal for all member countries. Common monetary policy is therefore a one of a low interest rate for a catching-up country. After adoption of the euro, a catching-up country faces a low interest rate monetary policy. We shall assume that the investment is a function of the real interest rate, r, and expected income, Y^e.

$$I = I(r, Y^e)$$

Further on we shall assume that a national real interest rate is a function of the national inflation rate, π, by a given common nominal interest rate, i.

$$r = r(\pi).$$

The higher the inflation rate, the lower is the real interest rate by given nominal interest rate.

The interest rate may be low for middle developed country adopting euro for two reasons: one is due to higher growth rate, the other is the higher inflation rate. The consequence for common monetary policy is accentuated by the differential inflation. As we shall argue later in this article, the middle developed countries in the euro area may have higher differential inflation. Such higher inflation reduces the real interest rate by a given nominal interest rate.

As a result, a boom–bust cycle may develop in the catching-up countries. In the boom phase, households borrow in the credit market to smooth consumption. The output gap ($Y - Y^*$) is closing, employment and wages rise, and the markup is squeezed. Firms will eventually start raising prices in order to protect their markups. The pressure for additional inflation mounts, until eventually it rises. The real interest rate in the catching-up country falls. The gap between the actual real interest rate and the common nominal interest rate (and the implied average real interest rate in the euro area) widens further. One would expect an increase in asset price inflation that would fuel a boom through the wealth effect. Then the demand pressure would spill over into a negative current account balance. And there would be accelerated economic growth due to demand pressure.

The boom may be followed by a bust phase in the euro-adopting, catching-up country. Lending expansion based on overly bullish expectations about future income may eventually become unsustainable. The debt-to-GDP ratio may increase and the current account position may deteriorate. These may lead to an increase in the cost of debt servicing. An eventual rise in prices and the comparative price level would be needed in order to restore macroeconomic equilibrium. The price competitiveness would dissipate and the slow-down of GDP growth may be a consequence.

Such a scenario may be relevant in the EMU, where monetary policy cannot respond to a credit boom in a catching-up country. Adopting the euro is not an economically neutral act (Eichengreen, 2002; Wyplosz, 2006). The basic macroeconomic model changes, since the national economic policy loses its grasp on monetary policy. The core inflation rate, interest rate, and nominal exchange rate are determined for the whole euro area. The macroeconomic model for an individual member country in the euro area is no longer a closed system. This has important macroeconomic repercussions: a national economy cannot control its nominal interest rate or its inflation rate in the framework of the national macroeconomic model any more. Initial experiences after adopting the euro show that this could be a real problem and not just a hypothetical one. In the EMU, monetary policy cannot respond to a credit boom in an individual catching-up country. If the credit boom is not properly kept in check by relevant policies, the situation could leads, through increased aggregate demand, to greater inflation pressure, asset price inflation and unsustainable current account deficits, and such a situation may become unsustainable for a new euro-adopting country (MacDonald and Wójcik, 2008: pp. 12–13). Stability is not built into the model; the model is essentially unstable. Part of the explanation for Slovenian inflation, seen after it adopted the euro, lies in the overheating of aggregate demand due to the new macroeconomic conditions for a middle developed country that has just joined the EMU.[1]

The other part of the explanation will be presented in this chapter when analysing the inflation process by exploring the Phillips curve and the natural rate of unemployment before and after joining the euro. The assumption is that the inflation process in a national economy changes after it adopts the euro. By using the Phillips curve, one can analyse the inflation process before the euro was adopted. Empirical evidence is, of course, weak due to the short time periods involved. However, on the basis of analytical considerations and empirical evidence some conjectures can be made about the changed inflation process in a country (such as Slovenia) after it adopts the euro. It is expected that the Phillips curve will have to be modified, since differential inflation is a new adjustment mechanism for middle-income countries. However, higher inflation may have detrimental effects on demand-driven, catching-up growth (McCombie and Thirwall, 1994).

Inflation differentials has been the subject of recent economic literature (MacDonald and Wojcik, 2008; Angeloni, Aucremanne and Ciccarelli, 2006; Balasz, Ritzberger-Gruenwald and Antoniette Silgoner, 2004; Hammermann and Flanagan, 2009). The approach of this chapter differs because it deals with inflation by using the concept of the Phillips curve. A similar approach was adopted in the working paper of Borio and Filardo (2007).

This chapter is structured so that, after the introduction in the first section, section 11.2 presents the Phillips curve before the euro was adopted in Slovenia. Section 11.3 deals with comparative price levels in the European single market and with the Phillips curve after adopting the euro. Section 11.4 deals with the Balassa effect and the Phillips curve of a differential inflation rate. Section 11.5 considers the Samuelson effect and managed differential inflation. Some policy considerations are presented in the section 11.6. Conclusions are given in section 11.7.

11.2 The Phillips curve before adopting the euro

A conventional Phillips curve (Ball and Mankiw, 2002) has the following form:

$$\pi = \pi^e + \lambda\ (u - u^*) \qquad (1)$$

Taking into account an adaptive expectation, the Phillips curve takes the form:

$$\pi = \pi_{-1} + \lambda\ (u - u^*) \qquad (2)$$

u^* is the so-called NAIRU, the non-accelerating inflation rate of unemployment, or natural rate of unemployment (NRU).

With a linear regression we shall estimate the following equation:

$$\Delta\pi = B - b \cdot u \qquad (3)$$

B is equal to $b \cdot u^*$. Let us assume that u^* is a constant. In such a case we derive u^*. u^* is that rate of unemployment which keeps the inflation rate unchanged: $\Delta\pi = 0$. The constant $B = b \cdot u^*$ we divide by b, B/b, and we obtain the natural rate of unemployment. This is a derivation done in the simplest fashion (Gordon, 1997).

Staiger, Stock and Watson (1997) extended the basic Phillips curve with control variable (X_t) which is supposed to reflect shocks in supply:

$$\Delta\pi_t = b(u_{t-1} - u^*) + c \cdot X_t + v_t$$
$$\Delta\pi_t = B_2 + b \cdot u_{t-1} + c \cdot X_t + v_t \quad (4)$$

Taking into account the control variable, the Phillips curve might take the following form:

$$\pi = \pi_1 + \lambda (u - u^*) + b \text{ gNEER}. \quad (5)$$

The growth of the nominal effective exchange rate (gNEER) is an instrumental variable of economic policy to manage the real exchange rate (RER) in order to keep the export competitiveness of the economy and sustain a high growth rate.

Based on yearly data for Slovenia in the 1993–2006 period, the regression (with *t* statistics in parentheses) of (3) is as follows:

$$\text{DgCPI} = \underset{(2.44)}{194.60} - \underset{(-2.64)}{29.03} \text{ UR} \qquad R^2 = 0.37 \quad (6)$$

where UR is the registered unemployment rate; DgCPI is the delta of the rate of growth of the consumer price index.

The results are statistically satisfactory. A natural rate of unemployment might be calculated from these results:

NRU is $u^* = 194.6/29.03 = 6.7$.

This is a sensible result.

The regression (with *t* statistics in parentheses) of (5) is as follows:

$$\text{CPI} = \underset{(1.00)}{85.90} - \underset{(-0.92)}{11.50} \text{ UR} + \underset{(2.19)}{3.88} \text{ gNEER} \qquad R^2 = 0.56 \quad (7)$$

where DgCPI is the delta of the growth rate of the consumer price index, UR is the unemployment rate, gNEER is the growth rate of the nominal effective exchange rate of the Slovenian currency, the tolar.

The estimates show that the specification of the equation might be good, the signs of parameters are as expected, whereas the statistical significance is not the best. Having $B = 85.9$ and $\lambda = 11.5$, the NAIRU would be $u^* = 7.5$ per cent. The estimated NRU is relatively high. The control variable, or a policy of a nominal exchange rate, has been increasing the NAIRU. The policy of a NEER compensated for a higher inflation rate and consequently it kept the NAIRU high too.

Since adoption of the euro, the inflation process has changed. We may therefore assume that the Phillips curve has also changed. For a national economy, which is part of the euro area, the Philips curve which is defined on the grounds of a non-accelerating inflation rate, $\pi - \pi_{-1} = 0$ will have new terms in the equation. We shall elaborate on which ones. On the other hand, in the new conditions the Phillips curve should be redefined in terms of differential inflation, that is, in terms of the difference of national inflation in comparison with average euro-area inflation: $\pi - \pi^{eu}$. In the next sections we shall elaborate on in which direction the inflation process has changed since the euro was adopted in a small middle-income country.

11.3 Price levels and the Phillips curve after adopting the euro

11.3.1 The law of one price and comparative price levels in a heterogeneous monetary union

We assume that in the framework of the European Single Market (ESM) there is a tendency towards the Law of One Price (LOP). LOP holds that the price of internationally traded goods should be the same anywhere in the world once that price is expressed in a common currency. Purchasing power parity (PPP) holds that the nominal exchange rate between two countries should be equal to the ratio of aggregate price levels between countries. A unit of currency in one country should have the same purchasing power in a foreign country. If the same goods enter each country's market basket used to construct the aggregate price level, then LOP implies that a PPP exchange rate should hold between the countries concerned (Taylor and Taylor, 2004).

The LOP states that for any good *i* the following rule holds:

$$P_i = eP^*_i, \quad \text{and} \quad e = P_i \,/\, P^*_i \tag{8}$$

where P_i is the domestic-currency price of good *i*, P^*_i is the foreign-currency price of good *i*, and *e* is the exchange rate, defined as the home-currency price of foreign currency. LOP states that once prices are converted to a common currency, the same good should sell for the same price in different countries (Rogoff, 1996).

A bilateral PPP exchange rate represents the hypothetical exchange rate that would be necessary to equalise price levels between two countries. The annual comparative price level (CPL) indices are computed as a ratio of the respective PPP exchange rate over the annual average of the respected nominal exchange rate, *e*, for country *i*:

$$CPL_{i/EU} = PPP_{i/EU} / e_{i/EU} \tag{9}$$

The CPL series can be used to test whether PPP holds, in which case the CPL equals 1 or 100. Thus, the deviation of a country's CPL index from the EU average (that equals 100) provides information about the price level of that country relative to the EU (Allington, Kattuman and Waldmann, 2005).

Movements in the CPL index depend on movements of the PPP and of the nominal exchange rate. The CPL series is dominated by changes in the nominal exchange rate which is much more volatile and amenable than the PPP. Price convergence can be achieved by changes in PPP and/or in the nominal exchange rate. Such is the case in a country before it joins the euro area.

For member countries of the euro area with a single currency ($e_{i/EU} = 1$) the comparative price level of an individual member country reflects the comparative purchasing power of that country:

$$CPL_{i/EU} = PPP_{i/EU} \tag{10}$$

In ideal conditions, the purchasing power of the euro should be equal in all member countries due to the LOP. If the CPL differs between countries, the LOP is not in full force.

Data (Table 11.1) show that there are significant differences in price levels among EU countries and that there is a sizeable gap in average price levels of the group of the old EU-15 and the group of new EU-12 member countries.

11.3.2 The convergence of price levels between old euro area member countries

We now consider the convergence of price levels between the original 12 member countries of the EMU. We may assume that the different price levels of individual member countries converge towards some equilibrium price level difference close to the LOP. There are two ways to measure convergence: σ- and β-convergence (Sala-i-Martin, 1996).

Table 11.1 Comparative price levels (EU-27 = 100), 2006

Country	CPL index
EU-27 (27 countries)	100
EU-15 (15 old member countries)*	108
max. level (Denmark)	138
min. level (Portugal)	85
EU-12 (12 'new' member countries)	61
max. level (Cyprus)	91
min. level (Bulgaria)	45

Source: Eurostat.
Note: The comparative price level of final consumption by private households including indirect taxes.
* Simple arithmetic average.

Sigma price level convergence

Comparative price levels are the ratio between purchasing power parities (PPP) and the market exchange rate for each country. Before adopting the euro in January 1999, the comparative price levels of individual countries also depended on national exchange rates. It is therefore sensible to distinguish two periods in the convergence of price levels: the period before and the period after adopting the euro by fixing conversion rates. The landmark date is 1998, the last year before adopting the euro. Eurostat publishes the coefficients of variations of comparative price levels of final consumption by private households, including indirect taxes. Eurostat's data show that in the 1996–2006 period there was no discernible trend in σ price level convergence. The coefficient of variation for the 12 euro area countries stabilised at around 11 per cent. A similar conclusion was reached by Lane (2006).

Our thesis would be that there is a tendency towards convergence of the CPL among EMU member countries, but only to a certain degree. Differences in the CPL may persist. We expect some persistent difference in the comparative level of prices will exist due to limitations in the European Single Market originating in the existence of national economies and the imperfections of the markets.

Beta price level convergence

The bigger the comparative price level gap the faster is the differential inflation. This is called β-convergence. The β-convergence equation can be written as follows:

$$\pi^{i} = a - \beta\,(P^{i}_{0}/P_{0}^{\,EU}/) \qquad (11)$$

π is the inflation rate, P^i_0/P_0^{EU} is the relative price level in an individual member country (P^i) and EU the average (P^{EU}) in base year 0, which is a nominal convergence variable. The coefficient β indicates the speed of convergence toward the equilibrium comparative price level of a country (Lein-Rupprecht et al., 2007).

For the empirical investigation we regressed the difference in logarithm (ln) of the CPL in the average of years 2005–6 and the average of 1995–6 against the average level of ln CPL in 1995–6. The data are taken for 12 euro member countries plus Denmark.

The regression (with *t* statistics) is as follows:

$$\ln(CPL06/CPL96) = \underset{(1.77)}{1.22} - \underset{(-1.78)}{0.26} \ln CPL96 \qquad R^2 = 0.22 \qquad (12)$$

The statistical results are weak (low R^2 and a significance level of less than 10 per cent), while the *β*-coefficient has the expected sign. *β* price level convergence among the old EMU member countries is weak, albeit present.

On the basis of the empirical results we may state that price level differences in the old euro member countries converged to normal- or equilibrium-level disparities before the fixing of national exchange rates against the euro. This explains why there was no differential inflationary pressure in these countries after they adopted the euro.

11.3.3 The convergence of the price levels of new EU member countries

We may expect the convergence process of 'new' EU member countries to differ from that of the 'old' member countries.[2] There are two reasons for this. First, the initial gap in comparative price levels is much larger (Table 11.1). Second, the level of development of newcomers is much lower and therefore there is catching-up growth. Both of these facts may have important consequences for the price level convergence process. We shall elaborate on this issue later on in this chapter.

The same equation is estimated for the 12 new EU member countries. The results (with *t* statistics in parentheses) are as follows:

$$\ln(CPL06/CPL96) = \underset{(9.66)}{2.14} - \underset{(-8.30)}{0.48} \ln CPL96 \qquad R^2 = 0.87 \qquad (13)$$

These estimates are statistically very strong and highly significant. On the basis of such empirical results we may assume there is a strong convergence of comparative price levels of the new EU member countries with the average of the EU-27.

For the new EU member countries it is possible to claim that there is a process of the catching up of price levels which is brought about by the higher inflation that is a function of the price level gap. The catching-up inflation of the new euro members is described by equation (11).

11.3.4 The Phillips curve after adopting the euro

After adopting the euro, the nominal exchange rate does not influence the national price equation, as was seen with the old Phillips curve (5). The role of the nominal exchange rate was to prevent the national price level converging towards the European price level or to prevent the LOP from working. After the removal of a national currency, the LOP will work fully and it should therefore be put into the price equation. We join equation (11) of β price convergence $\pi = a - \beta\ (P^i_0/P_0^{\ EU})$, and the original Phillips curve (2). We obtain the following new extended Phillips curve:

$$\pi = \pi_{-1} + \lambda\ (u - u^*) - \beta\ (P^i_0/P^{eu}_0) \tag{14}$$

Price equation could or should take two arguments into account: the unemployment gap $(u - u^*)$, which approximates the output gap, and the price level gap (P^i/P^{eu}).

Phillips curve (14) differs from Phillips curve (5) in one important respect: the Phillips curve before adopting the euro contains an instrumental variable, NEER, which was under the control of the national government. The CPL in (14) is not controlled by the national government and therefore the inflation rate is determined by an exogenous variable.

A country which adopts the euro with a large initial price level gap may expect a higher inflation rate due to the effect of the LOP. The NAIRU or u^* in such a Phillips curve is going to be high. This statement still cannot be verified empirically by the regression of equation (14) because the time series data are too short. However, such conjecture is possible on the basis of theoretical considerations and the empirical fact of past movements of inflation. Higher differential inflation is to be expected.

The prediction of higher differential inflation after adopting the euro needs further elaboration. The question is how to explain the price level gap, what the economic reasons are for it, and which factors control differential inflation. Below we shall explore two reasons for the sizeable price level gap of the new middle-income EU member countries. One is for structural and economic development reasons, or Balassa's effect. The other is for economic policy reasons, or Samuelson's effect.

11.4 The comparative price level gap due to Balassa's developmental and structural effect

In the original euro member countries there were no persistent inflation differentials after the euro was adopted. The reason for this lies in the fact that the LOP in the ESM works and that the original euro member countries achieved sustained (equilibrium) comparative price level disparities before fixing their national exchange rates vis-à-vis the euro. Yet there are good reasons to expect that differential inflation rates among EMU member countries would exist on a temporary basis. Differences in inflation rates reflect asymmetric, policy-related, cyclical and structural factors. When countries face asymmetric shocks, they will adjust through differential inflation. The equilibrium level of the average inflation rate in the euro area would be higher due to the area's heterogeneity. This thesis is not discussed in the present chapter.

On the other hand, the new euro-adopting countries, which are all middle developed countries, adopted the euro before their CPLs had achieved sustainable (equilibrium) comparative price level disparities. Hence, their differential inflations might persist for a long time. The persistent inflationary processes, which maintain persistent higher differential inflation, are in conflict with the need for catching-up growth and the need for a stable equilibrium. A persistent differential inflation rate is a persistent threat to economic growth prospects and the stability of the economy.

11.4.1 Differential inflation due to economic development reasons

A characteristic of the heterogeneity of the euro area is that there are significant differences in development levels as measured by GDP per person in PPS. We may assume that the EMU consists of two groups of countries: developed countries (DCs) and middle developed countries (MDCs). The MDCs are catching-up countries with high-trend productivity growth rates. Slovenia is such a country. For more about groupings and differential growth, see the article by Senjur (2007). Balassa (1964) claimed that comparative price levels depend on comparative income per capita levels. This argument is in favour of the thesis that there are long-term differences in price levels between the countries of the EMU.

Balassa (1964) saw 'purchasing power parity' as the real parity between two countries that is represented by the quotient between the purchasing power of money in one country and the other. Purchasing power parities are calculated as ratios of consumer goods prices for any pair of countries. Balassa made an important observation: the currency of the country with higher productivity levels (measured by per capita incomes) will be overvalued in terms of PPP, which means that its CPL is higher. The ratio of purchasing power parity to the exchange rate (e.g., the CPL) will be an increasing function of income levels (y):

$$\mathrm{CPL}_i = PP_i / e_i = F(y_i) \tag{15}$$

The greater the productivity differentials in the production of traded goods between two countries the greater will be gap between PPP and the equilibrium real exchange rate ($E = e.P^*/P$) (Balassa, 1964: p. 586). This has become known in recent literature as the Balassa effect or the Balassa-Samuelson effect (Égert et al., 2002; Égert et al., 2004; Jazbec, 2002; Masten, 2008).

For the new EU member countries the above statement can be expressed in the following equation:

$$P^i{}_t / P^{eu}{}_t = b\,(y^i{}_t / y^{eu}{}_t) \tag{16}$$

The relative price level of an individual country in comparison to the euro average is a positive function of the relative income per capita gap of an individual country in comparison to the euro average.

Balassa offered the following explanation.[3] The exchange rate should relate to the prices of traded goods. Inter-country wage differences in the sector of traded goods will correspond to productivity differences. Whereas the internal mobility of labour will tend to equalise the wages of comparable labour within each country, there is no international mobility of labour and no inter-country equalisation of wages. International differences in productivity are smaller in the service sector than in traded goods. Services will therefore be relatively more expensive in countries with higher levels of productivity. Since services enter the calculation of PPPs but do not directly affect exchange rates, the PPP between the currencies of two countries, expressed in terms of the currency of the country with higher productivity levels, would be lower than the equilibrium rate of exchange. The currency of the country with the higher productivity level will be overvalued in terms of PPP. The higher productivity growth in the lower income country would reduce the undervaluation of its real exchange rate by higher inflation rates.

The De Grauwe (2007) and Balassa models assume the international immobility of labour and no international arbitration of labour costs. The reasoning is as follows. There is an increase of productivity in tradable goods ($gq_T > 0$). Prices of tradeables remain unchanged ($\pi^T = 0$). Real wages increase in accordance with increased productivity ($g_{wT} = g_{qT}$). On the other hand, there is no productivity change in non-tradable goods (e.g., services). Since there is internal mobility of labour, real wages will have to increase in non-tradables as well ($g_{wN} > g_{qN}$). This requires an increase in the price of non-tradables ($\pi^N > 0$). Therefore, for the whole economy it is possible to claim that the growth in productivity drives inflation. The basic assumption behind this is that real wages grow faster than productivity, and that unit labour costs grow. It is presupposed that unit labour costs grow faster in the newcomers than in the old member countries.

De Grauwe (2007) asserted that the Balassa-Samuelson (BS) effect could be important for the 'new' EU member states and could lead to structurally (differential) higher inflation. New member states experience high productivity growth in their tradable sectors, which is part of their catching-up process with western Europe. Higher inflation is a result of the catching-up process and could be considered as an equilibrating process. If productivity growth is faster in the new member country than in the eurozone, that is $(g_q - g_{q*}) > 0$, then inflation in the new member state would exceed eurozone inflation. De Grauwe (2007: p. 221) predicts that, given the robust relationship between real GDP per capita and the price level suggested by the Balassa-Samuelson effect, we could expect that both the economic catching-up process and the differential increase in price levels would continue for some time.[4] Mihaljek and Klau (2008) provide recent empirical estimates of catching-up and inflation in transition economies.

11.4.2 Differential inflation as a result of differential growth rates

We may assume that there is a double catching-up effect for the new EMU countries, which are middle-income and open economies.

The catching up of the level of prices:

$$\pi = a - \beta\ (P^i{}_0/P_0{}^{eu}) \tag{17}$$

and the catching-up of development levels. The catching-up hypotheses of the growth rate of output could be defined by the following equation (Baumoll, 1986; Sala-i-Martin, 1996):

$$gy^i = A - a\,(y^i_0 / y^{eu}_0) \tag{18}$$

The growth rate in country *i* (gy^i) is positively related to the income gap in initial year (y^i_0 / y^{eu}_0). y^i is GDP per capita in PPS for country *i* and y^{eu} is for the euro area average, respectively.

Equations (17) and (18) imply Balassa's relationship, expressed in equation (19):

$$P^i_t / P^{eu}_t = b\,(y^i_t / y^{eu}_t) \tag{19}$$

Taking (17)–(19) into account, we can state the following:

$$\pi - \pi^{eu} = b\,(g - g^{eu}) \tag{20}$$

where ($g > g^{eu}$) and $\pi > \pi^{eu}$.

Differential inflation ($\pi - \pi^{eu}$) depends on the differential growth of the rate of GDP per capita ($g_y - g^{eu}_y$). An above-average rate of growth is associated with an above-average rate of inflation due to a double catching-up effect: the price level is catching up and the income level is also catching up. The thesis that differential growth rates ($g > g^{eu}$) are associated with differential inflation rates ($\pi > \pi^{eu}$) is based on the Balassa effect.[5]

We ran a cross-section analysis on data for 26 EU-member countries (without the UK). A dummy value 0 was given to the 'old' EU-member countries and 1 to the 'new' EU member countries. We estimated the following equations:

$$\text{CPL05-06} = A + a_1\text{CGDP06} + a_2\text{DUMMY} + a_3\text{CGDP06*D} \tag{21}$$

$$g\text{HICP} = B + b_1\, g\text{RGDP} \tag{22}$$

We regressed comparative price levels (EU-27 = 100) in the years 2000–1 to comparative GDP per capita in PPS (EU-27 = 100) in the year 2000, and the CPL in the years 2005–6 to comparative GDP per capita in 2005–6. The regression results for the two periods are very similar. Table 11.2 shows the results for 2006. The statistical results are good; the dummy variables are statistically significant. In the new member

Table 11.2 Summary of regression results

Models	Coefficients	Significance
Dependent variable: CPL0506		
Constant	94.31	0.00
CGDP06	0.11	0.15
DUMMY	–68.36	0.00
CGDP06*D	0.48	0.035
R^2	0.83	
Dependent variable: gHICP		
Constant	1.56	0.08
GRGDP	0.43	0.03
R^2	0.18	

countries the comparative price level (CPL05-06) is related to the comparative level of GDPs (CGDP06).

In the second regression we regressed the growth rates of harmonised indices of consumer prices (*g*HICPs) to real GDP growth rates (gRGDP) in the 2002–6 period. The statistical results here are not good: nflation rates are not strongly related to growth rates. This is the reason we shall use comparative GDP levels as a variable in the Phillips curve.

11.4.3 The Phillips curve of the differential inflation rate

We may assume that inflation in a small, open economy after it introduces the euro would depend on the inflation rate in the euro area and on the unemployment gap:

$$\pi = \pi^{eu} - b\,(u - u^*) \tag{23}$$

We may describe such a setting as demand-pull differential inflation (Samuelson & Solow, 1960).

Having in mind the importance of differential inflation, we could reformulate the Phillips curve:

$$\pi - \pi^{eu} = -a\,(u - u^{**}) \tag{24}$$

Such a Phillips curve implies a reformulated natural rate of unemployment. The natural rate of unemployment is that rate at which there is no differential rate of inflation. Instead of the NAIRU (u^*), we would have a NDIRU (non-differential inflation rate of unemployment), u^{**}.

By combining the basic Phillips curve and the Balassa effect we can obtain the following combined equation of differential inflation:

$$\pi - \pi^{eu} = a_1(u - u^{**}) + a_2 \,(y/y^{eu}) \qquad (25)$$

Taking relation (19) into account, the reformulated Phillips curve could be written as:

$$\pi - \pi^{eu} = a_1(u - u^{**}) + a_2 \,(P^i/P^{eu}) \qquad (26)$$

The idea is that differential inflation is affected through the separate effect of the unemployment gap and by the double catching-up effect (the catching-up of the price level and the catching-up of the income level). Compare relation (26) to the Phillips curve in (5).

Price competitiveness. A higher differential inflation rate has important economic policy repercussions. The growth rate is demand-driven and depends on price competitiveness, which is defined by real exchange rate (E) and differential inflation ($\pi - \pi^{eu}$).

Price competitiveness: $E = (eP/P^{eu})$, and $g_E = g_e + \pi - \pi^{eu}$. (27)

where g denotes the growth rate of a variable, *e* is the nominal exchange rate, *E* is the real exchange rate, *P* is the price level, whereas P^{eu} is the average price level in the EMU area. Higher differential inflation reduces the price competitiveness of exports and may therefore reduce the growth rate. The question is thus not only how to explain differential inflation but also how to manage it.

11.5 Managed comparative price levels: The Samuelson effect

Samuelson (1964) considered several ways to compare PPP between two countries. There may exist arbitrage in price levels, the cost of living, and production costs. There could be a comparison of labour costs per unit of product. If real wages correspond with productivity there is no additional competitiveness of exports. If wages lag behind productivity levels then this may be an additional reason for the undervaluation of the country's currency. Samuelson (1964, p. 153) noted: 'The productivity improvements abroad since 1949 have not yet been matched by commensurate rises in foreign money wages relative to ours'. This contributed to the overvaluation of the dollar. The Samuelson effect could be defined as follows. When comparative wages are lower than productivity this contributes to the undervaluation of the currency, and if the growth of productivity exceeds the growth of wages this contributes to the competitiveness of the country's exports.

11.5.1 Differential inflation due to comparative unit labour costs (ULC)

The explanation of the CPL with comparative GDP levels is referred to in the literature as the Ballasa-Samuelson effect. For the purpose of this paper, I prefer to separate the Balassa effect from the Samuelson effect. The Balassa effect explains the CPL with developmental and structural factors. The Samuelson effect explains the CPL with economic policy factors: LDCs keep CPLs reduced in order to maintain the price competitiveness of their exports. The instrument to keep the CPLs lower is to keep comparative unit labour costs low. The Balassa and Samuelson effects may work in different directions as far as differential inflation is concerned. The first may work towards higher and the second towards lower differential inflation.

Lower comparative unit labour costs (ULCs) in LDCs are an instrument to keep the price competitiveness of their exports in markets of DCs. We may expect that LDCs would want to keep comparative labour costs lower than comparative productivity levels in order to keep the CPL low and therefore sustain export competitiveness.

In order to illustrate the point about the Samuelson effect we use the analytical framework of price determination, which enables us to include relative labour costs in the analysis. Domestic prices (P_d) and wages are determined by the following price-setting relationship:

$$P_d = A\ (w/q)^{\theta} \qquad (28)$$

A is a constant and includes a mark-up; $w = W/L$ are wages per worker; $q = Q/L$ is output per worker or the productivity of labour; w/q is labour costs per output. Parameter θ reflects the elasticity of prices in relation to labour unit costs. We shall assume that the mark-up is constant. We express the price-setting relationship in growth rate terms:

$$\pi = \theta\ (g_w - g_q) \qquad (29)$$

Domestic inflation is determined by the difference between the growth of wages and productivity per worker. Expression $(g_w - g_q)$ reflect the growth of unit labour costs (*g*LUC). If all countries were to follow the wage policy rule $g_w = g_q$, there would be no differential inflation due to labour unit costs.

Since we are interested in differential inflation, $\pi - \pi^{eu}$, we may maintain it is a function of the difference in the growth rate of LUC of two countries under comparison or groups of countries.

$$\pi^i - \pi^{eu} = c(g\,ULC^i - gULC^{eu}) \tag{30}$$

A higher differential growth of ULC contributes to a higher differential inflation rate. This is a cost-push differential inflation rate (Samuelson and Solow, 1960).

11.5.2 The Phillips curve of a managed differential inflation rate

Our conclusion is that there may be tendencies toward a higher unemployment rate and toward a higher inflation rate for a middle-income EMU member country. A similar conclusion was reached by Calmfors (2001), who established the existence of a national inflation bias and higher equilibrium unemployment inside the EMU. One option for policymakers is to manage aggregate demand in order to manage the unemployment gap in such a way as to affect differential inflation, and to implement income policies to restrain unit labour costs.

Equations (24) and (30) could be combined to form an extended and reformulated Phillips curve. Such an inflation equation includes the demand-pull and cost-push arguments of inflation:

$$\pi - \pi^{eu} = a\,(u - u^{**}) + c(g\,ULC - gULC^{eu}) \tag{31}$$

In such a formulation differential inflation is a result of the unemployment rate and the differential growth of unit labour costs.

There is a tendency towards LOP and the catching-up growth effect, which accelerate differential inflation in middle-income countries. As a result, the equilibrium or natural rate of unemployment tends to be higher. A country may manage (or restrain) differential inflation by managing the rate of unemployment through demand management, and by managing relative unit labour costs by incomes policy (Tobin, 1972).

11.6 Policy implications and discussion

Conversion rate. The original euro member states achieved 'normal CPL disparity levels' before they adopted the euro. The CPL disparities were normal in the sense that they were not a source of differential inflationary pressure after adoption of the euro. I am unaware of any study that calculates a sustainable or even an equilibrium price level gap for Slovenia at the time of it adopting the euro. The existing official exchange rate of the Slovenian tolar (SIT) of the Bank of Slovenia in relation to the euro on 31 December 2006, which was EUR 1 = SIT 239.64, was taken as the actual conversion rate of tolars into euros on 1 January 2007, the time the country adopted the euro. At such a conversion rate, the average level of prices in Slovenia was 26 per cent lower than in the eurozone. At a lower conversion rate, the price level gap would have been lower and there would have been less of a need for higher differential inflation to equilibrate price levels (Weyerstrass 2008). The question is should the conversion rate upon adoption of the euro follow the rule of purchasing power parity? This question is even more relevant since Eurostat regularly provides data on comparative price levels and on GDP in purchasing power standards. Not taking PPP into account at the time of adopting the euro may cause inflationary pressure after the euro has been adopted.[6]

Nominal exchange rate adjustment in order to keep sustained price competitiveness. The higher inflation rates seen in 2007–8 in Slovenia after the euro was adopted can be attributed to two factors: (1) the comparative price level in Slovenia at the time of adopting the euro (around 75 per cent) was too low and it needed to converge further towards the average. The equilibrium or sustainable price level for Slovenia might be somewhere around 85 per cent of the average. Higher differential inflation is needed to achieve such a level. (2) The country's adoption of the euro abolished the national exchange rate as a shelter for the national price level. After the euro was adopted such a situation was simply unsustainable. Prices had to rise faster. The law of one price was at work in Slovenia in 2007 and 2008, after the country's adoption of the euro.

In order to illustrate the problem I will use comparative data of Portugal, Slovakia and Slovenia. Portugal became a member of the EMU in 1999, Slovenia in 2007, and Slovakia in 2009. These three countries reveal three different paths of their comparative prices levels before and after they adopted the euro.

Tables 11.3, 11.4 and 11.5 reveal three different price level paths in the 1995–2006 period, reflecting three different policies of adjustment to euro conditions. Portugal increased the price level by four percentage points from 1996 to 1998. This was achieved with slight depreciation and with slightly higher differential inflation rates. Portugal started its adoption of the euro with a comparative price level of about 82 per cent of the average in the euro area. Its price level remained at that level for

Table 11.3 Comparative price level of final consumption by private households: Portugal, Slovakia and Slovenia (euro area – 12 countries = 100)

Year	Portugal	Slovenia	Slovakia
1995	77.1	69.8	37.0
1998	81.6	72.0	40.7
2003	83.0	73.6	48.9
2005	82.7	73.5	54.8
2006	83.3	73.8	56.7

Source: Eurostat.

Table 11.4 Harmonised annual average consumer price indices (1996 = 100), 1996–2006: euro area (12 countries), Portugal, Slovenia, Slovakia

Year	Euro area (12)	Portugal	Slovenia	Slovakia
1996	100	100	100	100
1999	104	106	124	125
2006	121	132	181	194

Source: Eurostat.

Table 11.5 Indices of national exchange rates against the euro (1995 = 100), 1995–2005: Portugal, Slovenia, Slovakia (EUR 1 = ... national currency)

Year	Portugal	Slovenia	Slovakia
1995	100	100	100
1999	102	126	113
2005	102	155	99

Source: Europe in Figures – Eurostat yearbook 2006–7.

all of time afterwards up until 2006. This means Portugal did not have positive differential inflation after it adopted the euro. The adoption of the euro was not inflationary. Slovakia was rapidly increasing its comparative price level: from an index of 37 in 1995 to 57 in 2006. This was achieved by above-average inflation rates. In the 1995–9 period, Slovakia was nominally depreciating its national currency against the euro and nominal appreciating it in the time afterwards up until 2005. Slovakia has increased its CPL by 20 percentage points in just 10 years with a combination of nominal appreciation of currency and higher differential inflation. Slovakia is adopting the euro in 2009 with a comparative price level of around 60–5 per cent of the average in the euro area. It remains to be seen what will happen to its inflation rate after it adopts the euro.

Slovenia reveals a different policy. Slovenia had an inflation rate that was triple of that of the euro area. However, the gap in the price level remained at approximately the same level: Slovenia had an average level of prices (expressed in euros) which was 25 per cent lower than that in the euro area. It is obvious that Slovenia used to employ the national exchange rate as a shelter for the national price level. We notice that the index of CPL increased by just three percentage points in the 1995–2006 period. Accession the EU and the ESM did not affect the comparative price level of Slovenia. Slovenia adopted the euro in 2007 with a comparative price level of 74 per cent of that in the euro area. Comparative price levels in Slovenia remained stable despite the higher inflation in comparison with the euro area. The policy of a nominal exchange rate has neutralised the effect of inflation on the CPL.[7]

An income policy should retain labour cost competitiveness. In the period before adopting the euro, namely 1996–2006,[8] labour unit costs were kept low: the growth of productivity exceeded the growth of real wages, and labour unit costs were decreasing. However, this was not enough to maintain cost competitiveness in comparison with the EU-15 over the whole period. In the 1996–9 period the negative growth rate of Slovenian ULC was higher than that of the EU-15, and the Slovenian economy was gaining in relative cost competitiveness. In the 2000–6 period the negative growth rates of LUC of the EU-15 area were higher than that of Slovenia, and the Slovenian economy was losing its comparative cost competitiveness. There is a real danger that Slovenia might have to face the end of the catching-up growth process inside the EMU area after it has adopted the euro.

11.7 Conclusions

In the 1993–2006 period, Slovenia managed the nominal exchange rate in such a way as to keep the real exchange rate stable. Inflation was thereby not detrimental to export competitiveness or to growth. At the same time, Slovenia kept its unit labour costs low. After losing its monetary policy, which determined the interest rate and exchange rate, the burden of policymaking has shifted to structural policy (of the labour market) and incomes policy (of unit labour costs). Since joining the euro area incomes policy has been taking on an increasingly important role. Low unit labour costs are a major precondition of the export competitiveness of the economy. This situation could last only for the middle-term period, as it is not sustainable in the long run.

Notes

1. Slovenia shows some signs of such movements in 2007–9. Investment grew in 2007 by 17 per cent, while the current account deficit increased by close to 5 per cent. Gross foreign debt rose from EUR 15 billion in 2004 to over EUR 40 billion in 2008. GDP grew by 6.8 per cent, which is above the potential growth rate of the last decade. Such movements on the demand side, caused by the new situation of the euro, contributed to higher inflation in Slovenia in 2007 and 2008. In 2009 the economy turned into a bust situation.
2. Concerning purchasing power parity in transition economies, see Bekö and Borsič (2007).
3. Balassa assumes that invisibles and capital movements do not enter the balance of payments.
4. A similar structuralist explanation of inflation was used in the economic development literature (Canavese 1983; Johnson 1984). It is of some interest that this literature does not refer to Balassa (1964), a source which dominates present-day discussions of structural inflation in catching-up countries.
5. This is not the whole of the explanation. Catching-up growth is frequently demand-driven. Higher differential growth rates are associated with higher differential inflation where growth is demand-driven. Such countries would see higher growth rates and higher inflation rates simultaneously.
6. De Grauwe (2007) deals with the question of how to set the conversion rate but does not refer to principle of PPP as one to follow in setting the conversion rate.
7. The policy of NER increased the NAIRU by around 1 percentage point as is implied by estimates of the Phillips curve (compare equations 6 and 7).
8. Data are taken from a publication by the government's Institute for Macroeconomic Analyses and Development (UMAR) called the Development Report 2009 (Poročilo o razvoju), Ljubljana, 2009.

References

Allington, Nigel F. B., Paul A. Kattuman, and Florian A. Waldmann (2005). One market, One Money, One Price. *International Journal of Central Banking* 1(3): 73–115.

Angelini, Paolo and Francesco Lippi. (2007). Did Prices Really Soar after the Euro Cash Changeover? Evidence of ATM Withdrawals. *International Journal of Central Banking* 3(4): 1–22.

Angeloni, Ignacio, Luc Aucremanne and Matteo Ciccarelli. (2006). Price Setting and Inflation Persistence: Did EMU Matter? *Economic Policy* 21(46): 353–87.

Ball, Laurence and N. Gregory Mankiw. (2002). The NAIRU in Theory and Practice. *Journal of Economic Perspectives* 16(4): 115–36.

Balassa, Bela (1964): The Purchasing-Power Parity Doctrine: A Reappraisal. *Journal of Political Economy* 72(6): 584–96.

Baumol, William J. (1986). Productivity Growth, Convergence, and Welfare: What the Long-Run Data Show. *American Economic Review* 76(5): 1072–85.

Bekö Jani, and Borsič Darja. (2007). Purchasing Power Parity in Transition Economies: Does it Hold in the Czech Republic, Hungary and Slovenia? *Post-Communist Economies* 19(4): 417–30.

Blanchard, Oliver. (2009). *Macroeconomics*. Fifth edition. New Jersey: Pearson Prentice Hall.

Borio, Claudio and Andrew Filardo. (2007). Globalisation and Inflation: New Cross-Country Evidence on the Global Determinants of Domestic Inflation. BIS Working Papers No. 227.

Canavese, Alfredo J. (1982). The Structuralist Explanation in the Theory of Inflation. *World Development* 10(7): 523–9.

Calmfors, L. (2001). Unemployment, Labor Market Reforms, and Monetary Union. *Journal of Labour Economics* 19(2): 265–89.

Coricelli, Fabrizio and Boštjan Jazbec. (2004). Real Exchange Rate Dynamics in Transition economies. *Structural Change and Economic Dynamics* 15(1): 83–100.

De Grauwe, Paul (2007). Precondition for a Successful Euro Adoption. In E. Basci, S. Togan and J. von Hagen (eds). *Macroeconomic Policies for EU Accession*. Edgar Elgar: Cheltenham, pp. 206–27.

Ėgert, Balász, Drine, Imed, Lommantzsch, Kirsten and Rault, Christophe. (2002). The Balassa-Samuelson Effect in Central and Eastern Europe: Myth or Reality? William Davidson Working Paper Number 483, July 2002.

Ėgert, Balász, Ritzberger-Gruenwald, Doris, and Antoniette Silgoner, Maria. (2004). Inflation Differentials in Europe: Past Experience and Future Prospects. *Monetary Policy & The Economy*, Issue 1(May), pp. 47–72.

Eichengreen, Barry (2002). The Enlargement Challenge: Can Monetary Union be Made to Work in an EU of 25 Members? *Australian Economic Review* 35(2): 113–21.

Gordon, Robert J. (1997). The Time-Varying NAIRU and its Implications for Economic Policy. *Journal of Economic Perspectives* 11(1), 11–32.

Hammermann, Felix and Mark Flanagan. (2009). What Explains Persistent Inflation Differentials across Transition Economies? *Economics of Transition* 17(2): 297–328.

Jazbec, Boštjan. (2002). Balassa-Samuelson effect in Transition Economies: The Case of Slovenia. William Davidson Working Paper Number 507, October 2002.

Johnson, Omotunde E. G. (1984). On Growth and Inflation in Developing Countries. *IMF Staff Papers* 31(4): 636–60.

Lane, Philip R. (2006). The Real Effects of European Monetary Union. *Journal of Economic Perspectives* 20(4): 47–66.

Lein-Rupprecht, Sarah M., Miguel A Leon-Ledesma, and Carolin Nerlich. (2007). How is Real Convergence Driving Nominal Convergence in the New EU Member States? European Central Bank, Working Paper Series, no. 827, November.

MacDonald, Ronald, Cezary Wójcik. (2008). Catching-Up and Inflation Differentials in a Heterogeneous Monetary Union: Some Implications for the Euro Area and New EU Member States. *Economic Systems* 32(1): 4–16.

Masten, Igor. (2008). Optimal Monetary Policy with Balassa-Samuelson-Type Productivity Shocks. *Journal of Comparative Economics* 36(1): 120–41.

McCombie, J. S. L. and A. P. Thirwall. (1994). *Economic Growth and Balance-of-Payment Constraint*. The Macmillan Press.

Mihaljek, Dubravko and Marc Klau. (2008). Catching-Up and Inflation in Transition Economies: The Balassa-Samuelson Effect Revisited. BIS Working Papers, No. 270, December 2008.

Rogoff, Kenneth. (1996). The Purchasing Power Puzzle. *Journal of Economic Literature* 34(2): 647–68.
Sala-i-Martin, Xavier X. (1996). The Classical Approach to Convergence Analysis. *The Economic Journal* 106(July): 1019–36.
Samuelson, Paul A. (1964). Theoretical Notes on Trade Problems. *Review of Economics and Statistics* 46(2): 145–54.
Samuelson, Paul A., Robert M. Solow. (1960). Analytical Aspects of Anti-Inflationary Policy. *The American Economic Review, Papers and Proceedings*, 50(2): 177–94.
Senjur, Marjan. (2007). A Development Club and Groupings in Europe, and Growth Strategies. *Comparative Economic Studies* 49(4): 660–82.
Staiger, Douglas, James H. Stock, and Mark W. Watson. (1997). The NAIRU, Unemployment and Monetary Policy. *Journal of Economic Perspectives* 11(1): 33–49.
Taylor, John B. (2000). Teaching Modern Macroeconomics at the Principle Level. *American Economic Review* 90(2): 90–4.
Taylor, Alan M. and Mark P. Taylor. (2004). The Purchasing Power Parity Debate. *Journal of Economic Perspective* 18(4): 135–58.
Tobin, James. (1972). Inflation and Unemployment. *American Economic Review* 62(1): 1–18.
Weyerstrass, Klaus. (2008). Economic Policies on Slovenia's Road to the Euro Area. *Economic Systems* 32(1): 92–102.
Weyerstrass, Klaus, and Reinhard Neck. (2007). A Simulation of the Macroeconomic Effects of Introducing the Euro in Slovenia. Ljubljana: Proceedings of the 6 EUROSIM Congress on Modeling and Simulation. B. Zupančič, R. Karba, S. Blažič (eds).
Wyplosz, Charles (2006). European Monetary Union: The Dark Sides of a Major Success. *Economic Policy* 21(46): 207–61.

12
Implications of Volatility for Uncovered Interest Parity Testing

Alexandra Horobet, Sorin Dumitrescu and Dan Gabriel Dumitrescu

12.1 Introduction

The concept of interest rate parity is an important component of the macroeconomic analysis for open economies and one of the basic models used in international finance. The validation of interest parity has important implications for both international corporate finance decisions and international investments. Interest rate parity has been developed in two forms, known as covered interest parity (CIP) and uncovered interest parity (UIP), which provide simple relationships between money market variables, more specifically interest rates, and foreign exchange market prices.

Investors have at their disposal two basic alternatives in terms of holding assets: one refers to holding assets denominated in their domestic currency, whereas the other refers to holding assets denominated in foreign currencies. The covered interest parity identifies a relationship between the forward premium or discount on the foreign currency against the home currency and the interest rate differential between the two currencies. On the other hand, the uncovered interest parity links the interest rate differential to the appreciation or depreciation of the foreign currency against the home currency between t and $t + 1$.

When the CIP condition ignores entirely credit risks, capital and exchange controls, and taxes in domestic and foreign currency environments, it is generally confirmed by market data. Herring and Marston (1976) and Levich (1985) provide evidence that the CIP condition is used as a formula for determining the exchange and interest rates at which trading takes place. Taylor (1989) finds no evidence of unexploited profit opportunities during relatively calm periods in foreign exchange and money markets, although potentially exploitable profitable arbitrage opportunities did occur during periods of market turbulence. Also, Dooley and Isard (1980) point out that in circumstances when one cannot ignore capital controls and risks empirical research has confirmed that deviations from CIP can be systematically related to the effective taxes imposed by capital controls and to non-currency-specific risk premiums associated with prospective controls.

The aim of this chapter is to explore the relationship between exchange rate changes and interest rate differentials in the uncovered interest parity framework, by taking into account the implications of capital market and foreign exchange market volatility on the UIP validation. Following previous lines of research, we advance the hypothesis that capital and foreign exchange market volatility has a significant influence on the UIP validation. Since one may employ GARCH models to forecast volatility, our findings may provide the basis for an improved forecasting ability of foreign exchange market models.

We contribute to the research in the field in a number of ways. First, we pursued a three-step procedure for testing UIP that initially involved the use of more traditional econometric models such as OLS regressions. Then we explored the influence of capital market and foreign exchange market volatility on the validation of uncovered interest parity using the regime-switching methodology, which can better explain the relationship between exchange rate changes and interest differentials in a changing volatility environment. Secondly, we investigated the influence of financial market volatility on the UIP validation by effectively incorporating volatility in regression models, but also by identifying high-volatility episodes and testing for UIP in each of these periods. Thirdly, our research examined not only the foreign exchange market volatility, but also the volatility in the capital market. Finally, we addressed the issue of UIP validation for emerging market currencies, which represents a significant contribution, given the fact that a rather limited body research has been focused on emerging markets compared to mature markets. The chapter is structured as follows: section 12.2 presents the data used in our analysis and the research methodology, section 12.3 outlines the main results and section 12.4 offers conclusions.

12.2 Data and research methodology

We use the exchange rates against the US$ and the interest rates reported by the European Central Bank, all collected from Datastream, for five currencies from Central and Eastern Europe (CEE) – Polish zloty

(PLZ), Czech koruna (CZK), Romanian leu (RON), Turkish Lira (NTL), and Russian ruble (RUR) – and for three developed markets currencies – Japanese yen (JPY), Swiss franc (SWF) and British pound (GBP). We also use VDAX as a measure of capital market volatility.[1] The analysis has been conducted over the period between 13 April 1994 and 13 April 2009, but is different from one currency to the other, depending on data availability. All returns are logarithmic.

Our testing of UIP follows a three-step procedure: first, we use OLS regressions to summarise the empirical facts about interest rate differentials and changes in exchange rates; secondly, we explore the influence of capital market and foreign exchange market volatility on the validation of UIP; thirdly, we employ the regime-switching methodology to explore better the relationship between exchange rate changes and interest differentials in a changing volatility environment. Before explaining our methodological approach we discuss the difficulties in effectively testing CIP and UIP and the main results obtained in the previous research.

12.2.1 Short review of empirical evidences from testing CIP and UIP

Investors have at their disposal two basic alternatives for holding assets: one refers to holding assets denominated in their domestic currency, whereas the other refers to holding assets denominated in foreign currencies. When the domestic alternative offers an interest rate denoted by r between times t and $t + 1$, the payoff of this investment equals $(1 + r)$. To benefit from the interest rate provided by the foreign investment alternative, denoted by r^*, the investor must first convert the amount in the domestic currency into foreign currency units using the spot exchange rate at time t, s_t,[2] then invest into foreign assets, obtaining at time $t + 1$ a payoff equal to $s_t \times (1 + r_t)$, which is afterwards reconverted in domestic currency units. If the domestic and foreign assets differ only with respect to the currencies of denomination, and if investors have the opportunity to cover their exposure to currency risk by converting their proceeds in foreign currencies at time $t + 1$ at the forward exchange rate for maturity $t + 1$, f_t, then market equilibrium leads to the *covered interest parity*:

$$\frac{f_t}{s_t} = \frac{1+r}{1+r^*} \quad \text{or, rewriting,} \quad (1+r) = f_t(1+r^*)/s_t \tag{1}$$

When investors leave their positions uncovered and wait until time $t + 1$ to convert the amount $s_t \times (1 + r_t)$ in the spot market, at the spot rate prevailing at time $t + 1$, s_{t+1}, markets will reach an equilibrium point when the return on the domestic currency equals the expected value of the return provided by the uncovered position in the foreign currency – this condition is known as *uncovered interest rate parity*:

$$\frac{E_t(s_{t+1})}{s_t} = \frac{1+r}{1+r^*} \text{ or, rewriting, } (1+r) = E_t(s_{t+1})(1+r^*)/s_t \tag{2}$$

Rearranging the terms of equation (1) above, we obtain:

$$\frac{f_t - s_t}{s_t} = \frac{1+r}{1+r^*} - 1, \text{ or for small values of } r^*, \frac{f_t - s_t}{s_t} \approx r - r^* \tag{3}$$

Equation (3) may be interpreted as the observable premium or discount on the foreign currency implied by the interest rate differential between the two currencies, as follows: whenever the interest rate in the domestic currency is higher than the foreign currency interest rate, this implies a forward premium on the foreign currency and a forward discount on the domestic currency; conversely, whenever the interest rate in the domestic currency is smaller than the foreign currency interest rate, this implies a forward discount on the foreign currency and a forward premium on the domestic currency.

On other hand, rearranging the terms of equation (2) leads to

$$\frac{E_t(s_{t+1}) - s_t}{s_t} = \frac{1+r}{1+r^*} - 1, \text{ or for small values of } r^*, \frac{E_t(s_{t+1}) - s_t}{s_t} \approx r - r^* \tag{4}$$

Equation (4) follows the interpretation for equation (3), only that now the interest rate differential between the two currencies is linked to the spot exchange rate prevailing in the market at time t and the expectations related to the value of the spot rate at time $t + 1$: whenever the interest rate in the domestic currency is higher than the foreign currency interest rate, an appreciation of the foreign currency and a depreciation of the domestic currency occurs; conversely, whenever the interest rate in the domestic currency is smaller than the foreign currency interest rate, investors expect a depreciation of the foreign currency and an appreciation of the domestic currency.

UIP examination raises an immediate obstacle, as the variables in equations (2) and (4) above are not directly observable: the expected future spot rate is not easily quantified and is in any case inherently subjective. Thus, assumptions have significant implications for the results obtained when testing UIP[3]: when UIP is found not to be supported by the facts, this may be explained either by the fact that UIP does not hold or that the assumption one makes about market expectations is at fault, or both. Owing to the difficulty of testing UIP, this condition has been tested jointly with the assumption that participants in the foreign exchange market form rational expectations, typically in such a way that future calculations of the spot rate will equal the value expected at time *t*, plus an error term that is uncorrelated with all information known at time *t*. The two assumptions imply that

$$s_{t+1} = f_t + u_{t+1} \tag{5}$$

and, consequently,

$$s_{t+1} - s_t = (r_t - r^*) + u_{t+1} \tag{6}$$

where u stands for the a prediction error. Therefore, UIP has been tested empirically by estimating the values of α- and β-coefficients in model specifications such as:

$$s_{t+1} = \alpha_0 + \alpha_1 f_t + u_{t+1} \text{ or } s_{t+1} - s_t = \beta_0 + \beta_1 (r_t - r^*) + u_{t+1} \tag{7}$$

where it is assumed that the error terms have zero means and are serially uncorrelated.

Isard (2006) distinguishes two issues in the empirical assessment of UIP: the size of the prediction errors and the question whether the predictions are systematically biased. In the case of the first issue, research conducted by Isard (1978), Mussa (1979) and Frenkel (1981) shows that interest rate differentials could explain only a small proportion of the subsequent changes in spot rates, whereas the hypothesis of unbiasedness can be assessed by testing whether $(\alpha_0, \alpha_1) = (0,1)$ or $(\beta_0, \beta_1) = (0,1)$. Tests generally support the value of α_1 as being equal to unity, but do not support the same value for β_1, at least for prediction horizons of less than one year. When prediction horizons are increased to between five and 20 years, the evidence is much more favourable to unbiasedness (see, e.g., Flood and Taylor (1997)). The interpretations offered to the rejection of the unbiasedness hypothesis are rather diverse. One interpretation is that market participants are risk averse and require risk premiums to hold uncovered foreign currency positions – this interpretation rejects the UIP condition, but does not discard the rational expectations assumption – see, in this respect, the influential paper of Fama (1984). Other explanations emphasise the so-called peso problem (Rogoff, 1980; Krasker, 1980), the simultaneity bias (Isard, 1988; McCallum, 1994), the incomplete information with rational learning

(Lewis, 1988; 1989), and the self-fulfilling prophecies of rational and risk-neutral market participants (Mussa, 1990).

Lothian and Wu (2003) argue that the failures of UIP that have been so widely documented are a coincidence of two empirical artefacts: the unique sample period of the 1980s and the noise induced by small UIP deviations. They contradict the so-called UIP puzzle overwhelmingly evidenced by literature (see, e.g., Bakshi and Naka, 1997; Bekaert, 1995; Flood and Rose, 1996; Wu and Zhang, 1997). More recently, authors have addressed a series of circumstances that may influence the validation or invalidation of UIP. Besides the specificities of the 1980s, other possible circumstances may play a role in the UIP testing, such as the integration of financial markets, interest rate defences of fixed exchange rates or changing levels of financial market volatility.

The issue of capital market volatility as a factor influencing UIP validation has been researched, with a rather general finding that UIP holds better in times of high market volatility and/or large interest rate differentials, whereas in times of lower volatility tests seem to reject the UIP condition. In one of the few attempts to test UIP on emerging markets, Cairns et al. (2007) conclude that in times of heightened global equity and bond market volatility, high-yielding currencies tend to depreciate, whereas low-yielding ones tend to serve as a 'safe haven', but the entire spectrum of currency sensitivity to global volatility could be found among Asia-Pacific currencies. The influence of volatility on UIP validity has also been tested using regime-switching models that allow for exchange rate switches between volatility regimes over time. The use of regime switching models to exchange rate data has been proposed by Engel and Hamilton (1990), Bekaert and Hodrick (1993), Bollen et al. (2000), Dewachter (2004), Huisman and Mahieu (2006), and Ichiue and Koyama (2008). Huisman and Mahieu (2006) use weekly data for the 1992 to 2006 period for the currencies of developed countries against the US$ and allow the exchange rate to switch between two regimes over time: the first regime is a UIP regime, in which changes in exchange rates are described by the observed interest rate differential between the two currencies involved, whereas the second regime is a random walk with drift. Based on the estimated regime probabilities, the authors investigate whether specific interest rate market conditions can be related to the periods with a high probability of being in the UIP regime. They conclude that an exchange rate switches between periods in which it is likely to be in a random walk regime and periods in which it is likely to be in an UIP regime, but the exchange rate is more likely to be in the UIP regime in high volatility periods and periods with large absolute interest rate differentials. Ichiue and Koyama (2008) advance as a possible explanation for the UIP invalidation in low volatility times carry-trade activities of market participants, and as an explanation for the UIP validation in high volatility times the rapid unwinding of carry-trade. They also observe that low interest rate currencies appreciate less frequently, but once the appreciation occurs, its movement is faster than when they depreciate; the authors also see here the result of carry-trade unwinding.

12.2.2 OLS regressions

We first test the UIP in a classical way, using a regression of the form:

$$(s_{t+1} - s_t) \cdot 52 = \alpha + \beta \cdot (r_t - r_t^*) + \varepsilon_{t+1} \tag{8}$$

where s denotes the exchange rate of the selected currency against the US\$, r is the domestic interest rate and r^* is the US interest rate. We run the regressions for a null hypothesis of $\alpha = 0$ and $\beta = 1$. We use non-overlapping weekly data for the OLS analysis with one-week interest rates to avoid possible estimation biases in standard errors that typically arise from the use of overlapping data. The regression of the form (8) tests for a relationship between the change in exchange rate and interest rate differential such as

$$E(s_{t+1} - s_t) = (r_t - r_t^*) \cdot n / 52 \tag{9}$$

which means that an arbitrage relationship should exist where the expected exchange rate return compensates for the return provided by the interest rate differential.

As noted above, previous tests on UIP failed to identify a relationship between the change in the exchange rates and interest rate differentials as indicated by theory. Specifically, a low-volatility environment might support the counter-intuitive relationship of the depreciation of lower-interest currencies. To test this supposition, we add another term to the regression in (8), which captures the influence of volatility on the relationship between exchange rates and interest rate differentials. The new regression takes the form:

$$(s_{t+1} - s_t) \cdot 52 = \alpha + (\beta_0 + \beta_v \cdot v_t) \cdot (r_t - r_t^*) + \varepsilon_{t+1} \tag{10}$$

where v_t is the annualised historical volatility calculated using daily exchange rate returns for approximately 20 business days up to the end of the month. The uncovered interest parity theory stands if we cannot reject the null hypothesis of $\alpha = \beta_v = 0$ and $\beta_0 = 1$ in (6). The parameter $(\beta_0 + \beta_v)$ reflects the extent to which currency returns are related to interest rate differentials depending on the exchange rate volatility. Thus, a positive β_v would indicate that a lower volatility leads to a lower value of $\beta_0 + \beta_v$, which means a higher deviation from that implied by UIP.

12.2.3 High volatility episodes and uncovered interest parity

When considering the impact of market volatility on the relationship between the changes in exchange rates and interest rate differential, it is important to investigate the influence of higher than normal volatility episodes on the UIP validity. Looking back at the 1994–2009 period,[4] Figure 12.1 shows several significant episodes of high market volatility, as indicated by swings in the VDAX indicator.

Out of all these episodes of high volatility, we selected nine periods, following a threshold in three-month (60 days) moving average of VDAX values (we used monthly data). If the daily increases in VDAX were equal to at least two standard deviations up from the moving average and were occurring in at least eight days out of any consecutive 20 days (or 1 month, approximately), we considered it as showing the debut of an episode of high volatility. The end of the high-volatility episode (or its peak) was defined in such a way the daily declines in VDAX are above one standard deviation of the moving average. Of these episodes we considered only those that have the percentage range (the difference between the highest value and the lowest value of VDAX) above

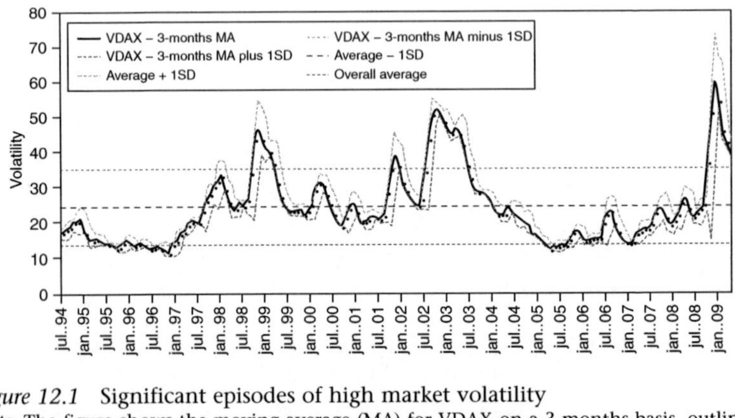

Figure 12.1 Significant episodes of high market volatility
Note: The figure shows the moving average (MA) for VDAX on a 3-months basis, outlining the thresholds for ±1 standard deviation (SD) from the average

the distance between the standard deviation and the average of VDAX over the entire period (44 per cent). Table 12.1 shows the remaining six episodes identified and the range in the VDAX value for each.

For the six episodes of high volatility in terms of VDAX we considered the average daily interest rate differential of the currencies against the US$ interest rate and the change in the exchange rates of currencies against the US$. We test the uncovered interest rate parity validity for the eight currencies using regressions of the form:

$$(s_{t+1} - s_t) = \alpha + \phi \cdot (r_t - r_t^*) + \varepsilon_{t+1} \tag{11}$$

where s denotes the exchange rate of the selected currency against the US$, r is the domestic interest rate and r^* is the US interest rate. We run the regressions for a null hypothesis of $\alpha = 0$ and $\beta = 1$. This part of our analysis also includes the euro, besides the eight currencies mentioned above. The daily changes in exchange rates are logarithmic and annualised.

12.2.4 The regime-switching models

To investigate more thoroughly the previous results and the influence of volatility on the UIP validation we use two regime-switching models, following Ichiue and Koyama (2008) and Bekaert and Hodrick (1993). The simplest regime-switching model is employed by Engel (1994) and is specified as

$$s_{t+1} - s_t = \alpha_i + \sigma_i \eta_{t+1} \tag{12}$$

Table 12.1 Episodes of high volatility, 1994–2009

Episode	Beginning day	Ending day	Maximum value of VDAX	Minimum value of VDAX	Percentage range in VDAX
1	13 August 1998	21 September 1998	54.23	29.92	81.25%
2	30 August 2001	25 September 2001	54.59	26.30	107.57%
3	4 June 2002	25 July 2002	58.76	28.61	105.38%
4	12 June 2006	13 June 2006	27.42	17.26	58.86%
5	10 July 2007	16 August 2007	31.42	20.42	53.87%
6	12 September 2008	28 October 2008	83.23	25.34	228.45%

where $i \in \{1,2\}$ denotes the regime (or state), α_i and σ_i denote the trend of exchange rate and the volatility of exchange rate change under regime *i* (or state *i*), respectively, and $\eta_{t+1} \sim N(0,1)$ i.i.d.

Ichiue and Koyama (2008) use a four-state model, specified in (13), which includes the interest rate differential and thus indicates the number and persistence of swings in exchange rates, and also periods when the UIP might hold. These periods should correspond to the higher volatility state of the regime-switching model.

$$s_{t+1} - s_t = \alpha_i + \beta_i \cdot (r_t - r_t^*) + \sigma_i \eta_{t+1} \tag{13}$$

Bekaert and Hodrick (1993) modify the model proposed by Engel and add an interest rate differential and a lag of exchange rate return in the model specified by (13), as follows:

$$s_{t+1} - s_t = \alpha_i + \beta_i \cdot (r_t - r_t^*) + \gamma_i \cdot (s_t - s_{t-1}) + \sigma_i \eta_{t+1} \tag{14}$$

Our model adds a lag of the exchange rate return to the set of explanatory variables and assumes simultaneous switches in the intercept α_i, the slope coefficient β_i, the volatility parameter σ_i and the interest differential coefficient γ_i. To estimate these models we use monthly data.

12.3 Results

12.3.1 Results of OLS analysis

We find that all estimated slope coefficients from equation (8) are statistically different from one at the five per cent level, which indicates that for all currency pairs and for the entire period the UIP is not validated. The same is true for β-coefficients from equation (10), which reinforces our findings. Table 12.2 reports the results from regression equations (8) and (10).

There are a few points to be noted. First, of all β-coefficients, only four are statistically different from zero (for RON, NTL, RUR and GBP), but all of them are positive, although their values are very close to zero. This indicates that, despite the fact that UIP does not hold, for the direction in the exchange rate change indicated by the interest rate, the differential follows the UIP framework. Overall, the relationship implied by UIP between interest rate differentials and exchange rate changes is weak and the inclusion of foreign exchange market volatility does not significantly alter this result. We observe that when volatility is taken

Table 12.2 Results of UIP test regressions

	UIP test without volatility – equation (8)		**UIP test with volatility – equation (10)**		
	α	β	α	β_0	β_v
Poland	–0.058	0.010	–0.127**	–0.025***	0.472**
	–(0.90)	(1.394)	–(2.01)	–(2.895)	(6.53)
Czech Republic	–0.053	0.016	–0.056	0.020	–0.019
	–(1.31)	(1.977)	–(1.36)	(1.618)	–(0.46)
Romania	0.007	0.004***	0.026	0.002*	0.014**
	(0.14)	(3.653)	(0.56)	(1.719)	(2.49)
Turkey	–0.145	0.009***	–0.174*	0.005*	0.036
	–(0.95)	(3.009)	–(4.53)	(1.873)	(0.13)
Russia	–0.165	0.038*	–0.072	0.020***	0.023***
	–(1.76)	(7.505)	–(0.87)	(3.310)	(5.15)
Japan	–0.053	–0.012	–0.062	–0.081***	0.655***
	–(0.70)	–(0.624)	–(0.83)	–(3.128)	(3.89)
Switzerland	–0.065	–0.022	–0.065	–0.051	0.315
	–(1.17)	–(1.098)	–(1.15)	–(1.520)	(1.08)
UK	–0.020	0.023*	–0.004	–0.148***	1.811***
	–(0.51)	(1.054)	–(0.10)	–(4.465)	(6.76)

Note: This table reports the results from the regression equations (8) and (10). *T*-statistics are reported in parantheses.
The values with ***, ** and * are different from zero at the 1 per cent, 5 per cent and 10 per cent significance levels. The sample is 30 December 2006 to 6 April 2009 for the CZK, JPY, PLZ, RUR and CHF; 26 May 1996 to 6 April 2009 for RON; 30 December 1996 to 2 January 2006 for NTL; 6 January 1997 to 6 April 2009 for GBP.

into account, its coefficients are statistically significant, at least at the 10 per cent level in the case of five currencies (PLZ, RON, RUR, JPY and GBP). Since β_v-coefficients are all positive, this indicates a higher deviation from what is implied by UIP. Nevertheless, the volatility addition to equation (10) leads to statistically different from zero interest rate differential coefficients in the case of PLZ and JPY. Interestingly, though, both these coefficients are negative, implying that the exchange rates for these two currencies change in the opposite direction compared to the one indicated by the interest rate differentials. For three of the high-yielding currencies (RON, NTL and RUR) the inclusion of volatility does not amend the positive relationship between exchange rate changes and interest rate differential.

12.3.2 High volatility implications for UIP validation

Figure 12.2 plots the annualised average depreciation of the US$ against the eight currencies plus the euro versus the annualised average interest rate differentials for the six high-volatility episodes identified in Table 12.1; Table 12.3 shows the results of the regressions specified in (11).

For all high-volatility moments we find that UIP does not hold, as all ϕ-coefficients are statistically different from 1. Still, for each of the six episodes of high volatility in the capital market, we found an overall positive relationship between the average daily interest rate differential and the changes in exchange rates against the US$. This means that in moments of increased capital market volatility the higher the interest rate differential, the higher the change in exchange rates: more specifically, when volatility in capital markets is high, low-yielding currencies tend to appreciate and high-yielding currencies tend to depreciate against the US$.

12.3.3 Results of Markov-switching models

Tables 12.3 and 12.4 comparatively present the results of applying the regime-switching models specified in (13) and (14). The estimation results of model (13) for high-yielding currencies are given in Table 12.4. The RON and the PLZ tend to appreciate when volatility is low and depreciate when volatility is high, although the rate of depreciation is lower than the rate of appreciation. In contrast, the CZK and the NTL depreciate slightly when volatility is low and appreciate when volatility is high. An unusual pattern is observed for the RUR, as in this case both β_1- and β_2-coefficients are significant at the 5 per cent level and positive. However, we note that for four out of five low-yielding currencies, the

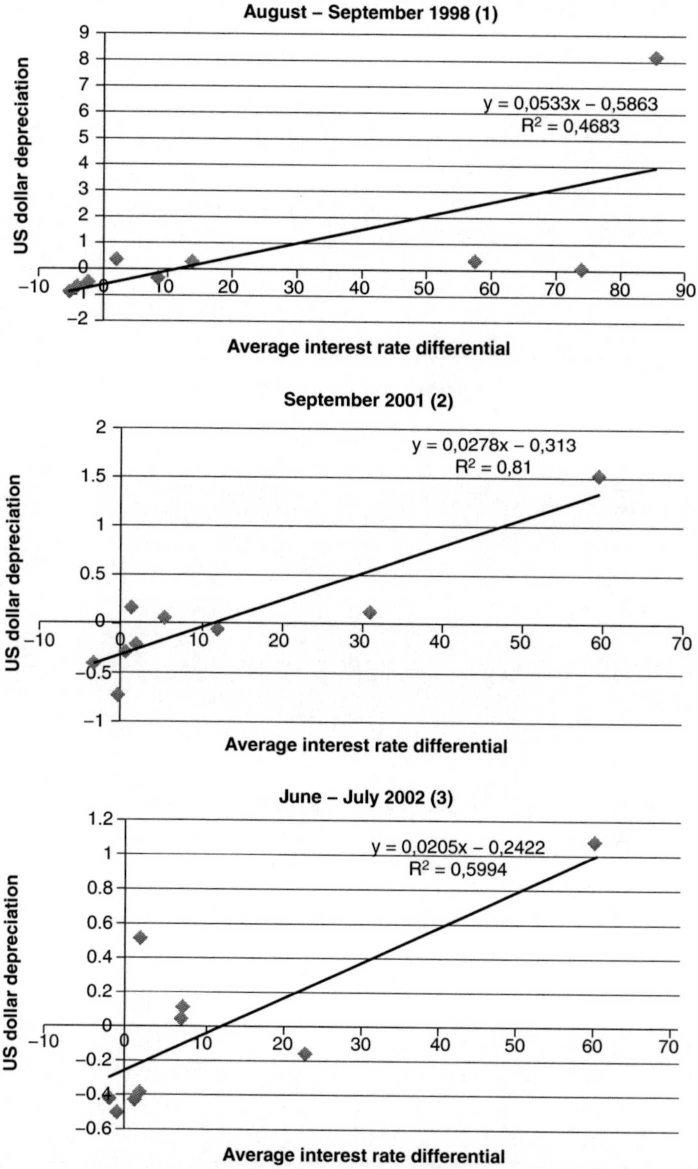

Figure 12.2 US dollar depreciation and interest rate differentials in volatile periods

Note: Numbers (1) to (6) refer to high-volatility episodes identified in Table 12.1

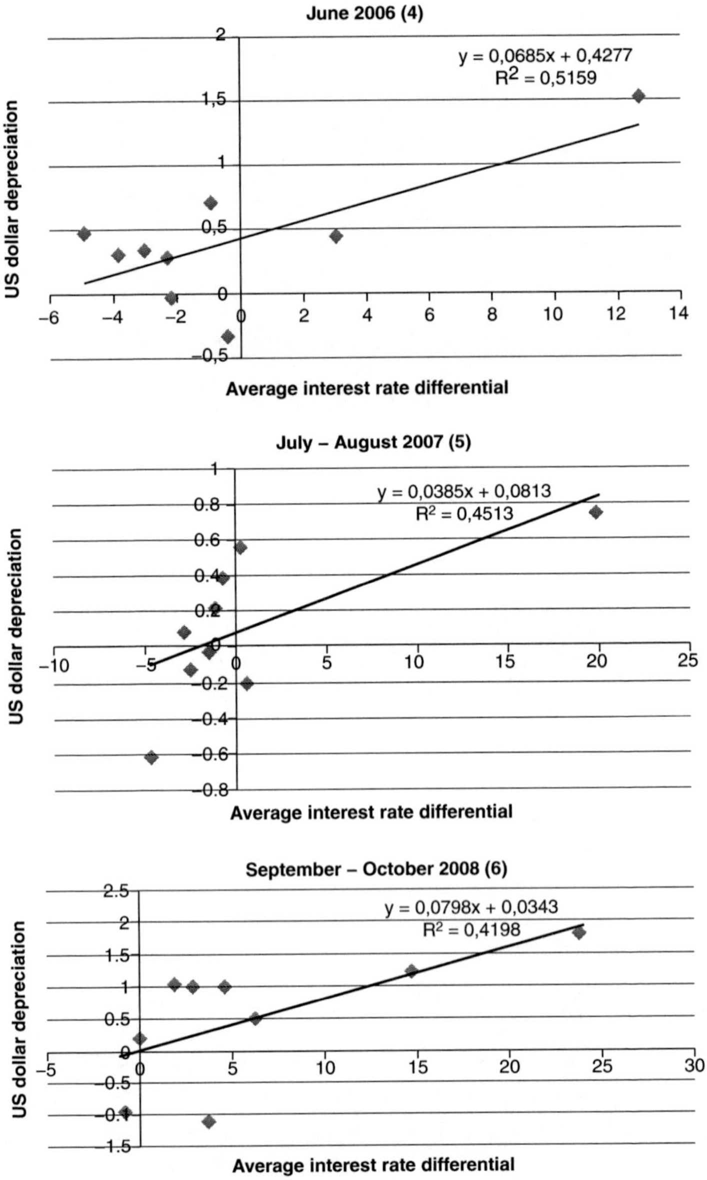

Figure 12.2 Continued

Table 12.3 Results of regressions for high-volatility episodes

High-volatility episodes	ϕ	R^2	Adj. R^2
1	0.0533** (2.4830)	0.4683	0.3923
2	0.0278*** (5.4631)	0.8100	0.7829
3	0.0205** (3.2366)	0.5994	0.5422
4	0.0685** (2.7313)	0.5159	0.3730
5	0.0385** (2.3996)	0.4513	0.3730
6	0.0798* (2.2503)	0.4198	0.3369

Note: This table reports the results from the regression equation (11). *T*-statistics are reported in parantheses.
The values with ***, ** and * are different from zero at the 1 per cent, 5 per cent and 10 per cent significance levels. High-volatility episodes numbers are taken from Table 12.1.

interest rate differential coefficient is significant only in the lower volatility state. Judging from the expected duration of each state, it appears that high-volatility episodes are brief and that a model such as (13) is, in general, unable to capture the relationship between exchange rates and interest rate differentials that governs these periods.

Table 12.5 comprises results from the Markov-switching model estimates of low-yielding currencies. Of these currencies, the JPY is the most interesting, appearing to depreciate at a much faster pace in the higher-volatility regime than in the lower-volatility one. The SWF depreciates when volatility is lower and appreciates when it is higher, but the speeds of adjustment are comparable. The GBP displays a different behaviour, with a tendency to appreciate much faster in the higher-volatility regime.

The evidence above indicates that high-yielding currencies appreciate and low-yielding currencies depreciate in low-volatility periods, whereas in high-volatility periods the model is unable to support or refute the UIP. Ichiue and Koyama (2007) explain similar findings with reference to the carry trade activities that take place in a low-volatility environment. According to them, the depreciation of low-interest rate currencies is influenced by the carry trade, whereas the fast appreciation is influenced by its rapid unwinding.

Model (14), which explicitly incorporates autoregressive dynamics, retains the two-state Markov process, with transition probabilities p_{11}

Table 12.4 Maximum likelihood parameter estimates of class one Markov-switching models for high-yielding currencies

Coefficient	RO		PL		CZ		TU		RU	
	State 1	**State 2**	**State 1**	**State 2**	**State 1**	**State 2**	**State 1**	**State 2**	**State 1**	**State 2**
$P_{i,i}$	0.98	0.00	0.99***	1.00***	0.97***	0.89***	0.24	0.93***	0.88***	0.97***
	0.09	–	0.08	0.39	0.08	0.09	0.18	0.12	0.22	0.09
α_i	−0.01**	0.17***	−0.01**	0.06	−0.01**	0.02	0.26***	−0.01	−0.06	0.00***
	(0.00)	(0.03)	(0.00)	(0.10)	(0.00)	(0.01)	(0.01)	(0.01)	(0.07)	(0.00)
β_i	5.54**	−1.51	10.37**	−6.88	−0.06	0.09	−0.77	0.03	0.52**	0.02***
	(1.06)	(5.02)	(4.42)	(264.87)	(0.10)	(0.17)	(0.02)***	(0.04)	(0.24)	(0.01)
	2.85%	3.46%	3.19%***	8.49%***	3.18%***	5.48%***	0.66%	3.32%	18.74%***	0.87%***
σ_i	(0.00)***	(0.02)*	(0.00)	(0.02)	(0.00)	(0.01)	(0.00)	(0.00)	(0.03)	(0.00)
Expected duration in number of periods	58.74	1.00	139.58	–	38.27	9.07	1.31	13.42	8.09	34.64

Note: Model description is given in equation (13). Standard errors are reported in parentheses and values with *, ** and *** are different from zero at the 10 per cent, 5 per cent and 1 per cent significance levels, respectively.

Table 12.5 Maximum likelihood parameter estimates of class one Markov-switching models for low-yielding currencies

Coefficient	SW		UK		JP	
	State 1	**State 2**	**State 1**	**State 2**	**State 1**	**State 2**
p_{ii}	0.76	0.02	0.99	0.99***	0.96***	1.00***
	–	0.10	–	0.08	0.23	0.09
α_i	−0.02***	0.04***	−0.03*	0.00	−0.38	0.00
	(0.00)	(0.01)	(0.02)	(0.00)	(0.42)	(0.01)
β_i	−0.40**	0.48	4.24	−0.14	−7.71	−0.05
	(0.18)	(0.31)	(0.96)	(0.16)	(8.55)	(0.14)
σ_i	2.69%***	1.27%***	2.59%**	2.13%***	5.33%***	2.86%***
	(0.00)	(0.00)	(0.01)	(0.00)	(0.01)	(0.00)
Expected duration in number of periods	4.25	1.02	81.42	133.68	25.92	–

Note: Model description is given in equation (13). Standard errors are reported in parentheses and values with *, ** and *** are different from zero at the 10 per cent, 5 per cent and 1 per cent significance levels, respectively.

Table 12.6 Maximum likelihood parameter estimates of class two Markov-switching models for high-yielding currencies

Coefficient	RO		PL		CZ		TU		RU	
	State 1	**State 2**	**State 1**	**State 2**	**State 1**	**State 2**	**State 1**	**State 2**	**State 1**	**State 2**
p_i	0.97***	0.91	0.99***	1.00***	0.99***	1.00**	0.24	0.96***	0.87***	0.97***
	0.07	–	0.08	0.38	0.09	0.43	0.24	0.12	0.23	0.09
α_i	−0.01***	0.01	−0.01**	0.12	−0.01*	0.08	0.34***	0.00	−0.08	0.00*
	(0.00)	(0.01)	(0.00)	(0.14)	(0.00)	(0.06)	(0.01)	(0.01)	(0.06)	(0.00)
β_i	9.06***	0.33	10.70**	−117.79	0.12*	−2.93	−1.56***	−0.01	0.77***	0.02***
	(1.18)	(2.85)	(4.50)	(319.80)	(0.06)	(2.75)	(0.06)	(0.04)	(0.23)	(0.01)
γ_i	−0.12	0.07	−0.03	−0.34	−0.02	−0.24	0.32***	−0.04	−0.47***	0.31**
	(0.10)	(0.19)	(0.09)	(0.58)	(0.09)	(0.50)	(0.04)	(0.10)	(0.19)	(0.13)
σ_i	2.16%***	5.56%***	3.19%***	8.28%***	3.45%***	6.99%***	0.47%***	3.76% ***	16.51%***	0.82%***
	(0.00)	(0.01)	(0.00)	(0.02)	(0.00)	(0.02)	(0.00)	(0.00)	(0.02)	(0.00)
Expected duration in number of periods	30.78	10.97	139.81	–	138.85	–	1.32	27.98	7.55	32.30

Note: Model description is given in equation (14). Standard errors are reported in parentheses and values with *, ** and *** are different from zero at the 10 per cent, 5 per cent and 1 per cent significance levels, respectively.

Table 12.7 Maximum likelihood parameter estimates of class two Markov-switching models for low-yielding currencies

Coefficient	SW		UK		JP	
	State 1	**State 2**	**State 1**	**State 2**	**State 1**	**State 2**
$p_{i,i}$	0.26	0.97***	1.00***	0.99***	0.58***	0.95***
	0.20	0.03	–	0.07	0.14	0.07
α_i	−0.06***	−0.01	−0.06***	0.00	0.07***	−0.01***
	(0.00)	(0.00)	(0.02)	(0.00)	(0.03)	(0.01)
β_i	−2.18	−0.18	4.64***	−0.15	2.86***	−0.35**
	–	(0.17)	(0.90)	(0.15)	(0.56)	(0.14)
γ_i	−1.12	0.08	0.48**	−0.05	−0.70***	−0.03
	–	(0.08)	(0.23)	(0.09)	(0.14)	(0.09)
σ_i	0.06%	2.88%***	2.10%***	2.13%***	2.79%***	2.81%***
	–	(0.00)	(0.01)	(0.00)	(0.01)	(0.00)
Expected duration in number of periods	1.35	29.42	–	138.02	2.38	18.75

Note: Model description is given in equation (14). Standard errors are reported in parentheses and values with *, ** and *** are different from zero at the 10 per cent, 5 per cent and 1 per cent significance levels, respectively.

(p_{22}) of remaining in State 1 (State 2), given that the economy is in State 1 (State 2), but the conditional means in each state are allowed to depend auto-regressively on lagged values of the exchange rate. Model (14) best captures regime changes for the RUR, in the high-yielding currencies panel, and the JPY in the low-yielding currencies panel. For these two currencies, the parameter estimates of the model in each state are significant at the 5 per cent level. The RUR tends to appreciate much faster in the high-volatility regime, whereas the JPY depreciates when volatility is somewhat higher.

The results in Tables 12.6 and 12.7 indicate that high-yielding currencies appreciate in low-volatility periods, with the exception of the NTL, which depreciated faster in the low-volatility state. Studying the expected duration of each state, we come to the conclusion that in the case of high-yielding currencies the depreciation is swift and the appreciation is slow, whereas the reverse holds for the low-yielding currencies.

12.4 Concluding remarks

Our paper explores the relationship between exchange rate changes and interest rate differentials in the uncovered interest parity framework, by taking into account the implications of capital market and foreign exchange market volatility on the UIP validation. The purpose of this research was to test whether volatility on capital and foreign exchange markets could predict when the UIP theory may hold. Since volatility can be forecast reliably with GARCH models, consistent validation of the parity relationship in times of turmoil on these markets would provide the basis for the creation of foreign exchange market models with an improved forecasting ability.

We have used nine currencies in our analysis, of which five were from CEE – Polish zloty, Czech koruna, Romanian leu, Turkish Lira, and Russian ruble – and four were developed market currencies – Japanese yen, Swiss franc, British pound, and euro. Our testing of uncovered interest parity followed a three-step procedure: first, we have used OLS regressions to summarise the empirical facts about interest rate differentials and changes in exchange rates; secondly, we have explored the influence of capital market and foreign exchange market volatility on the validation of uncovered interest parity; thirdly, we have employed the regime-switching methodology to capture in a better manner the relationship between exchange rate changes and interest differentials in a changing volatility environment.

We found that the uncovered interest theory was not validated over the entire period, but the direction in the exchange rate change indicated by the interest rate differential followed the UIP framework. Overall, the relationship implied by UIP between interest rate differentials and exchange rate changes is weak and, taking into account foreign exchange market volatility, does not significantly alter this result. When capital market volatility is considered, UIP is again not validated, but for each of the six episodes of high-volatility in the capital market that we identified, we found an overall positive relationship between the average daily interest rate differential and the changes in exchange rates against the US$. This means that in moments of increased capital market volatility, the higher the interest rate differential, the higher the change in exchange rates: more specifically, when the volatility in capital markets is high, low-yielding currencies tend to appreciate and high-yielding currencies tend to depreciate against the US$.

The regime-switching models we used in our analysis are unable to support or refute the uncovered interest parity in times of high volatility. Still, in periods of low volatility, we find that high-yielding currencies appreciate and low-yielding currencies depreciate, but the sizes of appreciation versus depreciation are different. Studying the expected duration of each state, we came to the conclusion that in the case of high-yielding currencies the depreciation is swift and the appreciation is slow, whereas the reverse holds for the low-yielding currencies. Our results confirm previous evidence and a possible explanation may reside in the carry-trade activities that take place in low-volatility environments and the subsequent unwinding of these in high-volatility times.

Notes

This chapter presents results achieved within the research project 'Modeling the interaction between the capital market and the foreign exchange market. Implications for financial stability in emerging markets', Project code IDEI_1782, funded by CNCSIS, PNII/IDEI.

1. VDAX expresses the implied volatility of the Deutsche Börse DAX Index anticipated on the derivatives market. The VDAX indicates in percentage points the volatility to be expected in the next 30 days for the DAX. The basis for the calculation of this index is provided by the DAX option contracts.
2. The spot exchange rate is denominated in units of the domestic currency per one unit of the foreign currency.
3. See Copeland (2005), for a detailed discussion on assumptions' implications for testing UIP.
4. From 13 April 1994 to 13 April 2009.

References

Bakshi, G., Naka, A. (1997) On the Unbiasedness of Forward Exchange Rates, *Financial Review*, 32: 145–62.

Bekaert, G. (1995) The Time-Variation of Expected Returns and Volatility in Foreign Exchange Markets, *Journal of Business and Economic Statistics*, 12: 115–38.

Bekaert, G., Hodrick, B. (1993) On Biases in the Measurement of Foreign Exchange Risk Premiums, *Journal of International Money and Finance*, 12: 115–38.

Bollen, N. P. B., Gray, S. F., Whaley, R. E. (2000) Regime Switching in Foreign Exchange Risk Premiums, *Journal of Econometrics*, 94: 29–276.

Cairns, J., Ho, C., McCauley, R. (2007) Exchange Rates and Global Volatility: Implications for Asia-Pacific Currencies, *BIS Quarterly Review*, March 2007, 41–52.

Copeland, L. (2005) *Exchange Rates and International Finance*, Fourth Edition, Harlow, England: Pearson Education Limited.

Dewachter, H. (2001) Can Markov Switching Models Replicate Chartist Profits in the Foreign Exchange Market? *Journal of International Money and Finance*, 20: 25–41.

Dooley, M. P., Isard, P., (1980) Capital Controls, Political Risk and Deviations from Interest-Rate Parity, *Journal of Political Economy*, 88: 370–84.

Engel, C., Hamilton, J. D. (1990) Long Swings in the Dollar: Are they in the Data and do Markets Know it? *American Economic Review*, 80: 689–713.

Engel, C. (1994) Can the Markov Switching Model Forecast Rates?, *Journal of International Economics*, 36, pp. 151–65.

Fama, E. (1984) Forward and Spot Exchange Rates, *Journal of Monetary Economics*, 14: 319–38.

Flood, R. P., Taylor, M. P. (1997) Exchange Rate Economics: What's Wrong with the Conventional Macro Approach? in J. A. Frenkel, G. Galli, and A. Giovannini (eds): *The Microstructure of Foreign Exchange Markets*, Chicago: University of Chicago Press.

Flood, R., Rose, A. (1996) Fixes: Of the Forward Discount Puzzle, *Review of Economics and Statistics*, 78: 748–52.

Frenkel, J. A., (1981) Flexible Exchange Rates, Prices and the Role of 'News': Lessons from the 1970s, *Journal of Political Economy*, 89: 665–705.

Herring, R. J., Marston, R. C. (1976) The Forward Market and Interest Rates in the Eurocurrency and National Money Markets in C. H. Stern, J. H. Makin, and D.E. Logue (eds): *Eurocurrencies and the International Monetary System*, Washington: American Enterprise Institute.

Huisman, R., Mahieu, R. J. (2006) Revisiting Uncovered Interest Rate Parity: Switching between UIP and the Random Walk, ERIM Report Series Reference No. ERS-2007-001-F&A. Available at SSRN: http://ssrn.com/abstract=957412.

Ichiue, H., Koyama, K. (2008) Regime Switches in Exchange Rate Volatility and Uncovered Interest Parity. Available at SSRN: http://ssrn.com/abstract=1106790.

Isard, P. (1978) Exchange-Rate Determination: A Survey of Popular Views and Recent Models, in: *Princeton Studies in International Finance*, No. 42.

Isard, P. (1988) Exchange Rate Modeling: An Assessment of Alternative Approaches, in R. C. Bryant, D. W. Henderson, G. Holtham, P. Hooper, and

S. A. Symansky (eds): *Empirical Macroeconomics for Interdependent Economies*, Washington: Brookings Institution, pp. 183–201.

Isard, P. (2006) Uncovered Interest Parity, IMF Working Paper, WP/06/96, April 2006.

Krasker, W. S., (1980): The Peso Problem in Testing the Efficiency of Forward Exchange Markets, *Journal of Monetary Economics*, 6: 269–76.

Levich, R. M., (1985) Empirical Studies of Exchange Rates: Price Behavior, Rate Determination and Market Efficiency, in R. W. Jones and P. B. Kenen, (eds): *Handbook of International Economics*, Amsterdam: North-Holland.

Lewis, K. K, (1988) The Persistence of the Peso Problem when Policy is Noisy, *Journal of International Money and Finance*, 7: 5–21.

Lewis, K. K, (1989) Changing Beliefs and Systematic Rational Forecast Errors with Evidence from Foreign Exchange, *American Economic Review*, 79: 621–36.

Lothian, J. R., Wu, L. (2003) Uncovered Interest Rate Parity over the Past Two Centuries (June 12, 2003). Available at SSRN: http://ssrn.com/abstract=585462.

McCallum, B. T. (1994) A Reconsideration of the Uncovered Interest Parity Relationship, *Journal of Monetary Economics*, 33: 105–32.

Mussa, M. (1979) Empirical Regularities in the Behaviour of Exchange Rates and Theories of the Foreign Exchange Market, Carnegie-Rochester Conference Series on Public Policy, Vol.11, pp. 9–57.

Mussa, M. (1990) Exchange Rates in Theory and Reality, *Essays in International Finance*, No. 179, Princeton: International Finance Section, Department of Economics, Princeton University.

Rogoff, K. (1980) Tests of the Martingale Mode for Foreign Exchange Future Markets, *Essays on Expectations and Exchange Rate Volatility*, doctoral dissertation, Cambridge, MA: Massachusetts Institute of Technology.

Taylor, M.P, (1989) Covered Interest Arbitrage and Market Turbulence, *Economic Journal*, 99: 376–91.

Wu, Y., Zhang, H. (1997) Forward Premiums as Unbiased Predictors of Future Currency Depreciation, *Journal of International Money and Finance*, 16: 609–23.

Index

Page numbers in *italics* refer to figures and tables.